THE INSATIABLE DRAGON

HOW CHINA TOOK CONTROL OF HOLLYWOOD - *A CAUTIONARY TALE*

Greg Rabidoux

The Insatiable Dragon: How China Took Control of Hollywood – A Cautionary Tale

First Edition: December 2022
Library of Congress Control Number: 2022920827
ISBN 978-1-7352716-4-4

Front and back cover design by Greg Rabidoux and Valentin Lencina-Rabidoux

Printed in USA by ValMar Books
(a division of ValMar Productions, Inc.)
Myrtle Beach, South Carolina

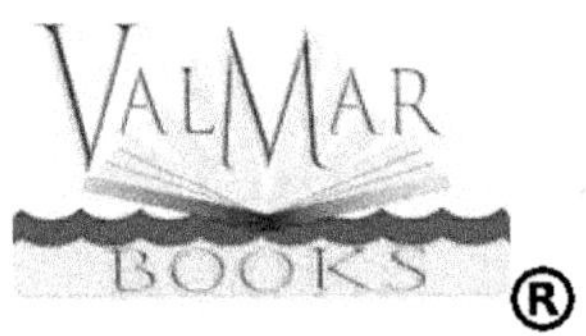

DEDICATION

This book is dedicated to Maravillas and Valentin, for all they do to help inspire, support, and love me throughout what is always an arduous and challenging process of making a book. They make it all worthwhile. This book is also dedicated to freedom loving people everywhere whose voices are silenced, whose lives and dreams are suppressed, and who pay a heavy price for indifference by those who could, but choose not to, make a difference.

"Three Things cannot long remain hidden-
The Sun, the Moon, and the Truth."-Confucius

TABLE OF CONTENTS

PREFACE

This book is a cautionary tale about the need to be careful, cunning, and courageous when dealing with the Chinese dragon. Even when, maybe, especially when you know why the dragon behaves the way it does. Knowing the why does not make you immune from its ferocity nor protect you from the reach of its mighty tail. It's not that the dragon is completely evil. No, but what the dragon wants, and what it is ready, willing, and more than able to do to sate its desire is not necessarily going to be what others want. Or need. Stand up to the dragon at your own peril.

This book is also a cautionary tale about how, over many years, and despite many obstacles in its path, the Chinese dragon came to assert its control over Hollywood. The stories that the world would now be told about China through film would be only those stories which pleased the mighty dragon. And what pleases it the most?

Stories told in a good way about China, its people, its purity, bravery, and generosity, of course. Stories that glorify its past, celebrate its present, and look forward with unbridled optimism about its future. Stories that talk about things and people that displease the dragon are taboo. Off-limits. Never to be told. Being controlled by the dragon means not being able to freely pick and choose which stories you tell or how you tell them.

But this book is not merely a tale about the past and how it came to be. It is also a map of sorts. A map representing new hope, and new beginnings. It all starts with making different choices than the ones that got you under the control of the dragon in the first place. This is what it fears. This is how it will be slayed.

WHAT THEY SAY ABOUT CHINA'S INFLUENCE OVER HOLLYWOOD

"Hollywood is now China's puppet…China has bought our silence with their money"[1]-*Judd Apatow, Hollywood Film Director*

"Hollywood now regularly censors its own movies to appease the Chinese Communist Party, the world's most powerful violator of human rights."[2]-*William Barr, Former US Attorney General*

"Now more than ever we need to talk to each other, to listen to each other and understand how we see the world, and cinema is the best medium for doing this."[3]-*Martin Scorsese-Hollywood Film Director*

"As a writer, I demand the right to write any character in the world that I want to write. I demand the right to be them, I demand the right to think them, and I demand the right to tell the truth as I see they are."[4]- *Film Director, Quentin Tarantino.*

"I applaud Quentin Tarantino's refusal to recut his film to appease China's censorship. Unalienable rights such as free speech should not be for sale."[5]-*US Secretary of State Mike Pompeo (2020-2024)*

"We made a stupid mistake in releasing *Kundun*. The bad news is that the film was made; the good news is that nobody watched it. Here I want to apologize, and in the future, we should prevent this sort of thing, which insults our friends, from happening."6-*Former Disney Studios CEO, Michael Eisner*

"They (China) have amazing influence… China will penalize the studio or filmmakers involved with that particular movie, so that they can't get other movies in…And that's definitely something we need to stop."7-*Chris Fenton, former President, DMG Entertainment Motion Picture Group*

"It is shameful that no US companies and very few politicians speak up about concentration camps in China. The United States has abandoned the world when it comes to human rights."8-*Judd Apatow*

"There is a fine line between censorship and good taste and moral responsibility."9-*Steven Spielberg*

"I'm a writer and, therefore, automatically a suspicious character."10-*Alfred Hitchcock*

"When you are appealing to people's fears and anxieties you can make some gains."11-*President Joe Biden*

INTRODUCTION
A TALE OF TWO CINEMAS

"Better a Diamond with a flaw, than a Pebble without."- Confucius

Chinese cinema was conceived, born and grew up in a perpetual state of chaos and conflict. Throughout its development, it endured profound crises, both foreign and domestic.

China's war with Great Britain over opium resulted in the British control of Hong Kong for over 156 years. Invasion of mainland China by the Empire of Japan and European aggression resulted in the carving up of Shanghai to the West and the bitter loss of Taiwan.

The bloody end of the Ming Dynasty resulted in a nearly 40-year struggle for control of mainland China.

Forced acceleration of an agrarian economy into an industrialized nation by the Chinese Communists resulted in the deaths of millions of their fellow Chinese, many by starvation.

Ill-advised cultural "revolutions" resulted in more deaths and disappearances of thousands of Chinese artists, performers, and filmmakers who were deemed to be not "revolutionary" enough in their craft.

These crises, imposed and self-inflicted, reveal both the burning desire of China to become a modern nation, a "superpower," and its deep resentment of all things foreign. A resentment, paranoia really, which was baked into the Chinese psyche with the Communist victory in 1949. China would never be the same again, nor would its domestic cinema. By design.

Political upheaval doesn't come along by mere chance, luck, or happenstance.

And lasting political change and domination by one party, one ideology, like communism in China, isn't fortune cookie fate. It is by design. It is manipulated, monitored, and regulated by ruthless leaders. Leaders, in truth, dictators who are hell-bent on ensuring that, in their case, their nation is never again suppressed or invaded by foreign armies, or even unacceptably influenced by foreign beliefs, values, or ideas.

The Chinese Communists recognized early on that cinema, the unstoppable magic of movies, must be harnessed, controlled, and manipulated for their own use. Communism and state-run propaganda do go together like a hammer and a sickle, it is tough to imagine the existence of one without the other.

But China faced an issue of epic proportions. A challenge the scale of which even Hollywood directing legends like Cecil B. DeMille or Dino DeLaurentis could appreciate. Hollywood owned movies. They owned the market. They owned most of the technical wizardry. They owned the stars.

And Chinese resentment and ambition grew.

But at this point, Hollywood was reveling in its prolonged "Golden Age" (1920-1962), an age of filmmaking when dazzling musicals, rugged cowboys, wartime heroes, glamorous gals, femme-fatales, and fast-talking private investigators ruled the screen. How on earth could anyone ever compete with, let alone wrestle away cinema's jeweled crown from that Hollywood? Well, like any great quest it first starts with an idea. So, let's look now at when Chinese cinema started and how it grew from a fledgling idea into a 21st century industry powerhouse.

More accurately, when cinema scholars and historians speak of the early days of Chinese Cinema, they talk of three rather distinct yet connected cinematic centers, a "three- headed-dragon" of Chinese cinema. And like the classic dragon which adorns and animates so many Chinese parades, this cinematic dragon also required several separate entities inside its body, ideally moving in harmony, to create the illusion of power and a single-minded purpose of movement.

Yet, as we shall see, this Chinese cinematic dragon hardly ever moved with a single, coordinated sense of purpose, power, or harmony. Its heads or centers of cinema consisted of Shanghai, a key city on mainland China, which ushered in the first golden age of Chinese film, Hong Kong, a vital port city controlled by British ruler, and was, for many years the number two export of films behind Hollywood, and Taiwan, ruled first by Japan and later, by the Kuomintang (Chinese Nationalists). This tiny island once known as Formosa, would become home to world class directors like Ang Lee and Academy Award winning films like *Crouching Tiger, Hidden Dragon* (2000). To this day, the Academy Awards still accepts three different entries for Chinese film-Mainland China, Hong Kong, and Taiwan.

Yet, where Hollywood's incredible growth was almost inevitable, given its twin blessings of nearly uninterrupted peace and prosperity, Chinese cinema grew not because of, but rather, despite its hostile surroundings. Shanghai, the first epicenter of Chinese cinema, was a foreign dominated, partitioned city of breath-taking opposites. Foreigners and Chinese. Incredible wealth and astonishing, abject poverty. Artistic freedom in foreign sectors, strict control in the Chinese sectors. Modern progress and peace versus unchecked tribalism, gang wars and endless violence. An urban ethos of hard-work and a can-do spirit alongside a cynical, fatalistic, opium-den addled underbelly of human refuse. Start with Charles Dickens' *A Tale of Two Cities* and multiply it about 100 times and then somehow confine it all into one tightly confined city, Shanghai, and you begin to get the picture.

Hong Kong, the second dragon head, was ceded to the British after the first of two opium wars, both of which ended in an utterly humiliating defeat of the Imperial Qing Dynasty at the hands of the British Empire. The price of these defeats was three-fold, territorial loss, huge financial debt, and a generation of Chinese opium addicts. The roots of resentment of all things foreign and a paranoid need to control its own affairs may not have entirely started with its loss of Hong Kong but this deep-seated and seething hatred and xenophobia certainly was mightily stoked during these defeats. And things only got worse during the final years of the last imperial Chinese dynasty.

And Taiwan, the final head of the cinematic dragon endured decades of repressive, foreign control of its beautiful island and native cinema. First, at the hands of the invading Japanese and then, after the mainland Chinese Civil War ended, a decades-long martial law and virtual lock-down at the hands of the losers of this civil war, the Kuomintang and their authoritarian leader, Chiang Kai-Shek.

Yet, somehow, as we shall see, Chinese cinema did grow and succeed despite an intensely hostile and perilous environment. Culminating with its control over the former, undisputed King of Cinema, Hollywood.

Equal is just a placeholder for the Chinese until a better place of advantage, even dominance can be obtained.

And it will become evident that if there was any intentional "model" used to achieve this success it seemed to follow very closely the same model or approach which modern-day China has taken while growing its dominance in nearly every arena which attracts global competition, like business, trade, politics, technology, and military.

First, the Chinese signal an openness or willingness to serve as student to whichever "master" asserts dominance in any given sector the Chinese covet at any given moment.

Next, as the student grows in stature and confidence, often because of benevolence by the "master" or industry leader in exchange for goodwill and peace in return by the student, a request is made by the student. This involves a supposedly more fair and equitable cooperation, even collaboration between now roughly equal partners.

Finally, while China has, with single-minded purpose, been acquiring the capacity, whether legally and ethically or illegally and unethically, to gain an advantage of superiority over its once master and then partner, it next exerts a one-sided control and dominance. By then, its co-collaborator has learned the painful and costly truth about doing any kind of business with the Chinese-all actions, all goals, and all actors under the power of China ultimately and exclusively serve only one master-The Chinese Communist Party. Unlike their western rivals who frequently see collaboration and cooperation as a rational and desired state of affairs between two entities, perhaps leading to a rough parity and harmony between equals, the Chinese Communist Party sees such a dynamic as a mere placeholder, a temporary though necessary step to take to set its foot upon the ultimate goal which is always the same- dominance.

When we discuss the current state of affairs between Hollywood and China in later chapters, this "model" and approach taken by the Chinese will become evident, even patently and profoundly obvious. But just because it's obvious to those of who choose to look upon the Hollywood-China relationship with a critical yet objective eye, does not mean it is obvious or avoidable to those deeply invested in the relationship. What is so apparent to impartial observers is either being willfully ignored or intentionally dismissed by today's movers and shakers of Hollywood.

Regardless, the fate of Hollywood and the fact it has gone from being mentor, co-collaborator, and now, subservient to China does not change one iota. In fact, knowing the roots of an adversary's paranoia and compulsion to exploit and dominate you doesn't mean you are obligated or compelled to collaborate with or appease this same rival. And, arguably, this is exactly what Hollywood has done with China. At a great cost. To them and to the rest of us who prefer our films uncensored and not pre-approved by China.

Put another way, a drowning victim does not drown any less if he is conscious of being drowned. But maybe he at least puts up a fight if he does not go willingly. So far, Hollywood, except for a few maverick film directors like Quentin Tarantino who seems more than willing to swim upstream, continues to not put up much of a fight as the water rises above its head.

But let's not get too ahead of ourselves in this modern-day, cautionary tale.

If there is any chance of combatting the insatiable Chinese dragon, then one must first know how it came to be and how it can be vanquished. Or, at least tamed.

CHAPTER 1

CRISIS AS OPPORTUNITY: A THREE-HEADED CINEMA

HONG KONG, CHINA, TAIWAN

危机

While early Chinese cinema struggled to develop with chaos, foreign and domestic, swirling all about, on the other side of the planet, a magical place called Hollywood was attracting talented and visionary filmmakers, actors, cinematographers, producers, and venture capitalists to make movies under relatively, serene, stable circumstances. The ideal situation from which to build an entertainment empire.

How a sleepy little town in southern California called Hollywood, founded in 1925, the same year that Charlie Chaplin's *The Gold Rush* premiered, became the cinematic epicenter of the world is, indeed, an astonishing story. Celebrating the talent, the vision, and the technological prowess of these early, film entrepreneurs seems fitting, even obligatory.

Of course, Hollywood movie magic has always been part good fortune. And well before Hollywood dazzled audiences with its irresistible storytelling and star power, this American success story also enjoyed several inherent advantages which its early global rivals like China, did not.

Time. Space. And Distance. Just to name a few.

Hollywood had the time to develop, innovate, experiment, fail and ultimately, succeed without much, if any governmental oversight, regulatory laws, or other, externally imposed deadlines.

Especially in its early days, the only deadlines, or regulations Hollywood faced were largely self-imposed. And those were market driven. More movies meant more money.

Hollywood also had the space, literally and figuratively, to grow. Decades before digital and even before portable cameras, Hollywood enjoyed unlimited physical space to build numerous and massive sound stages throughout California. Under sunshine and palm trees came epic blockbusters, rough and tumble westerns, silly comedies, sassy romances, film noir thrillers. Long before the US HUAC "invited" the leaders of Hollywood to DC to discuss its alleged communist leanings, the film industry enjoyed unlimited political space to be concerned only with making films, putting "fannies" in the seats, and making enough profit to make more films.

Hollywood also enjoyed a sort of un-encumbered "psychic" space from any real upheaval or tumult which could have threatened its incredible growth. Even real, global events like the Spanish Civil War, the Russian Revolution, and the spread of Communism, World War I and World War II somehow managed to stay far enough away from Hollywood to not stop or even slow its charmed roll.

Only later, when its own greed, market manipulation and ideological sympathy to communism finally awakened external forces like the US Congress to look closer, did Hollywood have to even contemplate the nature of real threats to its growth. To its industry dominance.

And while a few filmmakers during this time dabbled with political and social commentary like *A Corner in Wheat* which depicted the excesses of capitalism and *The Red Man* which showed the plight of Native Americans, dominance meant churning out Errol Flynn swashbucklers, escapism, and lighthearted romantic comedies. Audiences packed theaters across America. As Jack Warner once ruefully noted, "they sit down, and my account sits up."[2]

Halfway across the world another cinematic epicenter was slowly starting to awaken and emerge.

Chinese cinema, unlike Hollywood, which until the rise of Indie filmmaking faced no real competition, domestic or foreign, was, from the start, a three-headed dragon. There was Shanghai, which, located in mainland China, oversaw the Golden Age of Chinese cinema but never enjoyed complete or exclusive industry dominance. Hong Kong, ceded to the British in 1842 because of a humiliating dynastic defeat to the British forces in the First Opium War, developed its own unique brand of filmmaking. This cinema engaged in a fierce rivalry over which would be the dominant language of film for the Chinese-speaking audience-Mandarin, preferred in Hong Kong, or Cantonese, preferred in mainland China. Ironically, Hong Kong filmmakers, whether native to it or moving there with intent, all enjoyed an artistic freedom under British rule that their Taiwanese or Shanghai cinematic brethren did not.

The third head of this three-headed-dragon, Taiwan, developed its own unique brand of filmmaking as it was conquered and controlled by the Japanese invaders from 1895, just as cinema, around the world was first starting to emerge in black and white fits and starts. For nearly 50 years, Taiwan served its cinematic Japanese masters. Later, in the years immediately after the People's Republic of China (Communist Party) victory over the Kuomintang Nationalists (1949) and for decades after, Taiwan endured a complete lock-down of its island and saw its filmmaking tightly controlled by the Nationalist Party who took refuge there.

So, while Hollywood enjoyed largely unimpeded growth with many of its movies of glamor and glitz reflecting this protected and privileged viewpoint, Chinese cinema grew mostly encumbered and threatened. Not surprisingly, its filmmakers and films expressed this viewpoint.

The early days of Chinese cinema saw the crumbling of the Chinese Qing Dynasty in 1911, the Xinhai revolution, the Boxer Rebellion, the rise of the Republic of China, a decades-long civil war between Nationalist and Communist forces for control over Mainland China, and not one but two costly defeats at the hands of Imperial Japan. It also saw its cinematic capital, Shanghai, partitioned into literal Chinese walls which denoted foreign control and Chinese control. A tale of two, very distinct cities confined into one, rather schizophrenic area.

So, in fairness, it is difficult, if not impossible, to at least not recognize when and where the current Chinese paranoia over foreigners and a near-obsessive need to infiltrate, monitor, and control its own citizenry began. And, how the collective consciousness of foreign resentment and xenophobia, cultivated by the Communist Party and stoked in part by Chinese Cinema, helps to give animation to modern-day Chinese imperialism and expansionism. None of which justifies it from a global perspective but then if the motives and mindset of one's rival remains cloaked in shadows it is impossible to ever confront it fully.

So, when Chinese Cinema, now mostly but not exclusively centered in Beijing, churns out heroic, historical films like *800 Heroes* about the glory of the Chinese warriors fighting the Japanese "devils"[3] with a heavy dose of revisionism and a glossy, patina of communist party glory, we, in the west, may find it hard to swallow. But we at least know why such films continue to be made. And why they continue to rule the Chinese box office.

Similarly, we also know why early American films like *The Alamo* (1960), which celebrated American heroes with a heavy dose of John Wayne revisionism were made to "give the people what they wanted"[4] and studio heads the money they needed to keep making more.

Each gives us some insight into the business of making for-profit films to a largely, domestic audience but it is only a sliver of the story to be told to describe the current relationship between Hollywood and China.

But this story of how two cinematic centers halfway around the world from each other grew up and became competitors is not just about crowd-pleasing action movies with distinctly ethnic heroes. No, the story of Hollywood and the Chinese cinema wouldn't be nearly as compelling if it was just about having different heroes and heroines. Thankfully, it's not.

In the beginning.

Shanghai.

Mysterious. Intriguing. Chaotic. Conflicted.

This "cosmopolitan metropolis," and "Paris of the East," this incredibly bustling city teeming with immigrants, refugees, and foreigners, which would become the epicenter of Chinese cinema for the first several decades of its growth began in humble surroundings.[5] Shanghai was originally a small, fishing, and agricultural port city located on the east coast of China across from the East China Sea. Throughout the Qing Dynasty (1644-1911), it grew in strategic, military, financial and cultural significance and by the late 1800s Shanghai emerged as China's most prosperous and important city. It would also become a city which in some sectors of China would never be seen as "legitimately Chinese" due to its foreign, most notably, western, influence.[6] Even at its apex of influence and power, Shanghai would never fully shake this cloak of suspicion and distrust from the rest of the mainland.

In August of 1896, in what was perhaps a telling harbinger of things to come, it was a foreigner, a Spaniard, Galen Bocca, who first introduced China to moving pictures, film. At the Xu Gardens in Xuyan, just outside of Shanghai proper, the first film (*Sing Song Girl: Red Peony*) was screened to an appreciative audience who watched in approval as they partook of their afternoon tea. About the same time, upon special invitation, Louis Lumiere, considered the inventor of modern cinematography, sent his cameraman to Shanghai. The visit was part filming, part informational sharing. These "moving pictures"[7] and the lore surrounding them soon became popular and, at least for the elite crowd, decorative tents and outdoor screens were set up for paid viewings.

The entertainment world was never again going to be the same.

Neither was China.

Just a year before this first film screening, China had suffered a humiliating and costly defeat at the hands of the Japanese invaders during the First Sino-Japanese War of 1894-1895. Both money and territory (The island of Formosa/Taiwan) was the price of peace. This was not the first nor the last such defeat during the Qing Dynasty. The scars would never fully heal.

In 1847, the Qing Dynasty suffered a swift and embarrassing defeat to the British over the opium and tea trade between their two nations. The price of peace for China was large sums of money to be paid to the English Crown annually as well as turning over the possession of Hong Kong to the British. Just a few years later, in The Second Opium War (1856-1860), China's outdated imperial guard again proved no match to the advanced warfare of the British and French naval fleets. More gold and more territory, in short, more foreign control and influence in China, was the price of peace yet again.

Domestic resentment of foreign invasion and its lasting influence had already turned to outrage and violence across China. In addition to fighting foreign invaders, the Qing dynasty was also fighting the enemy from within, finding itself trying to put down civil uprisings like The Taping Rebellion of 1850-1864 and later, The Boxer Rebellion of 1899-1901. Around the same time (1898), the Qing Dynasty experienced a true palace coup, as the Empress Dowager Cixi ended the young Emperor Guangxu's ill-fated attempted at reform (The 100 Day Reform) by placing him under house (really, palace) arrest until his death, which many believed was due to orders by the Empress to have him poisoned some 10 years later in 1908 and just a day before the Empress succumbed to old age at 73.

Talk about having all the elements of an epic drama! In fact, this and more was depicted in Bernardo Bertolucci's 1987 Academy Award winning film, *The Last Emperor*, the only movie up to that point allowed to film in the Forbidden City (Dongchen District, Palace Complex of Beijing). With formal power now resting in the very young hands of the "Boy Emperor,"[8] the much younger half-brother of Guangxu, Aisin-Gioro Pu'Yi or simply "Puyi," heir to the imperial throne, the destiny of China had been irrevocably changed. Pu'Yi was not destined to reign for long.

Many Chinese, including scholar and western-educated nationalist leader, Dr. Sun Tat-Sen, in exile at the time, and founder of the secret Chinese Revolutionary Alliance in 1905 (*Tongmenghui)* saw what had become painfully obvious to so many-The Qing Dynasty was gasping on its final fumes. Its own excesses, internal corruption, bureaucratic inefficiency, and refusal to modernize, had cost all of China dearly. The Qing dynastic dinosaur which had ruled China for over two centuries was now ripe for extinction.

By 1911, after a series of armed uprisings the stage was set for the newly formed Kuomintang or Nationalist Party founded by Sun Yat-Sen to seize power. The Qing Dynasty finally crumbled under the weight of its own venal corruption and the fervor of domestic revolutionaries who wanted a western-style democratic state assembled in its place. In fact, the "Father of China," Dr. Sun Yat-Sen, had developed three guiding revolutionary principles, which to some extent, both the Nationalists and later, the Communists would borrow freely from and adapt as their own. He even credited Abraham Lincoln's Gettysburg Address and its "Government of the people, by the people and for the people"[9] as an inspiration. The first of these principles was *Minzu Zhuyi* or an "independence from foreign domination." Centuries of suffering foreign incursion had finally led to the demise of the imperial rulers and warlords who had allowed this to go on virtually unchecked and unchallenged, even profiteering with foreigners at the expense of ordinary Chinese.

The second principle was *Minquan* or the "rights of the people" that must be preserved and finally, *Minsheng*, or prioritizing the "welfare of the worker" over all other considerations.[10] Not squarely falling into the democratic or socialist camps, Sun Yat-Sen was elected provisional president of the new Republic of China Assembly in December of 1911. However, Sun Yat-Sen, despite having cornered the Chinese market on principle and populism, lacked the military might to once and for all rid China of the Manchu Dynasty. For this, he turned to a retired military chief, Yuan Shi-Kai, who had recently, in November of 1911, been appointed Prime Minister by the surviving Empress Dowager on behalf of the child emperor, Pu'Yi.

Yuan Shi-Kai, a self-serving opportunist, saw the handwriting on the wall and entered into an armistice with the newly formed, opposition government led by Sun Yat-Sen. The ideology of the revolutionaries now became fully armed.

The last nail had been hammered into the dynastic coffin. Seeing no options, the last surviving Empress signed the formal abdication of power of the ruling Qing Dynasty on February the 12th, 1912 on behalf of young Pu'Yi. With the stroke of a pen, 267 consecutive years of Qing Dynasty rule and over 2,000 years of Chinese imperial system abruptly and permanently came to a halt.

Amid this tumultuous backdrop, with many worrying out loud what the "New China" would look like and become, filmmaking entrepreneurs like Russian-born émigré, Benjamin Brodsky, and his Chinese business partner Ren Qing Tai, saw an unprecedented opportunity. An opportunity to meet the growing demand for movies from an emerging new class of Chinese citizens and the growing foreign presence.

In 1909, as his counterparts across the globe in the serene, hills of Hollywood were starting to dot the landscape with studios and film sets, Brodsky and his partner, Ren Qing Tai founded The Yaxiya (Asia) Film Production Company in Shanghai. Just four years earlier, in 1905, *Dingjun Mountain* became the first domestic Chinese film ever made. Directed by Ren Qing Tai, the film featured then-Chinese opera singing sensation, Tan Xinpei, dressed in character as Huang Zhong from the Peking Opera of the same name. The opera and film were based on an account of the Battle of Mount Dingjun (219 AD) and an episode from the 14th century novel, Romance of the Three Kingdoms.

This film, based on Chinese Opera, was typical of what would dominate early Chinese filmmaking. For the first few decades of its infancy, Chinese cinema, especially centered in Shanghai, would show opera productions as well as adapt stories from the so-called "Mandarin Duck and Butterfly School"[11] of fiction for the big screen. These were largely fiction and romance novels but, like Chinese opera, had very distinct notions of good and evil, and socially acceptable versus unacceptable behavior, with clear consequences, usually death, for disobedience or deviancy. Early on, the Chinese viewed cinema as a very powerful tool to inform, educate and indoctrinate the masses with lessons of what was and what was not to be emulated.

If the preferred values and way of life for typical Chinese seemed clear on-screen, it was anything but, off-screen.

Student protests which had begun in earnest on May 4th of 1919 and continued well into the mid-1920s, in response to the appeasement of China to Japan's territorial demands (Japan kept its occupation of the Shandong region) challenged traditional and imperial Chinese values, beliefs and what they saw as political elitism.

Not merely protests, the May 4th Movement led to a permanent change to China's political landscape. In 1921, two May 4th leaders, Li Dazhao and Chen Duciu, founded the modern day Chinese Communist Party in Shanghai, originally with close ties to the COMINTERN which helped provide the new party with funding, resources, and strategy.

As this dynamic shook age old Chinese institutions, the struggle to control China raged on between the Nationalists, the Imperial loyalists who wanted a return to at least regional feudalism, the warlords and now the more organized and funded

Communists which were joined by former KMT progressives who had broken away from the Nationalist movement early on.

Despite this hyper-instability, or perhaps in part, because of it, Chinese cinema continued to grow.

In numbers, popularity, influence and even in social criticism of contemporary China.

In 1927, the same year of the Shanghai Massacre where KMT conspired with the notorious "Green Gang" to kill hundreds of Chinese Communists at the Port of Shanghai, there were 179 Chinese owned film companies. While Chinese opera and fictionalized romance still dominated this fledgling film industry, there was the emergence of a new film genre which was already competing for top billing.

And, led by film studios like The Tianyi Film Company (The Shaw brothers), a new-old art form was gaining in popularity on-screen. This was referred to as Wuxia (Wu=martial or armed and Xia=chivalrous or heroes) or fantasy swordplay and martial arts action genre.

Adapted from a long and rich line of Wuxia literature, films like *The Swordsman Li Fei Fei* (1925) and *The Burning of the Red Lotus Temple* (1928) not only helped the emerging cinema of China grow but studios like Mingxin and later, Lianghua, become industry powerhouses.

Tianyi studios proved especially adept at making dramatic and (for that time) quite believable choreographed fight sequences and sophisticated stunts using wire and trampoline assisted acrobatics, as well as sped-up camera techniques. Both combined to dazzle early audiences.

However, this new-old genre was viewed as a threat by the emerging new Republic of China and its governing party, the Kuomintang.

Why?

What was so wrong about films that mixed traditional Chinese Opera with fantasy swordplay, spirits of past warriors and heroic, mythical deeds of chivalry and courage?

Well, for one, elevating the individual, even a heroic one, over the many, the collective, seemed to fly in the face of traditional, Confucian values. Maybe worse, these heroic screen warriors, embodying the Xia or personal freedom and independence openly defied and ran contrary to the real-life teachings and doctrine of both the KMT and the emerging communist party of China. Both recognized the need to indoctrinate the nearly 500 million rural Chinese, many of whom were illiterate, into what they each viewed as the duties and responsibilities of full-fledged citizens in a "New" China.

In short, it was to be collectivism and conformity not individuality and independence that should be celebrated and emulated in all forms of media, including film.

So, while each, the KMT and Communists, wanted to instill different values into the citizenry and wanted exclusive loyalty, they agreed on one thing-the emerging film industry could be a potentially powerful medium to teach millions of Chinese their proper role in a nation that had just thrown off over 2,000 years of dynastic rule. And Wuxia films, regardless of their popularity, were viewed as anathema. The KMT in fact, banned all Wuxia films, fantasy swordplay and any film deemed not "appropriately upholding" Chinese values.[12] The KMT leadership blamed such films, especially being produced in Shanghai in the 1920s and, to a lesser extent, Beijing, for brewing anti-government sentiment and further fueling the May 4th inspired student protests and uprising.

Near the end of the decade, in 1928, the Kuomintang, now led by Chiang Kai-Shek with the passing of Sun Yat-Sen, seized full control of China. Banning Wuxia films on the mainland of China, production shifted to the British controlled Hong Kong cinema and the Japanese controlled Taiwan cinema throughout the late 1920s and well into the 1930s up to the second Sino-Japanese War of 1937.

Despite these and other restrictions placed on film production, we will see that Shanghai Cinema was on the cusp of entering its "First Golden Age of Cinema"[13] about the same time as Hollywood halfway across the world.

The Second Cinematic Dragonhead

Meanwhile, south of Shanghai along the eastern coast of China, across from the Philippine Sea and below Taiwan, the British territory of Hong Kong, which China had ceded to the Royal Crown after losing the First Opium War of 1839-1842, was also developing its own, distinct cinema.

If an industry could ever have a "King" and a "Father," one Caucasian and one Chinese, then Hong Kong cinema was just such an industry.

Ben Brodsky, who was one of the early film pioneers in Shanghai, was arguably, even more influential in helping develop the Hong Kong cinema. A cinema which would, for decades, be the third largest film center in the world after Hollywood and Bollywood (India) and the second largest exporter of films after Hollywood, especially at its peak in the 1960s and 70s with the beloved Bruce Lee martial arts films leading the way.

But before there was Bruce there was BB and company.

Arriving in China in 1909, Brodsky wasted no time in leaving his mark on this new, very fledgling film industry. That same year he produced two notable films, *Revealed by the Pot,* and *The*

Widowed Empress. Just four years later in 1913, he co-founded with Li Minwei (who would be dubbed by Chinese commentators later as the "Father of Chinese Cinema") The Huamei Film Company. Its soon produced the first Hong Kong dramatic film, *Zuangzi Tests His Wife*. This was a film of the Hong Kong based Mirror Stage Club's production of a play by the same name. Early on, Brodsky and his technical assistant, Rolan Van Velzer, a NYC based cameraman, negotiated a creative and financial deal with the Mirror Club. Brodsky's film company would have full access to the actors, props, and equipment for filming and in exchange they would finance the stage productions by the Club.

It seemed to work out well for both.

But Brodsky and his Chinese colleagues had even more lofty goals in mind.

The same year (1913), The Huamei Film Company was founded, Brodsky also established the Variety Film Exchange Company and the Variety Film Manufacturing Company, in part, setting up a film laboratory at an abandoned warehouse with equipment bought and borrowed from NYC.

Taking it one step further, Brodsky along with 9 Chinese Board of Directors which included economists, businessmen and high-ranking government officials, founded The Chinese Cinema Company (1914). An ingenious business model in many ways, Brodsky in part, helped to legitimize film as a viable industry, worthy of close business and governmental sectors' support and sponsorship.

Shortly thereafter, Brodsky produced his first original film, *The Sport of Kings* (1914), a depiction and celebration of Hong Kong's annual horse race and the international attention and prestige it attracted. This film, along with the Chinese Government sponsored *A Trip Through China* (1916), (Yuan Shi-

Kai personally endorsed the film and had his three sons take part in the documentary) helped catapult Brodsky in the public arena and earned him accolades. The Chinese media at the time dubbed him the "King of Chinese Cinema."[14]

But the "King" had an unfulfilled dream. He wanted to produce a grand, epic film, a "Ten-Reeler" like D.W. Griffith's *The Birth of a Nation* (1915), the controversial yet still significant motion picture depicting Black-White relations during the American Civil War. Brodsky's film would give similar treatment, at least in scope, to China, a sort of "Birth of China." However, the death of his chief sponsor in 1916 (Yuan Shi-Kai) and the ongoing struggle between 1917-1928 for control of China, which included Chinese warlord violence and pitched battles between dynasty loyalists and the KMT Nationalists soured Brodsky on China. At the onset of violence, Brodsky chose to relocate to Japan for several years and showcase the reviled Japanese in his next film projects.

However, the "King" had a more than able "Court."

Led by the Li brothers (Li Minwei, Li Beihai, and Li Haishan) who founded the China Sun Film Company (Minxin) in 1923, making it the first fully owned Chinese film venture, Hong Kong cinema proved to be in good hands.

It did, however, continue to face stiff hurdles. Films in Cantonese were banned on the mainland by the KMT and competition from Shanghai was intense.

For example, Minxin (not to be confused with the Shanghai-based, Mingxin) set about to film an epic adventure story based on the Mulan ancient poem. Entitled *Mulan Joins the Army*, the idea was to bring a beloved tale to the screen while also building nationalistic sentiment for joining the military and ridding China of foreign invaders. Directed by Hou Yao, the Li brothers invested over 30,000 Yuan (about $75,000 purchasing power at the time) in the film, which had a 20-member film crew, access to 400 soldiers by the KMT and was filmed on-site, with protection assured, in Northern China.

It was indeed an epic and stirring film of its time.

However, a smaller-budgeted, similar film, shot by The Shanghai-based Tianyi Film Co., beat Minxin to the box-office punch.

Late 1927 saw the release of *Hua Mulan Joins the Army* just a few months before Minxin released its own *Mulan Joins the Army*.

The upside?

Chinese audiences apparently didn't tire of *Mulan* stories either then or decades later, as 2020 saw the release of an epic, action *Mulan* film by Disney targeted for China. We'll get to why the much beloved *Mushu* character was not anywhere to be found in the 2020 version. Promise.

As the 1920s came to an end, a new film studio, Lianhua, was founded by Lai Man-Wai and Luo Mingyou. Though it was established in Hong Kong but relocated its operational headquarters to Shanghai in 1931, it is notable in that its stated mission illustrates how some, like Li Man-Wai, were already looking to supplant Hollywood as the film center of the world.

In late 1929 Lianhua took out splashy, full-page ads in trade journals calling on all filmmakers to resist the "invasion of American films"14 that were dominating the Shanghai and Hong Kong box offices. Films like Greta Garbo's *The Single Standard*, Gary Cooper's *The Virginian*, The Marx Brothers in *Cocoanuts* and of course, a mouse named Mickey in *Steamboat Willie*.

Lianhua promoted itself as a modern film company which would help create a "Chinese Hollywood."[15]

Lai Man-Wai's goal was to create an integrated management of all the elements in the film business, from script development to filming to distribution and box-office sales based on the Hollywood organizational model at that time. Towards this end, Man-Wai envisioned studios and film sets on location in Hong Kong, Shanghai, and Beijing.

Lai Man-Wai's close contacts with the Nationalists helped the studio quickly break into the "The Big 3" studios (along with Mingxin and Tianyi), but when the KMT Nationalist forces withdrew from Shanghai in late 1937 due to the Japanese invasion and occupation of most, though not all, of Shanghai, Lianhua studios along with Man-Wai's dream of supplanting Hollywood, collapsed.

The Third Cinematic Dragonhead

The *Ilha Formosa*, the beautiful island.

Situated just a little over 100 miles from the coast of Mainland China, measuring in at just over 13,000 square miles to China's 3.7 million square miles, Taiwan, aka, The Republic of China (I'll explain in a moment) sure has attracted a lot of attention over the years.

Portugal was the first European nation to explore the island in 1552. Mesmerized by its natural beauty, Portuguese sailors called it *Ilha de Formosa* (The Beautiful Island). Shortly after honoring its natural beauty in their own language, the Portuguese then conquered the island and claimed it as their own for the Portuguese crown. They ruled the island between 1554-1624. Since that period, Taiwan has lived under Dutch, Spanish, Tungning, Qing, Japanese, and Kuomintang rule. Its indigenous people even had a brief independence movement after the Qing Dynasty signed a peace treaty with Imperial Japan in 1895, which turned the island over to the Japanese. It came to be known as the

Republic of Formosa independence and lasted about as long as it takes one to ferry from Taiwan to China. Hint: Not long.

But when it comes to Taiwanese Cinema, we are rightly most concerned with, at least initially, the period of Japanese rule between 1895-1945.

Why?

Because just as Chinese cinema was beginning to emerge in Shanghai and Hong Kong, this third and final head of the three-headed dragon was being tightly controlled by a foreign entity with a wholly different and self-serving agenda.

Japan saw Taiwan as a colony of the Imperial Empire of Japan. Consequently, they also viewed the emerging film industry as a tool to ensure conformity of all the Taiwanese to the greater good of serving Japan. Unlike Hong Kong, which ironically enjoyed more creative freedom under British rule than their counterparts in Shanghai did under first, the KMT and then, the Chinese Communists, Taiwanese filmmakers enjoyed no such creative space to operate and grow. Independent film studios did not thrive in Taiwan and the films the Taiwanese watched were almost all imported from Japan, Mainland China, or Hollywood.

Homegrown films were produced under Japanese control and were intended to teach the Taiwanese how to become proper Japanese citizens and to appreciate its culture, traditions and the behavior expected of all Japanese.

An early example was *Eyes of Buddha* (1922). This film told the story of a young Taiwanese virgin who is rescued from the evil clutches of a corrupt Chinese government official by a young, heroic Japanese soldier. As the Chinese official "savagely attempts to marry the girl, he is frightened away by the flashing eyes of a nearby statue of Buddha."[16]

A later, semi-documentary film, shows the "savage and uneducated Taiwanese,"[17] accepting supervision from a Japanese policeman and learning and modeling the proper behavior expected of all Japanese imperial citizens. It also depicts how Taiwanese farmers who adopt preferred farming techniques taught by their Japanese overlords prosper and those that do not, fail.

Another technique employed by the Japanese for over three decades towards these same ends was the use of a *Benshi* or in Taiwanese, a *Benzi* when showing films. The *Benzi* was a live narrator who would instruct the audience how to react during the film and what lessons to take and apply from each film. Audience members who did not follow the *Benzi's* instructions or seemed indifferent were removed for more strict teachings elsewhere.

Decades later, Taiwanese filmmakers would re-visit both the Japanese attempt at forced cultural annexation as well as the abuses during the KMT imposed martial law on Taiwan in films like *City of Sadness* (1989), *The Puppetmaster* (1993), and *A Borrowed Life* (1994).

Without getting too far afield too fast, let's just say this-Given the incredible challenges which the Taiwanese historically faced, it's astonishing that their cinema has yielded both the highest grossing foreign language film ever in the US and another of its films voted as the Greatest Chinese film ever (*Crouching Tiger, Hidden Dragon*, and *City of Sadness*).

Carefully placing the three heads of the dragon back together to make it whole once more, the early days, especially the 1920s, saw Chinese cinema start to come into its own. While still dominated by Chinese Opera and Wuxia with some light comedies thrown in for good measure, and still reliant on American films to meet growing demand, Chinese cinema was already taking calculated steps to become independent.

Fears that Hollywood would re-shape China in its "morally bankrupt and sinister, western view"[18] were, by the end of the decade, fast becoming unfounded.

As scholar Zhian Qian, argues;

"The promotion and consumption of American films in the 1920s in Shanghai at least, did not result in a homogenous American culture. The Chinese re-deployed, re-invented and appropriated American (Hollywood) films for local political, cultural, and social purposes."[19]

A clear example of what would become a case of Chinese appropriation and re-invention for its own "local" purposes is the 1928 Hollywood Fox Film *Street Angel.* Starring Janet Gaynor, the film tells the story of a prostitute in an abusive situation who struggles to pay rent and set aside enough money to buy medicine for her dying mother. Befriended by a street painter, she tries to escape her surroundings. At its core, it is a story of a corrupt and abusive system that offers very little real options for many to succeed, especially, women.

In 1937, Mingxin Film Studios, a studio which became very closely tied to leftist and Communist leaning films, released its own *Street Angel,* starring Xuan Zhao and Huishen Zhao. But this time the film told the story of a prostitute and her would-be singer sister, struggling against local, abusive street scoundrels and a repressive landlord, set in "Old Shanghai." The movie illustrated the clear gulf between the classes in Shanghai at the time (rich and poor, foreign, and Chinese) and tried to show the western colonialism prevalent in Shanghai with its segregated "foreign concessions," as well as a corrupt system that offered few legitimate options for women seeking a better way of life.[20]

In 2005 the Chinese Mingxin version of *Street Angel* was named one of the top 100 Chinese films of all time at the 24th Hong Kong Film Festival.

This wasn't the first nor last time that Chinese filmmakers appropriated, re-invented, and then re-deployed Hollywood film exports to better serve local, Chinese purposes.

As the 1920s ended, Hollywood's box office champs included the previously cited, a mouse (Mickey Mouse in *Steamboat Willie*), a recluse (Greta Garbo in *The Single Standard*), a Virginian (Gary Cooper), the Brothers Marx (no relation to Karl) in *Cocoanuts*, and a young girl who sees visions and saves France (*The Passion of Joan of Arc*).

To pick up on my previous "spoiler alert," the ending of the 1920s for Chinese Cinema ushered in its own "First Golden Age of Cinema"19 in about as tumultuous a time as could be imagined.

CHAPTER 2
THE FIRST GOLDEN AGE OF CHINESE CINEMA: THE JAPANESE CRASH THS PARTY

Hong Kong may have enjoyed more creative freedom, but it was still greatly hampered by producing films in Mandarin, and Wuxia (fantasy films), both things banned by the KMT across mainland China. Taiwan still labored under the thumb of its Japanese overlords, it would take decades for it to find and fully express its own voice. So, as the 1930s began it would have to be Shanghai, that mysterious, dazzling, and schizophrenic metropolis to carry the burden of growing the film industry in China. And it would not disappoint. But to say there were obstacles to overcome would be to kind of like saying that Hannibal, the Carthaginian general, not the erudite movie cannibal that scared poor Jodie Foster (and the rest of us) had a bit of a walk to endure with his elephant army before they fought the Romans.

In short, if it is true that art flourishes in times of tragedy then the First Golden Age of Chinese Cinema, (1930-1937), was all but inevitable.

First, the obstacles.

The very fragile stability that was beginning to take hold across China as the KMT strengthened its grip by 1929 began to literally go off the tracks by September of 1931.

Why?

Well, the Empire of Japan long had its expansionist eye on what was then called "Inner Chinese Manchuria"[21] or Mukden, its Manchu dynastic name. But it was largely controlled by warlords who tended to resent anyone or anything that threatened their control. One warlord in particular, Zhang Zuolin, controlled most of the territory since the end of World War I. The KMT had struck a mutually beneficial agreement of sorts with ZZ. The former did not try to militarily attack the warlord and his Manchu army, the latter served as a buffer against foreign (non-Chinese) enemies to the mainland.

Zhang had already evaded several Japanese attempts to assassinate him. But by 1928 they succeeded. The succession of power was murky at best and the Manchu warriors, while feared for their own brand of brutality were far from a modernized, fully trained unit.

In short, the prize of inner Manchuria was ripe for the taking.

On September 18th of 1931, the Japanese set in-motion a rather flimsy pretext for a military grab at territory disguised as a "response" to Chinese aggression. Suemori Kawamoto, an officer with the 29th Japanese infantry regiment, acting on orders from his superiors, had his men set dynamite to the South Manchurian Railway train tracks just outside of Mukden in the Southeast of Manchuria. It was a weak blast, not even up to the standards of one of Tom Cruise's *Mission Impossible* set-piece explosions. It didn't even interrupt railway service, but still, it did the job of its masters. The Japanese blamed Chinese dissidents of the May 4th Movement and Communist activists for this "cowardly attack"[22] and vowed swift retaliation.

Within days, the Imperial Japanese army had begun what would expand into a full-fledged invasion and conquest of inner Manchuria. Within six months they established the new "puppet state" of Manchukuo and had installed, you guessed it, the former child emperor of the Qing Dynasty, Pu'Yi, as the area's emperor. Japan would use this newly seized territory as a base of military operations for its later, more expansive invasion of mainland China in 1937.

Not content with its forced acquisition of Manchukuo, Japan quickly went further and deeper into Chinese territory. Starting with yet another "explosion incident" on January 1st, 1933, in Shanhaiguan (an area in the fortified eastern side of the Great Wall where it meets the Bohai sea), fighting quickly broke out between the Republic of China (KMT) forces and the Japanese. This time, a Japanese commander of a 200-man garrison still having a presence near the Great Wall since the 1901 Boxer Rebellion settlement, allegedly set-off several grenades and had his men shoot into the air to create a "conflict." So, sure enough fighting ensues. The Japanese Navy and air force engage and soon overwhelm the Chinese forces. Between January 1-May 10 of 1933, the Japanese push forward and eventually take the province of Rehe (a province on the Northern side of the Great Wall) and incorporate that into their newly established state of Manchukuo. Apparently, the Emperor Pu'Yi could not contain his glee at this "gift."23

Meanwhile, Shanghai, the emerging epicenter of Chinese cinema was not immune to Chinese-Japanese hostilities. In late January of 1932, organized protests broke out in the international settlement area of Shanghai (not under Chinese rule) against the Japanese invasion of Manchuria and what was seen as unchecked Japanese expansionism. Anti-foreign sentiments, already strong across China but especially intense in Hong Kong, Beijing and Shanghai were at a breaking point.

Clear enough, right? Here's where it gets muddy. The Chinese allege that the Japanese sent ultra-nationalist, militant Buddhists to the internationally controlled area of Shanghai to provoke even further violence (yep, you read correctly, militant Buddhists) and unrest there. Things got out of hand quickly. Chinese protesters apparently killed at least one of the monks while Japanese

Nationalists riot, burn down a factory and kill two Chinese in another part of Shanghai.

For the next nearly three months heavy fighting ensues between the Chinese and Japanese. An uneasy truce is finally called in early May. Not a final ending but merely a prelude of even worse hostilities to come.

Against this backdrop of violence and foreign incursion, the fledging film industry in Shanghai faced more threats from within. This time it wasn't coming from the end of a Japanese bayonet, it was from a Beijing bureaucrat with a censor's pen.

It wasn't the first time of course. Back in its infancy, in the early 1900s, the Qing Dynasty had established the Shanghai Autonomous Bureau to monitor and to ban any films considered to be "obscene." It wasn't stringently enforced though and the highly subjective nature of what was or was not "obscene" allowed for some wiggle room as well as films that were made and distributed to select theaters and districts of Shanghai.

As previously discussed, the KMT ramped up censorship efforts and categories that were to be banned in attempting to address the growing numbers and types of films, both domestic and imported. Wuxia and Shenguai (fantasy sword play and martial arts) films were specifically banned as were any films that showed "carnal desire" or advocated "superstition and unscientific thinking."[24]

One of the unintended consequences of these early censorship efforts was to encourage alternative market distribution on the part of Hong Kong filmmakers and producers as they picked up the slack of Shanghai's Wuxia films dwindling numbers. We'll see later that it wasn't mere coincidence that Bruce Lee's martial arts films originated from Hong Kong and exploded in popularity in places like San Francisco's (USA) Chinatown.

But by 1930 Chinese censorship efforts went from a somewhat subjective and haphazard approach to a serious, targeted one aimed at ensuring ideological, social, and political control by the Republic of China (ROC) through its governing party, the Kuomintang (KMT) Nationalists.

In November of that year (1930), the Chinese Assembly (Legislative Yuan) passed the Film Censorship Law. This new law spelled out in both broad and detailed terms which films, whether originating in China or being imported from places like Hollywood, would be banned and why.

Some of the criterion was highly subjective and overly broad by design. Any film that tended to or did hurt Chinese pride or in any way offended the Chinese race, went against Chinese morality and public order, taught or advocated superstition or heresy in any form as well as promote or advance Christianity was forbidden. While the ban on Christianity in films was a leftover from an earlier KMT order as well as banning the essence of Wuxia or Shenghuai films, the others were newly codified.

In addition, the Law banned any film which tended to or did violate the "Three Principles of the People" as expressed by former KMT and ROC leader, Dr. Sun Yat-Sen. Again, these were *Minzu* or a sense of civic Chinese nationalism, *Minquan* or "people power" and *Minsheng* or "social welfare for all."[25]

By January 1931, the Chinese Executive Branch (Executive Yuan) created the Film Censorship Committee with sweeping powers and authority to review and monitor any, and all films to ensure compliance with the newly passed censorship standards. By 1934, they changed the Committee to the even more bureaucratic sounding "Central Film Censorship Committee"[26] with some members now being appointed from the film industry itself. Those who did serve were denounced by colleagues who felt they had sold out their art for power.

Sound familiar? It should. As you may recall, this was pretty much verbatim what filmmakers, producers and actors thought of those who "ratted" out the "Hollywood Ten" to the US Congressional House Select Committee on Un-American Activities or HUAC, which come to think of it, is even more ominous sounding than its Chinese counterpart when it came to film censorship. And Hollywood, like their Chinese counterparts, were also trying to work within the confines of newly enacted censorship as applied by the Motion Pictures Production Code, *aka*, the Hays Code.

So, with violence, invasions, and warfare literally outside their studio doors and censorship spies peeping through their windows, it's a wonder any Chinese films got made during this period.

But somehow, art flourished.

With left leaning film studios like Linghua, Mingxin and Tianyi leading the way, the business of making film in China had, by the late 1920s and early 1930s begun to be a big and cutthroat business. Nearly 180 studios had been whittled down and consolidated into 10. There were now over 1000 movie theaters and the demand for both Hollywood imports and domestic films had never been higher.

And while the Chinese Communist Party (CCP) was on the retreat and would begin its now celebrated "Long March" (a 6000-mile trek from SE to NW China, including from Jianxi to Yan'an, Shaanxi province, fighting the troops of Chiang Kai-Shek along the way, 1934-35) which would cement Chairman Mao Zedong's leadership of the CCP for decades to come, communism in Chinese cinema was already establishing a firm foothold.[27]

Demonstrating that Mao was indeed correct that there is no such thing as art for arts' sake, the CCP early on targeted the art of filmmaking for infiltration. Throughout the 1930s the CCP helped finance budding careers to ensure that CCP members were well placed in positions as screenwriters, cinematographers, and directors. In other words, influence those in the industry who wrote, filmed, and directed what the actors would say and do on the screen.

Collectively, these filmmakers and industry professionals made up what we now refer to as the "Chinese Leftists Cinematic Movement."[28] In short, it was their aim to create films that were not for mere entertainment, but which also had a leftist and communist social, political, and cultural agenda. A message for the masses. The KMT and CCP were waging a war for the heart and soul of China and film was far too powerful an ally to ignore, or worse, allow the Nationalists to exert sole control over.

Sun Yu, a young leftist director and screenwriter was one of these at the heart of this movement. He was one of the core directors for the far-left leaning Lianhua Film company. His works during this period included *Wildflower* (1930), about an ill-fated romance between a young orphan girl and a street musician whose love is destroyed by traditional Chinese family intolerance and "misguided" values. And then they are corrupted by the Shanghai underworld with its capitalist greed and lust for power.

Daybreak (1933) also written and directed by Sun Yu, celebrates the National Revolutionary forces of the KMT making its successful 1926 northern expedition against regional warlords and feudalism. A clever film, on its surface it might seem to be supportive of the KMT and by consequence against its opposition. But as presented, the film makes clear that the next and most vital revolution is coming, and it will be a progressive (Communism) and not repressive or status quo (KMT) change.

But it is Sun Yu's 1935 work, *The Great Road* (aka, The Big Road) which cemented his legacy as an influential leftist film propagandist. Here, six men working on building an anti-Japanese, defensive highway, must learn that success against the enemy (the Japanese, but also all foreign invaders) can only come through collective (communist) action and group solidarity. There is no other option or path.

Along with *Wild Rose* (1931), *Little Toys* (1933), and those he directed post-1937, Sun Yu proved himself a master propagandist both for leftism and for his contributions to the body of films known as the National Defense Films of the 1930s and 40s.

A rival but politically like-minded Mingxin Film studios director Cheng Bugao was also busy helping to advance communist and far-left aims. His *Spring Silkworms* (1933) epitomizes this leftist cinematic movement through film. This film, co-written by Cai Cusheng and Xia Yan, both important figures in this movement, tells the story of Silkworm farmers in the Zhejiang province who desperately struggle for survival in the face of terrible market conditions as well as being sabotaged by their own traditional values and beliefs in superstition. Governmental incompetence and indifference are also a prevalent theme.

Cusheng went on to make *Song of the Fishermen* (1934), for Lianhua studios. Voted as one of China's Top 30 All-Time Greatest films, SOTF played for a record 84 straight days in Shanghai theaters. Here, the story is told through the perspective of a poor family who fish for their livelihood. Because of terrible weather, the economy and corruption, they all must sing in the streets of Shanghai for loose change to survive. There is another option of course and that is a dramatic shift in thinking and working. A shift that come only come through a revolution as powerful as a typhoon.

The mid-1930s also saw Chinese producers make good on their promise to create their own "Chinese Greta Garbo."[29] Actress Ruan Lingyu, still only age 24 but with several films on her resume, including The *Homecoming*, *Little Toys,* and *Wildflower*, was catapulted to stardom and all that it brought, good and bad, with her role in *The Goddess* (1934). Directed by Wu Yonggang for Lianhua studios, the film tells the story of a young and devoted mother who must sell her body as a prostitute in Shanghai to make enough money for herself and her infant son to survive. With a character named "The Boss," symbolizing the old and corrupt way, Ruan's Goddess (ka, *Shen'nu*, meaning both Goddess and slang for prostitute) struggles against a system that can never be fixed only replaced.

Ruan Lingyu in true "Hollywood" fashion endured increasing tabloid scandal and sensationalism off-camera as her career took off on-camera. Escaping a life of poverty, at age 16 she fled her home for Shanghai for a career in film and was soon discovered and signed by Lianhua studios. Off-camera, she was involved in a rocky relationship with a notorious gambler and womanizer who had been disinherited by his wealthy family. Tiring of supporting her lover and his luxurious lifestyle, she broke up with him to become the mistress of a very wealthy and still very-married, tea tycoon.

When she starred in *New Women* (1935), at the still tender age of 24, she was already being called the "Greta Garbo of the East,"[30] being sued by her former gambler-lover who claimed they had been secretly married, while fending off rumors that her married tycoon was domestically abusing her. Maybe it was destiny. Maybe just very clever casting. Either way the parallels between Ruan and the film's real-life inspiration, Ai Xia, were startling.

Like Ruan, Ai Xia left home at age 16 and came to Shanghai to pursue a career in film. In her case, she was escaping an arranged marriage to a much older man. She was signed on by Mingxin Studios. Like Ruan, Ai was already the subject of nasty tabloid fodder, in her case for her sexuality and her feminist streak. She starred in *A Modern Woman* (1933), the same year Ruan starred in *Three Modern Women* (1933).

Maybe it would have been best for Ruan if the parallels had ended there.

In Cai Cusheng's *New Women* (1935), Ruan portrayed Mei Wing, a character based on Ai Xia, who just the year prior, in 1934, citing abuse and depression, had committed suicide. In the film, Mei Wing achieves some overnight success as a writer just as Ai Xia had, and must raise money to help cure her sick, young child. She is manipulated by a corrupt system and a rich overlord who forces her into prostitution. In the film, Mei Wing watches helplessly as her efforts to cure her daughter fail. No longer able to bear the pain of her loss, Mei commits suicide. The movie ends with Chinese female factory workers, inspired by the life and feminist writings of Mei Wing, walking out of a factory, protesting unlivable conditions and wages.

While the film went on to become a feminist and leftist cinema sensation, Ruan was not as fortunate.

Not long after the release of *New Women*, and just shy of her 25th birthday, Ruan also committed suicide. Scandal swirled around her untimely death. Investigations found evidence she had been physically abused the night of her death and her alleged suicide note, though later brought into question, read "Gossip is a fearful thing."[31]

Ruan's legacy as a feminist icon seems even more assured as the day of her death (March 8th) coincides now with the United Nation's International Women's Day. A day set aside to celebrate female emancipation and to advocate for the end of repression and abuse of women everywhere.

China had indeed found their own "Greta Garbo of the East," but had lost her almost as quickly.

As tensions and hostilities continued to escalate between the Chinese and Japanese, Lianhua studios produced one of the more powerful "allegorical" films of the decade. *Blood on Wolf Mountain* (1936) directed by Fei Mu, who would later go on to direct what is often hailed as the greatest Chinese film ever made (*Spring in a Small Town*, 1948), tells the story of a small Chinese village that is beset and terrorized by a pack of out-of-town, blood thirsty wolves. Only by uniting, putting aside any petty or selfish interests will the village have any hope of turning back these invading animals. Given the time and context when the film was made it's tough not to "get" Fei Mu's message even if you wouldn't know an allegory if it bit you in the behind.

One of the last leftist films to be made before much of the film industry would "go dark" because of the coming second Sino-Japanese War, was *Crossroads* (1937). A Mingxin release, this film tells the story of young graduate students coping with worldwide economic depression and life under the threat of foreign incursion. Though one of its main characters, Xu, sees no way out and commits suicide, the remaining four students and friends are optimistic that under a new system (communism), happiness and opportunity will soon flourish.

Interestingly, during this same time, one of the only Chinese films to be screened in the US during the 1930s was *Song of China* (1935). It was a mostly propaganda piece for Chiang Kai-Shek and the KMT and positioned him and the Nationalists as perhaps the only real and best hope for a new and prosperous China. American audiences polled, not surprisingly, were solidly behind the Chinese Nationalists and Chiang Kai-Shek in their struggle against Mao's communists.

As far as films being sent to China from Hollywood, it was a much different story.

From 1930-1937 alone, Hollywood made nearly 50 films where China, specifically Shanghai and to a lesser extent, Hong Kong, was the primary setting. Mostly sympathetic to the "rebels" of the ongoing struggle between the KMT and the Communist rebels, the films portrayed China as exotic, romantic, and intriguing with an underbelly of crime and corruption midst a revolutionary upheaval.

Americans were often featured as well-meaning missionaries, military men rooting out crime, visionary pilots trailblazing new global routes, and in some instances, virtuous women breaking up illegal alien smuggling rings.

Some notable films included: *Shanghai Express* (1932) featuring Marlene Dietrich as Shanghai Lily, Swedish-Actor Warner Oland as Henry Chang (Oland would go on to play Honolulu Detective Charlie Chan in numerous franchise films) and the first Chinese-American film star Anna May Wong (born Wong Liu Tsong) as Hui Fei. *Bitter Tea of General Yen* (1932) which addressed the first interracial sexual attraction between Barbara Stanwyck's character, and a Chinese General played by Nils Asther, aka, "The male Greta Garbo,"[32] *Oil for the Lamps of China* (1935) which pitted a greedy, capitalist American company against a virtuous underdog (Pat O'Brien) and his young, communist assistant (Willie Fung) and the latter's quest to keep the lamps burning in China during the civil war.

Finally, Pearl S. Buck's much celebrated *The Good Earth* (1937) portrait of rural, traditional Chinese and the saving grace of a true, hearty, and resilient Chinese woman in the face of war and famine.

It wasn't too hard to tell which side Hollywood was on in the Chinese conflict.

Nor should this shock anyone.

As discussed earlier, the 1930s saw the continued deepening of communist sympathies and ties to the Communist International or COMINTERN in the American film industry, especially among its screenwriters, producers, and directors. The Communist Party of the USA formed the first-ever Hollywood Chapter in 1935, and the CP International helped fund "Popular Front" organizations throughout Hollywood which attracted the skills, time, and pocketbooks of several film heavyweights, including the so-called *Comisar*. This deepening of communist sympathies may have been best exemplified by John Howard Lawson, aka, "The *Comisar*," who, according to many at the time, "called the shots in Hollywood for the Kremlin."[33] He co-founded the leftist Writers Guild of America (WGA) and along with others like writers Dalton Trumbo, Lester Cole, Ring Lardner Jr., and director Edward Dmytryk, would lead the way in Hollywood to raise money and awareness of the leftist struggle in Spain, the coming fascism of Nazis and Hitler, and later, help shape the growing legend of the emerging leader of the Chinese Communist Party, Mao Zedong.

Even James Cagney, the Yankee Doodle Dandy himself, found himself "caught up" in the communist net of seduction and allure.

Yet, the business of Hollywood required putting paying "fannies in the seats" and that meant giving the people what they wanted. So, yes, Hollywood managed to make social commentary and interject its ideological sympathies and subtly, even not-so subtly "cheer" for the team they wanted to win but the 1930s Golden Age of Cinema in Hollywood meant large doses of escapism, romantic comedies, adventure, and fantasy fun.

So, movies like *The Wizard of Oz* (still the most watched movie ever), *Gone With The Wind*, *Robin Hood*, *The Buccaneer, The Three Musketeers*, *It Happened One Night*, *Philadelphia Story*, *Mr. Smith Goes to Washington*, *King Kong* and *Snow White and the Seven Dwarfs* along with stars like Judy Garland, Gary Cooper, Mae West, Fred Astaire and Ginger Rogers, Cary Grant, Clark Gable, Spencer Tracy, Katherine Hepburn, The Marx Brothers and Shirley Temple and her *Good Ship Lollipop* ruled the decade.[34]

In short, moviegoers in America didn't plunk down their hard-earned money to sit in a darkened theater next to strangers to be reminded of the depression, political upheaval and violence that was sweeping across the globe. With all this scary stuff in the real world, well, many simply wanted to be scared. But for fun only.

So, while the leftists in Hollywood may have swallowed hard as they typed out the scripts, it was still the decade of the studio system and the Big Three (Warner Brothers, MGM, and Paramount) continued to call the shots with Universal, Columbia and Disney studios hot on their heels.

Horror films it was then, with Boris Karloff leading the way, *Frankenstein*, *Bride of Frankenstein*, *Dr. Jekyll and Mr. Hyde*,

Vampyr and *The Hunchback of Notre Dame* all helped round out Hollywood's first Golden Age of Cinema both at the domestic and global box office.35

Yet, there was also no denying that change, dramatic change was coming. And soon. To Hollywood and to China. And it was making its way along the Marco Polo bridge towards Shanghai.

Sino-Japanese War: The Sequel

Between 1931-1937, The Empire of Japan continued its incursion into Chinese territory. Using its newly acquired state of Manchukuo as a base of operations, Japanese forces continued to encroach into the northern regions of Beijing and Tianjin, both sitting just south of Manchukuo. Forced relocation of thousands of refugees and Japanese citizens into the Manchukuo area was also designed to consolidate this area and fortify it against any possible counterinsurgency by the Chinese.

But subtlety was not part of their plan. And both the KMT Nationalists and the Chinese Communists, locked in their own internal civil war since 1927, realized that neither was guaranteed survival against continued Japanese expansionism if they remained divided. So, while it may have taken one of Chiang Kai-Shek's own field marshals to kidnap him so he could have some "quality" time to think it over, soon after, he approved a truce in late December of 1936 between his forces and Mao Zedong's Communists.

But the Japanese forced the Chinese to go one better.

On the evening of July 7th, 1937, a Japanese force which was occupying Fengtai, an area about 9 miles north of the Marco Polo (Lugou) bridge which connected into downtown Beijing, demanded entry into nearby Wanping. Apparently, the Japanese believed that one of their soldiers had gone missing into this tiny, walled town (Wanping) and wanted to conduct a door-to-door search. The Chinese guarding the town refused. Again, just like in previous "incidents," here's where the two sides vehemently disagree over what happened next. The Japanese claim they were fired at first, the Chinese say they heard shots from the Japanese soldiers which initiated their return fire.

Truth, as the war adage goes, is usually the first casualty of every war.

Ultimately, it may not have mattered.

Hostilities quickly escalated into a full-blown war between the Empire of Japan and the Republic of China, the second of its kind in modern times. The Central Chinese Government issued a proclamation which ordered the folding of the Communist Red Army (CRA) into the National Revolutionary Army (NRA) to defend all of China against Japan. Awkward, right? In reality, Mao's forces with few exceptions (Battles of Taiyuan and Wuhan of 1938), practiced guerilla warfare on their own while the Nationalists fought a more traditional campaign.

With issues of fighting style of defending the mainland aside for a moment, the more modern and better equipped Japanese land, sea and air forces rapidly overwhelmed the still largely antiquated and outgunned Chinese. Within two years the Japanese had seized control of nearly all the Chinese ports, major cities as far west as Hankou, and Beijing and Tianin. Despite determined and even heroic resistance, the Chinese controlled portion of Shanghai also fell by late November of 1937. This resistance included the now legendary "800 Heroes" battle at the Sihang Warehouse in Old Shangahi, where about 400 not 800 Chinese nationalist forces fought for nearly 4 full days against overwhelming odds before a cease-fire was agreed to.36

This resistance, which some western observers just across the river from the foreign concessions side of Shanghai would call the

"Chinese Alamo"35 has been immortalized on screen in several films, including the most recent, 2020 version directed by Hu Guan (*The Eight Hundred*). It has gone on to rival even the Mulan film franchise as the biggest box office draw to a Chinese and Chinese-speaking audience. Not without controversy though, we'll discuss later why the Chinese Communist Party sought to ban portions of, and even the entire film at various points in production and release.

Another wartime incident which has drawn comparisons to yet another American incident and film, this time, *Gone with The Wind* (GWTW) was the Japanese ransacking and occupation of the capitol of the Nationalists at the time (1937), Nanjing.

The Chinese have a different name for it, they call it simply, "The Rape of Nanjing."36 And their accusations against the Japanese here tend to make, from their perspective, the burning of Atlanta during the American civil war and portrayed in GWTW as well, a bit of a campfire gone bad.

The Chinese claim that nearly 300,000 Chinese civilians and troops that had surrendered, were murdered, as well as over 10,000 women raped and beaten. All this, in addition to claims that the Japanese had burned and laid waste to the city.38

While the Japanese still dismiss such claims as "wartime propaganda,"37 even today, one thing is clear, its memory has been burned into the psyche of the Chinese through films both commercial and documentary, formal anniversaries, books, teachings, and ceremonies. All these sources serve to powerfully reinforce and remind everyone of the savagery and brutality by the Japanese invaders at the expense of the Chinese. The "Rape of Nanjing"39 being the most notorious of many violations.

By 1938 the important trading port of Canton (Guangzhou) fell. By late 1940, the Japanese controlled most of Manchuria, Peking (Beijing), Nanking (Nanjing), Shanghai and Taiwan.

They reduced major parts of Shanghai to rubble. While the foreign concession areas remained largely intact, the Japanese increasingly tightened their hold. Private residences and villas were confiscated into wartime brothels, gambling centers and opium dens. British, American and Netherland citizens were forced to wear the letters B, A or N on their clothing in public. And though Jewish refugees initially had fled to Shanghai from Hitler's Germany, the Japanese under pressure from Hitler also rounded up Jews from the so-called "Jewish Ghettos" of Shanghai. Many were then executed on the spot or detained and relocated to Germany for "proper execution."[40] The atrocities committed by the Japanese during their occupation would later be powerfully portrayed in movies like *Purple Mountain* (2008).

As the Nationalist army retreated both west and south and the communists fled to the rural areas to continue strategic guerilla warfare resistance, the war came to a bit of a stalemate. The Japanese had seized control but had not achieved a full conquest. Vastly superior by land, sea, and air, they could and were bombing the Chinese population at will, but the sheer vastness of China with its decentralized command made it difficult for the Japanese to fully consolidate all its military gains.

Yet, by 1941, shortly after the Japanese bombing of Pearl Harbor (December 7th, 1941) when US aid finally began to flow to the Chinese, Japan had nearly destroyed the three-headed cinematic dragon.

Pre-war, major Shanghai film studios like Tianyi were destroyed. Leftist and Communist backed filmmakers fled the city. More conservative or Nationalist filmmakers made their way to the new KMT capital of Xinhua in Nanjing, after that fell, to Shengzhou. Xinhua remained the only major film studio standing. Operating from a small portion of Shanghai not fully controlled by the Japanese, the aptly nicknamed "Orphan Island,"[41] Xinhua, founded in 1934 and one of the most leftist studios of all, was able to produce the 1939 hit *Mulan Joins the Army* and a batch of national defense films aimed at resisting Japan and calling for a new communist regime until it ceased production in 1942.

Hong Kong, the second head of the Chinese cinematic dragon, formally surrendered to the Japanese just 18 days after Pearl Harbor. The Japanese seized the remaining archives and stock of film strips and melted them down for silver nitrate, a useful element in making military weapons. The Hong Kong film industry ceased to exist during the Japanese occupation.

Taiwan, the final head of the dragon, already under Japanese control, was restricted even further. Only a few films were produced and those were by the Japanese or at the specific orders of the Japanese. These films were either propaganda for the Japanese war effort or educational, aimed at ensuring the complete assimilation of the Taiwanese into the Japanese Empire.

These were indeed the darkest of the dark days of Chinese cinema.

Meanwhile, the sun could not have been shining much brighter on Hollywood.

While the HUAC hearings, the Hollywood Ten, McCarthyism and the Cold War all loomed on the near horizon, Hollywood didn't just survive the war years, it thrived. Attendance was at an all-time high, the big screen was making even bigger stars out of Bogie and Bacall, Stewart and Stanwyck, Rita, Lana, and Ingrid while directors Orson and "Hitch," were changing the way we saw movies. In just five years (1941-45), studios struck box office gold with films like *Citizen Kane* (1941), *The Maltese Falcon* (1941), *Casablanca* (1942), *Yankee Doodle Dandy* (1942), *Shadow of A Doubt* (1943), *To Have and Have Not* (1944), *Double Indemnity* (1944), and *Spellbound* (1945).

In fact, of the Top 100 Films of all time ranked by The American Film Institute, Hollywood during the war years can boast of landing 9 films in the top 100, and of having the #1 and #3 all-time greatest films (*Citizen Kane*, starring and directed by Orson Welles, and *Casablanca* starring Humphrey Bogart and Ingrid Bergman).

Like Kirk Douglas in the post-war film *Champion*, Hollywood welcomed the post-war years as the undisputed worldwide champ of modern cinema while its Chinese rival lay flat on its back on the canvas.

However, the smelling salts were provided in the form of an allied victory. Once the Japanese surrendered in 1945, Chinese cinema showed signs of life once again. In fact, despite the KMT re-establishing control in Shanghai, seizing all Japanese film studies as "enemy property," and re-instating its pre-war censorship, what filmmakers referred to as the "white terror," filmmaking thrived, at least briefly in a post-war China.[42]

Nationalist filmmakers emerged in Hong Kong and Taiwan, the latter now under KMT control, while leftists and pro-communist filmmakers found work at sympathetic film studios like Lianhua (which would become Kunlun Studios). KMT itself sought to dominate the film industry with its ownership of the newly created Central Film Studios 1 and 2, which produced strong Nationalist propaganda films and anti-communist "teaching" films.

But it was two Shanghai-based film directors and two Shanghai film studios that led the revival of Chinese cinema.

At the direction of Zhou Enlai, the number two communist party leader behind Chairman Mao Zhedong, a new film studio, called Kunlun Film Company was created in late 1946. Staffed with and led by communist party approved members, Kunlun was a melding of the former Lianhua studios and at least 7 other smaller, independent studios. All pro-communist party, all with a strong political agenda to get on the big screen.

Anticipating a People's Republic of China (communist) victory over the Republic of China's Nationalists and the Western, US-backed Chiang Kai-Shek, the PRC wanted to ensure dominance if not complete control of the film industry on the mainland immediately during the victory transition.

The same year Kunlun Film Company (KFC) was created, their plan was off to a very promising start.

The Spring River Flows East (1947), directed by leftist filmmakers Zheng Junli and Cai Cusheng, produced by KFC, was based in part on an ancient Chinese poem:

"How much sorrow can one have to bear?

As much as a river of Spring Water flowing East."43

The film, which was quickly proclaimed as "China's very own *Gone with the Wind*,"42 was indeed, a sweeping epic of a movie with a running time of well over 3 hours with an intermission. The film depicts the struggles of a young couple and their family, first, under Japanese occupation, then under repressive Nationalist corruption. Part One (Eight War Torn Years) focuses on the destruction and cruelty under the Japanese, Part Two (The Dawn) offers an ironic twist, a bittersweet chance at reunion for the young couple, whose lives now have been irrevocably changed by the war.

By the time the female lead Sufen (Bai Yang) declares that "Our generation will have to sacrifice, break away from the past so that he (their son, Kansheng) can have a better world,"[44] the film has made it abundantly clear that the Japanese are evil invaders, the Nationalists corrupt and opportunistic and that the real hope lies in a new way, a collective and unifying way (the PRC).

The movie played at theaters for three continuous months and an estimated 750,000 moviegoers came, both records for Chinese cinema at the time.

As the civil war between US-backed Chiang Kai-Shek's Nationalists and Soviet-backed Mao Zedong's Communists raged on, Wenhua Studios, which rejected the purely good v. purely evil narrative of Kunlun Films, took over the box office in 1948. Their surprise hit film *Spring in a Small Town*, directed by Fei Mu (*Blood Mountain*) was made on a shoestring budget and had only 5 cast members.

Despite these limitations, the film was proclaimed as the greatest Chinese film by the Hong Kong Film Critics Society in 2005. Fei Mu takes a minimalist plot of a family living in the ruins of their family compound post-Japanese occupation in Jiangnan Region (it encompasses the city of Shanghai) and infuses the film with both traditional Confucian values and progressive feminism. It portrays Shanghai as a broken city, gray, lifeless with simmering passion and longing bubbling below the surface.

It was this lack of dominant leftist politics and absence of Communist idolatry that no doubt caused the CCP to label the film as "reactionary and rightists in its politics."[45] Neither of which bodes well for any filmmaker post-Chinese civil war. In fact, despite Fei Mu's standing as a film grandmaster and his previous films likening the hated Japanese to bloodthirsty wolves, he would find himself the target of persecution in one of Mao's seemingly endless purges and cultural revolution years later. Fei Mu would flee to Hong Kong for safety to wait out the political "storm."

The following year (1949), Kunlun Films once again ruled the Chinese cinema.

Crows and Sparrows, an allegorical film directed by Zheng Junli, portrayed the greedy and corrupt KMT officials seeking to sell an apartment building and toss the poor renters onto the streets as the crows and the normal but helpless citizens being tossed out as the sparrows.

The film is unrelentingly negative of both the Japanese and the KMT party officials who collaborated with then during the war. And at the time of filming, as the civil war was beginning to come to an end, it portrays Nationalists as desperately seeking to maintain their former luxurious lifestyles at the expense of the poor but honest Chinese.

The film almost didn't get made.

Though the civil war was winding down and more and more it was becoming obvious that the KMT was on the losing side, it still asserted censorship over films and controlled the release and distribution of all films.

Junli and his screenwriter, Che Becheng, were able to skirt around such censorship as they gave the official, much-diluted screenplay to KMT censors and then filmed the actual screenplay in secret. To avoid scrutiny, a portion of the movie was filmed underground and in the evening. Only after the KMT control of Shanghai crumbled in 1949 did the crew come above ground and shoot the remaining scenes during the day and use natural sunlight.

Years later, when the Chinese Ministry of Culture awarded the film second prize at a prestigious competition both Zhou Enlai and Mao were displeased. They both were convinced that the courage of the film crew and its powerful story which not only excoriated the KMT but praised the Communists deserved first place. Apparently, the Minister of Culture could take a "hint." *Crows and Sparrows* was quickly named the winner and its previous rating was blamed on a "misunderstanding."

Its director (Junli) and his screenwriter (Becheng) though must have wished their being branded traitors by the ruling Communist Party was also merely a "misunderstanding."[46]

Both were eventually tortured and died in prison at the hands of their communist captors for supposed "mistakes," and lack of "absolute ideological purity" of communist thought.

For Junli who directed some of the most virulent and anti-Japanese films produced in Chinese cinema and infused his great works with pro-communism principles and vision, well, his "mistakes" included supporting the release of the film *The Life Wu Xun* directed by Sun Yu.

This film, released in 1950, was based on the true story of Wu Xun, a liberal educator during the Qing Dynasty who raised money for years through begging and then used that money to build a school for indigent and illiterate Chinese children. He was, for years, a beloved and admired figure in Chinese history.

But where others saw a noble and inspiring leader and example to follow, Mao's communists saw a threat.

Mao Zedong attacked the film upon its release, arguing that by encouraging the masses to revere the main character of the film it diminishes the great communist revolution. In fact, Mao went on to assert that the film implied that the great revolution and victory of communism was not even necessary. Not with such figures like Wu Xun begging for money and exploiting his benefactors.

Mao's wife and her close advisors quickly joined in the chorus of communist critiques of the film and its "secret" meaning. They found the worshipping of such figures during the Qing dynasty immoral and unacceptable.

While they were at it, his attackers took a closer look at one of Zheng Junli's earlier films, *The Married Couple*. Apparently, on second glance they found issues. Of course, they did.

Taking his cue from none other than Mao, who criticized communist officials who took mistresses while extolling the virtues of family and stability, Junli's film showed the damage which such infidelity caused to all involved. Or as it was called, "succumbing to the sugar-coated bullet (mistress)."[47]

Still, the many communist party officials who were engaging in such infidelity certainly didn't appreciate Junli's film. They couldn't really attack Mao, certainly not openly, so Junli became an easy target for their anger. The communist playbook for eliminating any critic employed a familiar and time-proven method-Label him as a "traitor," force him to admit his mistakes and then kill him anyways.

After being tortured while held captive, Junli died in 1969.

His confidante and screenwriter, Chen Baichen suffered a similar fate. He was imprisoned, tortured, and died for committing unforgivable "mistakes."[48]

Just one year prior to Junli's death, his colleague and co-director of *Spring River Flows East*, Cai Cusheng, were jailed by the CCP and forced to admit his "mistakes" and then punished for his lack of absolute ideological purity. These mistakes may have included fleeing to Chonqing (KMT Capitol) and working at the Nationalist Central Film Studio 1 during part of the Japanese occupation as well as helping launch a Mandarin language cinema in Hong Kong. None of which was approved by the Party leaders.

Cusheng, long revered as a beacon for progressive cinema, the director of beloved, pro-worker film *The Song of the Fishermen* and the only Chinese filmmaker to ever win an International Film Award (Moscow) at the time, died in 1968 after being tortured by his Communist captors.

In a strange twist, his ashes are now kept at the famed Babaoshan Revolutionary Cemetery in Beijing. This cemetery is reserved for only the highest-ranking revolutionary heroes and those individuals who made major, positive contributions to Chinese society.

Apparently, Cusheng was honorable enough to be "buried" alongside other revolutionary heroes, but not honorable enough to be allowed to live.

Mao's Communists Take Control, Chiang's KMT Flees to Taiwan

Unlike say, the American Civil War, which always envisioned a life after the war with both the warring sides playing important if not, equal roles in the rebuilding of the nation, neither the KMT nor the CCP was designed to operate within a two-party system. For one to ascend and assert control the other had to descend, or, in the Chinese case, be destroyed.

For a brief moment, there seemed some hope their shared hostilities might end in peace and defy the odds.

Shortly after the surrender of Japan to the allies, the CCP and the KMT entered into negotiations to explore a peaceful outcome of their ongoing civil war. With the backing of the US, the KMT and their primary negotiator, Wang Shijie and the CCP and its representative, Zhou Enlai, met over a period of nearly six weeks, starting on August 29th and ending on October 10, 1945.

Away from the negotiating table, the two sides continued to wage war.

Finally, on October 10th, the two leaders, Chiang Kai-Shek of the KMT Nationalists and Mao Zedong of the CCP People's Army met in-person. This would mark the last time they would meet in-person, the first such meeting in over 20 years.

The negotiations culminated with an agreement, known as "The Double-Tenth Agreement," (10/10 or October the tenth) where both sides agreed at least in principle to recognizing the legitimacy of the other and agreeing to at some future date, forming a governing coalition.[49]

In response, the US sent General George Marshall to help mediate a peaceful transition from civil war to peaceful governance. While the US had supplied the KMT with over 50,000 troops and some $4.5 billion in aid during the Sino-Japanese war, in recognition of this agreement, the US banned any further aid or weapons to either side.

Hailed as a new and peaceful era for all of China, the euphoria would not last long.

The civil war worsened. Both sides dug in. Mao referred to the negotiated and signed agreement as a "mere scrap of paper."[50] By early 1947, the US and the "Marshall Mission"[51] ended. The General came home, empty handed. US officials feared that the corruption, wartime mismanagement and strategic blunders by the Nationalists along with the growing support of the Communists with the average worker and peasant across China might spell doom for any hope of a democratic China.

Pessimism for the prospects of a future Chinese democracy or even a democratic-socialist nation would soon turn to realism.

In November of 1948, the People's Army launched the final large-scale, military campaign of the Chinese civil war, known as the Huahai campaign.

As the communists advanced to Shanghai, the Nationalists imposed a martial law across the city, summarily rounded up and executed known or suspected communists and emptied out the Shanghai bank, fleeing to Taiwan with gold. The end was near.

On May 27th, 1949, after 10 straight days of brutal fighting, the Communists seized control of Shanghai.

Nationalists and suspected Japanese collaborators were soon rounded up. The once elegant Canidrome ballroom, where lavish parties were held and screenings of the latest popular films shown, was turned into a temporary enemy detention and execution center. Political revenge was taken on civilians, bodies piled up.

By December of 1949 virtually all of China was under communist control. Only pockets of resistance remained. Chiang Kai-Shek and the Nationalists had fled to Taiwan where they seized control and imposed martial law.

The civil war had ended in a resounding Communist victory.

The cost was high for both sides. Some 1.5 million Communist soldiers and over 600,000 Nationalists died in a civil war that had lasted over 22 years with a brief truce during the defense against the Imperial Japanese. Chinese civilians bore an even greater burden. Over 5 million civilians died during the civil war due to a combination of combat, famine, and disease.[52]

As a new decade neared, Mao and his followers envisioned extraordinary and sweeping reforms across China. Economic, agrarian, educational, social, cultural, and political. Nothing it seemed would remain as it once was.

This included seizing control of the film industry and having it now exist only to serve the glory of the communist revolution and its agenda. Mao also planned on destroying the Nationalists in neighboring Taiwan. The CCP succeeded in the former while the Korean War and the US presence in the region stymied the latter.

The age of Chinese Communism had begun.

CHAPTER 3
THE CCP TAKES CONTROL OF CHINESE CINEMA: HOLLYWOOD GOES BIG

Art Must Have Purpose. And That Purpose is to Glorify the Revolution

Censorship by its very nature is negative. Subtraction not addition. Under the KMT censors, Chinese filmmakers labored under a regime of strict censorship. Specific and unyielding, filmmakers knew what would be approved and what would be rejected. What would be seen, what would remain on the cutting room floor.

Within this vise-like control though, several films did push the boundaries. Aided by a cadre of leftist filmmakers, writers, actors and crew, cinema, up to and during the civil war, reflected the same political divisions and enmity which split China in two warring camps. While many films seemed united in their common hatred of the Japanese and in their desire to immortalize the Chinese as heroic defenders, what lay beyond was not uniform. Communism not Nationalism was the answer to the question as many films, some subtly, some not so subtly, made clear. Leftist filmmakers made clear that in their vision and through their films, the future in China did not hold a return to feudalism or nationalism.

Besides, as many filmmakers also came to realize, the KMT had its collective hands full. Corruption, resisting Japanese invaders, an economy in shambles, the growing threat of communism, dwindling support, particularly in the countryside, and wobbly international support, all combined to weaken KMT's grip on the arts and culture. Film, while seen as an important tool for Nationalist propaganda and Japanese defense, was not the first nor sole priority of KMT and its embattled leader, Chiang Kai-Shek.

Under the new People's Republic of China (PRC) founded in 1949 by the Chinese Communist Party (CCP) led by its Chairman, Mao Zedong, film was no longer something to simply subtract from or influence its final form through specific codes and guidelines.

Film would now play a vital role in *political addition.*

Chinese filmmakers would now become active builders in the construction of a new and revolutionary society. Revolutionary fervor must be continually fed, new heroes must be created, new stories of the proletariat uprising must be told and made legendary. Any remaining fidelity to Nationalism, however small or isolated, must be crushed forever. And Mao realized early on that art, and especially the powerful medium of film, had no rival when it came to its ability to educate, indoctrinate, and animate the masses.

The CCP under Mao would not become distracted or divided in how it would harness the power of film for the glory of the great proletarian revolution.

In short, art must never exist only for art's sake. Art could only serve one master. And that master was the CCP.

The new regime wasted no time putting cinema to work.

The CCP Central Film Bureau consolidated all the previously independent film studios under one, state-run system. In doing so, the CCP patterned its control over films from the Soviets who featured a strong, centralized control of its film industry and an exhaustive list of censorship codes and ways which its films must help the party meet its production goals.

Over the next 17 years, leading up to the Great Proletarian Cultural Revolution of 1966-1976, known as "the disaster years"[53] for film, Chinese cinema would release over 600 films, over 8,000 reels of CCP produced documentary and news films and would boast the first wide screen film, made in 1960.

With few exceptions, films would exist, would be allowed to exist, to glorify the revolution and the People's Liberation Army, the communist party, workers, peasants, farmers who met their production goals and the leader of China, Chairman Mao.

With titles like *New Heroes and Heroines*, *Arise United Toward Tomorrow*, *Flowers of the Motherland*, *Red Children* and *The Red Lantern*, films that met specific ideological criterion and not diversity of thought found an audience.

Films that offended Chinese pride, were in any way subversive to communist party ideals or did not satisfactorily serve the CCP were either never completed or ever seen on screen.

In fact, some years, cinema on the mainland would suffer through periods of film famine, with only a handful of films being approved by the CCP, other years, no new films would be released. About the only Chinese cinema which benefitted during these lean times was Hong Kong cinema. Still, the greater good, not entertainment or box office, was the goal here.

And how best to ensure this goal was met?

The new regime also wasted no time appointing one of its most fervent and skilled propagandists to direct the powerful Film Agency of the Central Propaganda Department and secured her a seat on the powerful Ministry of Culture Steering Committee on Film.

Who was to fulfill this role?

None other than Jiang Qing, who also happened to be the wife of Mao Zedong at the time.

There was a clear upside of course. Appointing his wife guaranteed that Mao would have his most loyal confidante in position of power to implement his views on art. Jiang, nicknamed "Madame Mao"[54] for her fervent and unyielding defense of all things Mao, lost no time in immediately censoring and shaping the message the masses saw and heard on all those newly built screens. Art was both political and highly personal.

Hollywood films, a symbol of western decadence and amorality were banned.

Despite these moves, Chinese filmmakers did have some reason for optimism. Maybe, they might enjoy more creative freedom under the CCP than they had under the KMT. Jiang Qing was after all, a former film actress herself. She was a contract player with Lianhua Films and played a minor role in the anti-Japanese allegorical film *Blood on Wolf Mountain* and appeared in Ibsen's stage play *A Doll's House* just a few years before meeting Mao.

She didn't even have a storied past of being a hardline communist like Mao's previous wife who was one of a very few females to have made and survived the Long March. No, coming from a bourgeois and well-to-do family, Jiang had lived the life of an intellectual, even teaching dramatic arts at college. And when she fled Shanghai in 1937 during the Japanese occupation, Jiang briefly worked for the Nationalist controlled Central Film Studio 1 in Chongqing, the KMT stronghold and capital.

If anyone could understand the need for creative freedom in film and acting who better than a former actress and intellectual? Even better, one who had worked in film for both sides of the political fence. Maybe, there was justified reason for optimism moving forward, right?

Wrong.

Almost immediately, "Madame Mao" led the charge to "purify" Chinese cinema and art. She amplified the attack on the previously beloved film *Spring in a Small Town* (1948) for its wrongful "narcotic effect"[55] on viewers and lack of optimism in the coming revolution and denounced the adoration of Wu Xun (*The Life of Wu Xun, 1950*), as dangerous and unjustified. Jiang and her allies in the Ministry of Culture and propaganda department vehemently attacked the film's message as unacceptably encouraging the adulation of an elitist (Wu Xun) and in casting doubt on the need for a worker's revolution to shed a corrupt feudalist system She saw this as betraying the spirit of the glorious uprising.

In both instances, the new Chinese film propagandist was echoing Mao's own personal and political criticisms. She also went to work targeting traditional Chinese opera for reform, both live and in film.

Concluding that Chinese Opera was far too feudalist and lacked true proletarian heroes and heroines, over the next few years, Jiang created "Model Revolutionary Operas."[56] These were to be followed and applied to all future productions. Jiang even wrote her own basic operas which glorified Mao, the revolution, and the worker. Emperors, Chancellors, feudalism, intellectuals, and other elites were forbidden. The scope of Chinese Opera reform was "as great as the great wall and even wider."56

The glorification of the worker, the peasant, the farmer and the CCP was what audiences would now see; on stage, in magazines, in comic books, on matchbook covers, even on tea-sets.

And, of course, on film.

And when it came to adapting opera for the big screen or making films from scratch, filmmakers soon found out that it was not mere words or censorship codes to follow. It was the very hands-on approach which Jiang Qing took to ensure fidelity to party goals. She would review drafts of screenplays, rewrite scripts with copious notes making "suggestions" from everything to lighting of characters like workers or peasants that needed to be lit "worthy of their heroism"[57] to reviews of entire story and character development. In Su Li's *Fight with Flood* for example, Jiang concluded that the film did not show the inherent class struggle powerfully enough and the Su Li was "too reluctant" in glorifying the worker. Even after changes were made Jiang would then use her forum as head of the film propaganda to mobilize public scrutiny and criticism against the film, all but guaranteeing that it would sink after release.[58]

As Zheng Chunqiao, a Mao loyalist and leading ideologue of the cultural revolution noted, "There is a counter-revolutionary punishment from the party for changing even one word of the model revolutionary opera into film."[59]

And for years, when it came to film, the party was personified by Jiang Qing. And her directive to filmmakers was clear, "Don't lose the shape of the model operas even a little."[60] It was said that she used feature films as the prime weapon in her arsenal of propaganda.

As for Mao, while he had made his view on art and film quite clear years before, some wondered if he even liked any of the films his wife scrutinized so closely?

Well, Mao's communist counterpart in Russia, Josef Stalin, certainly did, he was an enthusiast film fanatic. He kept his projectionist and interpreter close to him at all times in his private residence for whenever he felt like a screening. His favorite flicks were *Volga, Volga*, a Russian musical comedy about patriotic villagers, and *Tarzan: The Ape Man*, which Stalin saw as a clear rejection of American capitalism. Hitler admired Charlie Chaplin, reportedly crying over Chaplin's portrayal of him in *The Great Dictator*.[61]

Before Stalin, the world's most feared dictator, Hitler, loved Disney animated films so much that Goebbels, his Nazi Party propagandist, gave "Der Fuhrer," Mickey Mouse original film prints as a Christmas present.[62]

When it came to his own favorite film, Mao was predictably, more inspired by party message than entertainment.

For the head of the CCP it was *The White Haired Girl* (1951) which brought him to tears.

Adapted from a Chinese folktale into both opera and ballet, TWHG told the story of a peasant girl who struggles under the abuse of a capitalist landlord, fleeing the woods to survive. A year later, her hair turned white from suffering, Xi'er is seen by the landlord during a terrible storm. He mistakes her for a reincarnated spirit sent to punish him. Justice is served.

Recrafted as one of Jian Qing's "8 Model Revolutionary"[63] opera and faithfully adapted to film, now Xi'er and the long-suffering peasants join the Communist Party and become revolutionaries. The lesson? Only the communist party has the capability to destroy evil capitalism and feudalism.

Along with a similarly crafted story in *The Red Detachment of Women* (RDOW), TWHG and RDOW for years were wildly popular, on stage, in the ballet, on screen, even in radio presentations.

During Jiang's reign as head of film propaganda, her "revolutionary models" were so omniscient that a popular yet underground quip at the time was "We are a nation of 800 million people who only watch 8 stories."[64]

Outside the film bureau, the CCP was rushing forward with their ambitious and extraordinary plans to rapidly transform the nation. Between 1949-1956, the CCP seized millions of acres of land from wealthy landowners and redistributed them to the masses. Crops identified as "evil" and "capitalist" like opium were destroyed. Mao also led an accelerated transition from a largely agrarian-based economy into an industrialized one.

Or at least, that was the plan.

If, seizing farming tools, dismantling farmlands, forcing families into state-owned and state-operated communes, while directing citizens to develop backyard smelts all sounds like a good idea to you then China in the 1950s was your kind of worker paradise.

Religion and religious ceremonies were banned, replaced by community-level communist party meetings and "action committees," and the notorious Hukou or internal travel passport was reinstated to better track and monitor all movement of citizens.[65]

The plan for rapid transformation was proving to be anything but as envisioned. Production targets were being missed and the death toll due to famine and flood was rising. Criticism of Mao and the CCP policies was beginning to grow from a low rumble into an audible roar.

Yet, predictably, mainland cinema was silent on the devastation and upheaval these CCP policies were causing across China. The handful of filmmakers and CCP approved films were still too busy reliving the defeat of the Japanese and celebrating the glorious revolution.

By 1956 when *The Battle of Shanggilang* was released, which celebrated the "incredible courage of the PLA" as they fought back the "American enemy" during the Korean War, China was heading in the opposite direction of growth and prosperity.[66]

Meanwhile, Hong Kong cinema was benefitting from the tumult on the mainland.

The Shao (Shaw) brothers reclaimed their pre-war film studio (Nanyang) and over the next decade, along with their chief rival, Cathay's MPRGI films, led a rebirth of Hong Kong film. Movies like *The Purple Hairpin* (1954) and *Mambo Girl* (1957), which was a blending of pop music, comedy and action took their place alongside a bevy of low budget "B" movies with lots of Kung Fu, Martial Arts, and Wuxia or fantasy sword play flicks. Hong Kong cinema was capturing both a growing domestic audience as well as developing a loyal international following. This would set the stage, marketwise at least, for a growing demand for more martial arts films. And this demand would in turn help launch the greatest martial arts star ever, Bruce Lee, whose films dominated that genre during the 1970s and beyond.

Though Taiwan cinema was still laboring under tight KMT control, China's mainland cinematic loss was, undeniably, Hong Kong's gain.

Meanwhile, back in the states, Hollywood and government at the highest levels was defending itself from accusations that it was either a hotbed of communism activity or a safe harbor for known commies. Yes, comrades, McCarthyism was in full swing.

Though HUAC had focused a good deal of its energy and resources on Hollywood, the Senate's sister committee led by US Senator Joe McCarthy (R-WI) and Marquette University alum, took aim at the US State Department and the US Army. Waving a paper, he claimed was a list of "known communists," the junior Senator, admiringly called "Tail-Gunner Joe" by his supporters, was challenging what he saw as the dangerous complacency of America deep within its own most respected and powerful institutions.[67]

In 1950, the Congress, over the veto of then-president Harry S. Truman, passed into law the McCarran Act (Internal Security Act).

This new law gave sweeping investigative and enforcement powers to the federal government to infiltrate and take-down subversive organizations aimed at overthrowing the US. Now, communist, and other subversive organizations would have to be registered in a data base and provide financial and personal information to the US Department of Justice to comply with the law. Entrance into the US, especially by known communists or communist agitators could be lawfully denied. Though several human rights groups, including the ACLU challenged the constitutionality of this new law and its provisions, it was upheld in 1954 in the landmark case *Galvan v Press*.[68]

In short, communist, or "red" hysteria was reaching a fever pitch by the time Senator McCarthy faced off against the US military in the highly publicized US v Army Senate hearings in 1954. McCarthyism, or "America with its sleeves rolled up,"[69] was spreading fear across a divided nation.

Hollywood was no exception. Still reeling from its own self-inflicted wounds over the notorious "Hollywood Ten," it seemed like it couldn't make up its cinematic "mind" whether to play the good solder in the fight against communism ("patriotism is our business") or make subtle and sometimes not so subtle statements about fear, hysteria and ratting out your friends.[70]

This schizophrenia in the studio showed up on the screen.

Several films during the late 1940s and during the 1950s, according to movie critic and writer, Nora Sayre, "depicted communists as all deviants, hypocrites and murderers."[71] Let's see, with titles like, *I Married a Communist* (1949), *The Red Menace* (1949), *I was a Communist for the FBI* (1951), *Big Jim*

McClain (1952), where John Wayne tries to break-up a communist ring subverting Hawaiians (what?) and Elia Kazan's (who famously tattled before HUAC) *Man on a Tightrope* (1953), she may have a point. It seemed at least part of Hollywood was trying to outdo HUAC in who could be more anti-communist and hysterical with fear of a coming "red wave" on the shores of America.

On the other hand, unlike mainland Chinese cinema, Hollywood rarely, if ever, spoke as one tightly controlled voice. So, there were also anti-paranoia and even pro-communist flicks like *Viva Zapata* (1951), *On the Waterfront* (1952), a not so-subtle metaphorical film about trust, loyalty and betraying your "brother," (HUAC tattling anyone?) and a few years later, in fact, two years after Senator McCarthy's death in 1957, a more subtle film about the real danger of communism may be sophisticated corruption in Hitchcock's *North by Northwest* (1959) and may also have signaled the end of Hollywood's communist hysteria phase.

As for censorship, well, Joseph Breen, the head of the Hays Code (Motion Picture Production Code) from 1934-1954, was no Jiang Qing.

Enforcing a code of sins to avoid, originally created largely by Daniel A. Lord (what else would he be named?), Breen was more concerned with lustful or excessive kissing and using the Lord's name (not Daniel but the other Lord) in vain. Fornicating not fascism was at the top of this code's concerns. Plus, with directors like Otto Preminger beginning to push the boundaries, the rise of television popularity and lowered costs of owning a set, and the end of the studio system all combined to weaken the notorious Hays Code and its censorship power over film. While the Chinese communist grip on mainland cinema was turning into a chokehold, Hollywood would soon be liberated by the end of the hated Hays Code. By 1968 the Code was formally replaced by the MPAA, a movie rating system for audiences.

In short, you could make whatever movie you wanted, it wouldn't be some censor troll in a darkened cave peering over each frame and deciding whether your movie would ever see the light of day.

Buyer beware. Buyer decides. And the free marketplace, filled with competition not communist directives, would shape the movie universe. At least west Of Shanghai. Way, way, west.

In 1956 very few movies on the mainland made it past the film bureau of propaganda and censorship in China. The most prominent films both involved a small but heroic band of Chinese soldiers overcoming formidable odds to keep the glorious communist revolution alive. Back home, yanks would call these "formula flicks."69 In the *Battle of Shanggaling Mountain*, the Chinese are seen battling back American aggression during the latter stages of the Korean War. Just three years later, Hollywood would release "what actually happened" on that small hill, called *Pork Chop Hill* starring Gregory Peck of *To Kill a Mockingbird* Fame. The other film to make it to the Shanghai screens relatively unscathed was *Chong Po li gian de hei an* which once again re-visited the Japanese aggression and the heroism of, you guessed it, a small but heroic band of Chinese soldiers.[72]

Artistically, these were lean times.

But this same year (1956), provided some hope. A tiny opening of the door of oppressive censorship and control seemed to occur.

Inspired in part by an ancient Chinese poem, "Let a hundred flowers bloom, let a hundred schools of thought contend,"[73] and the not so ancient truth that criticism of communism and Mao's policies was beginning to crest, Mao launched what he called "The Hundred Flowers Campaign."[74]

Officially the aim of this campaign was to encourage diversity of thought, a rainbow of ideas and to foster constructive criticism of the government. A sort of political pre-emption of his most vociferous critics whose main complaint was they couldn't openly complain.

Brilliant, right?

Unofficially, some of those same critics feared that the real aim of all these flowers blooming was to get critics and dissidents to self-identify so that they could then be weeded out and *purified*.

The Chinese soon got their answer.

Within weeks thousands then hundreds of thousands of notecards and letters flooded the CCP with complaints, concerns, criticisms, and a few viable suggestions.

Scientists complained of CCP assigned monitors who suppressed knowledge and prioritized ideology well above actual scientific breakthrough or common-sense application. Lawyers complained that laws and much needed reforms were too slow to come, bogged down in party mud. Teachers complained that they had no academic freedom and were forced to ignore or even refute known Chinese history in favor of state propaganda. The hypocrisy of party officials who promulgated directives for all to follow then violated their own directives like adultery, drugs, and alcohol in private. If, the hypocrisy of American politicians who gave clear, unimpeachable lock-down orders during the COVID pandemic like forbidding indoor dining or traveling and who then were seen, you guessed it, dining indoors and traveling to resorts and vacation spots, seems to be eerily similar, well, you aren't the only one who noticed. Humans in positions of near absolute power tend to act very predictably human, don't they?

But it wasn't just blatant double-standards and politician-hypocrisy which thousands of Chinese students protested. No, they erected what were called "Democratic Walls,"[75] which were huge posters on campuses that named names and alleged sins of leading CCP officials and loudly, perhaps, naively, interpreted this campaign of blooming flowers to mean this was the time to let their criticisms and calls for reform be known across China.

Did I say perhaps?

Once he got over the initial shock of the outpouring of criticism, which, let's face it, was really aimed at him and his policies since you couldn't really tell where Mao started and where the CCP ended, he set in motion a harsh crackdown of his most vociferous critics. Labeling well over 300,000 of these dissidents as extremists and rightists he began a CCP purging process that in some ways didn't really abate until his death.

So much for transparency and openness. Just under two years since the "100 Flowers" campaign bloomed ever so briefly, the next "great" campaign was already in motion, this time it was The Great Leap Forward (1958-1962), which honestly, was anything but for all of China.

The crackdown to reach the goal of nearly complete industrialization and banishing all single-family farms, went into overdrive. Millions more citizens were forced from their homes and relocated into communes, more children were taken from their parents and put into labor camps for "re-education," and even heavier reliance on Soviet-style farming and technocrats occurred. This all culminated in staggering numbers of dead due to famine, exaggerated production numbers from across China due to fear of not meeting pre-conceived party goals and an economy of promise now in peril.[76]

In the middle of all this self-imposed tragedy, the heavily censored Chinese cinema managed to produce one noteworthy film which entered the mainstream pop culture. *Women's Basketball Player #5 (1961)*. Based on the real-life achievements of Yang Jie, a basketball player on the Chinese National Women's team, the film, a favorite of Mao and Jiang, gave the Chinese a new and improved hero to emulate. Literally, a team player, who was loyal, played only for the glory of the party and sought no individual acclimation. Yang Jie was Wu Xun, a now disgraced former feudalist, folk hero.

The film also signaled what would be acceptable for years to come in China, athletes could now join the proletariat as heroic and worthy of mass adoration. The wave of anti-intellectualism, anti-academician, and anti-elite of any kind in film and art would also dominate for decades to come. The director of WBP#5, Xie Jin, would also score again with his *Red Detachment of Women* (1961). This film reinforced women as heroic and the true soldiers who were expected to carry forth the banner of communism. This movie was released near the end of *The Great Leap Forward.*

Undaunted by yet another unmitigated policy disaster, and despite dissent in their own ranks, Mao and his allies announced yet another "great" campaign.

This time, 1962-1966, marked an intensive effort to achieve an absolute socialist education, particularly, among the youth of China. Relying on the teaching and texts of Mao, this mass indoctrination effort was aimed at instilling only proletarian values in the next revolutionary generation and marking intellectuals and elites as anathema to progress. Visual arts, including film had a crucial supporting goal in this education campaign. As Jiang Qing made clear, "all visual art, including film, must become revolutionary art and must show our youth there is only one path in life. The communist path."

As Mao upped the ante by ordering some 275,000 CCP cadres, intellectuals, and students to the countryside to "shed any artifice or lingering elitism"[77] by participating in grueling workshops and training, sort of like a new employee's worst nightmare, two films that same year (1964) were praised for aiding the greater cause. *The 8th Company of Nanking Road* and *The White Tiger Regiment*.

But to greatly understate the case, if, independence of vision, was something you valued then these were not good times to be a filmmaker in China. And it was about to get worse.

In a move which indicated the nature of the times, Lu Dingyi, former head of the CCP central propaganda department and later the Minister of Culture, was accused of promoting reactionary, anti-communist policies because he had made his disagreement over the object of art public. Dingyi did not share Mao's view that culture must exclusively serve proletarian politics. He was ousted. In fact, the Minister he replaced, Mao Dun, the author of *Spring Silkworms*, the beloved novel then film, had just been ousted from that same post for "lack of full commitment to the party."[78]

There's a saying that revolutionaries tend to "eat their own"[79] due to the relentless, almost irrational insistence on perpetual ideological cleansing and purity. If, that's true, then these two former Ministers of Culture were mere appetizers.

You Can't Spell Cultural without Cult: The Great Cultural Revolution 1966-1976

And you can't spell *cultus*, which is Latin for "to worship and adore," without cult.

Not even 20 years had passed since the Chinese Communist Party's "glorious revolution" over the Kuomintang Nationalists in

1949 and Lin Biao and Mao Zedong sensed something was missing.

They feared that the energy and enthusiasm of the "glorious revolution" had already fizzled. Lost its zip under a barrage of dull, lifeless bureaucrats, technocrats, and corrupt party officials that were more concerned over their own status and power rather than the plight of the proletariat. The charisma of communism it seemed, had already dried up.

And, let's face it, both Biao and Chairman Mao hadn't exactly been lighting up the CCP scoreboard since assuming power. A forced and hyper-accelerated attempt at transforming a largely agrarian society into a modern industrialized one ended in disaster. Between 25-40 million dead from famine, an economy in shambles, millions of acres of crops destroyed. Soviet-style mismanagement and flat-out wrong farming methods, as well as incredibly short-sighted bureaucratic decisions, were all partially at fault.[80]

But the forced industrialization policy, that was entirely the brainchild of Chairman Mao.

A supposed softening and newly found openness to criticism during the "100 Flowers Campaign" which abruptly ended in an avalanche of criticism, again, that was pure Mao. That campaign ended with a ruthless backlash against his critics. Many were either rounded up for "ideological purification," jailed or simply "banished." The ambitious "social re-education" program had created more resentment than revolutionary fervor and seemed to only embolden his critics.[81]

In the aftermath of not one, not two, but three disastrous policies, Mao continued to rail against what he viewed as "corrupt complacency,"[82] while his critics, growing louder and more defiant daily, railed against his failures. In fact, his personal red star had fallen so much that following the failed "100 Flowers" campaign, Mao was being forced to the sidelines.

Benched maybe, but still calling some shots.

Culturally, his will was still being implemented by "Madame Mao."80 The arts, especially opera and film, which Mao had clearly stated were never created merely for "art's sake" but must have a purpose to serve the revolution and elevate the proletariat, continued to come under tightened censorship and suppression. But this area was also a disappointment. Not only was mainland Chinese cinema failing to produce enough films worthy of the revolution, but the entire industry was losing market share, domestically and internationally, to its chief rival, Hong Kong, the second cinematic dragon.

But the thing that was missing the most, the ingredient that was most needed, Mao and Lin Biao concluded, was the revolutionary fervor of 1949.

And this passion, this power, and this energy, well, it wasn't going to come from the intellectuals, or their political rivals nipping at their heels. Nor would it come from bureaucrats who had become fat, happy and corrupt.

No, it would come from where unbridled, unquestioned zealotry with boundless energy always seems to come from-the next generation of revolutionaries. The youngest of the young.

In 1966, Mao and Lin Bia launched The Great Cultural Revolution. This time, the goal was to completely purge what they saw as the impure elements of Chinese society, culture and politics and revive the revolutionary spirit of 1949.

Sound familiar?

Mao, Jiang, Biao and their allies concluded that China had styled itself too much as a near "satellite of the Soviet Union."83 And that it had cost them time, resources and progress. So, they decided that China must take a completely new path. Ideological purity, not political squabbles or bureaucratic jockeying must be the driver of such a new society. A true communist utopia was, they were convinced, within their reach.

In short, a cult of Mao must be created and celebrated through all forms of culture and societal norms. For he, and he alone, knew the path to enlightenment. And how did they know this to be true? Well, as Lin Biao stated, "All truth was there, for all to see"[84] in the teachings of Mao. Millions of copies of "The "Little Red Book of Mao"[85] were made and distributed. Reading was obligatory. A new generation of zealots were activated. The cult of Mao was conceived.

To ensure that there was no rival thought or confusion among the youth, all schools were closed. Directives were announced that all youth were to mobilize in "Red Brigades" and "Red Guards" to best serve the revolution. These paramilitary units were given license to attack and harass the "older, corrupt" communist party members and officials who had "betrayed" the revolution. Orders were given to these youthful "saviors" to attack the old customs and culture. [86]

Mao had unleashed a red fury.

Predictably, things got out of control fast.

Red Guard chapters across China, especially in the major urban areas, were quickly formed and activated. Competition between chapters over which were the "true" Mao acolytes took on a religious, cult-like fervor and intensity. They battled all those who they believed, had lost faith in Maoism, all the while, battling each other for supremacy.

This was not a battle between hardened, veterans of war and political struggles. This was fought by and between kids. The youth which Mao so coveted as the next generation of revolutionaries unquestioningly obeyed his directives.

As Yu Xiangzhen, a schoolgirl of only 13 years young when the GCR began, tells it, "We drank wolf's milk, and we were a generation which blindly followed orders." She recounts that one day in junior high school a voice came over their school loudspeaker and said, "Fellow students we must closely follow Chairman Mao, get out of your classroom now, devote yourself to the Cultural Revolution."[87]

In practice, Yu tells of how this meant beating elders, subjecting their teacher to unbased accusations which led to her being humiliated, tortured, assaulted, and sent to labor camps. How this meant being give a belt and told to whip adults who dared to question the teachings of Mao. How this meant making up charges against adults in their town, even neighbors, even their parents to prove their loyalty to Mao. She also recounts how she grew to hate Jiang Qing, whom she saw as one of the most committed to this disastrous campaign even long after it was clear the damage it brought to all of China.[88]

Within the first phase (1966-68) Chinese President Liu Shaoqi was removed from office, denounced as a traitor then imprisoned and beaten. He died shortly thereafter in 1969. Many urban areas in China rapidly spiraled out of control, on the brink of complete anarchy. The Chinese economy still wobbly from the previous misguided and disastrous policies of forced industrialization plummeted. By September of 1967 Mao had to call in the Chinese regular army to try and restore some order. Only partially successful, the Red Guards continued to grow in numbers and resolve. By 1969, with Mao's blessing, Lin Biao assumed control and implemented martial law. This included curfews, lockdowns, and a further suspension of individual rights in the name of security.

Though it had somehow managed to stay afloat during invasions, a world war and a civil war, Chinese cinema on the mainland all but went silent during these "disaster years." Only one feature film, *The East is Red*, a song and dance epic celebrating the Chinese Communist Party and Mao released just prior to the cultural revolution (1965) seems noteworthy. The much-respected Beijing Film Academy was closed between 1966-1978 and not coincidentally, during this same time period the so-called "Fourth Generation" of Chinese film directors simply stopped making films and cinema ground to a halt. The only films produced during these years were almost exclusively revolutionary operas approved by and in some case written by Jiang Qing. Re-boots of *The White Haired Girl* and *The Red Detachment of Women* as musicals, as ballets, as operas dominated. *Sparkling Red Star*, an overt propaganda film celebrating Maoism almost seemed fresh by comparison.[89]

In the middle of this "revolution," the very "un-revolutionary" leader of the United States at that time, Richard Nixon, made an historic visit to "Red China." Ironically, Mao and Jiang Qing held a private screening of the film *The Red Detachment of Women* for President Nixon but made sure that no film credits were shown. When he asked who the film's director, writer or music composer was, Jiang, the former theater teacher, actress and playwright responded, "It was created entirely only by the masses, the great proletarian workers."[90]

Blacklisted?

The pioneers of Chinese cinema must have wished that all they had to worry about during this cultural "revolution," was being blacklisted and unable to find work, as some of their

Hollywood colleagues faced during the 1950s. Or, maybe, having to set-aside their ego to write screenplays under a pseudonym as Dalton Trumbo did for several years as he was blacklisted for his own communist leanings. His Oscar winning 1960 script for *Spartacus* was his final and best parting shot at all those who he felt "ratted out" mutual friends before HUAC. In *Spartacus*, Trumbo has dozens of freed Thracian slaves as metaphorical stand-ins for his Hollywood colleagues and Kirk Douglas (Spartacus) playing the part of Trumbo and others who were betrayed before the HUAC "invaders." In an epic scene, the freed slaves one by one all claim that "I am Spartacus," to deceive the Romans and defend their friend and ally against unjust charges. For many, it was just a good, historical action movie. For the "Hollywood Ten," an on-screen moment to savor.[91]

But while Trumbo and other Hollywood talent were mostly still free to apply their craft somehow, even if, under the cover of darkness, Chinese intellectuals, writers, actors, film directors and other talent, were rounded up, imprisoned, beaten, and sent to labor camps to pay for their "bourgeois sins."[92]

Well-known and beloved figures of Chinese film like Zheng Junli and Chen Baichen, along with Xu Lai (actress), Wang Ying (actress), Xun Huisheng (a Peking Opera star), Ying Yunwei (Shanghai film director), Zhou Xinfang (a Peking Opera Grandmaster), Xie Xuehang (a feminist and founder of the Taiwanese Communist Party), Sun Weishei (the first female film director of a modern, spoken drama) and hundreds more, were all casualties of the "Great Cultural Revolution." Most died in prison, several were executed. A few lucky ones managed to simply disappear or escape into anonymous exile.

Once celebrated for their individual and collective talent, vision and contribution through film and art to the glorious revolution, they had, seemingly in an instant, become poison to progressives. Enemies of the Maoist state.

In short, mainland Chinese cinema had been beaten into silence and submission.

But, if cinema is like a drug with no ill side-effects, as one Hollywood producer once noted, then, shut down one supply chain and another will emerge somewhere else to meet the demand. 93

In this case, Hong Kong was all too eager to step up and take on the role of supplier.

Of the many profitable films they produced, and the many legendary actors and directors the Hong Kong based Shaw Brothers signed to contracts with over the years, it was the one that got away that they would regret forever.

In 1970, Raymond Chow and Leonard Ho, who had just left the Shaw Brothers Studio to join Hui Brothers, inked a deal with a former child actor and up and coming martial arts star named Bruce Lee. A young but "mature beyond his years actor"94 in the business, Mr. Lee had rejected an industry standard contract offered by the Shaw Brothers because, as he made clear, it was both creatively limiting and financially insulting. Executives Chow and Ho made sure that Lee was neither limited artistically nor exploited financially. And they sure did not want to insult this prodigy who they were convinced was the next big thing in film. The result was as cinematically magical and explosively popular as it was tragically short.

Between 1970-1973, Lee, the son of a Cantonese Hong Kong opera star, born in San Francisco's Chinatown and raised in Kowloon, Hong Kong, and schooled at the University of Washington in Seattle (USA), was the ideal movie star at the ideal time to bridge east and west, the cinema of China and Asia with the hills of Hollywood. Charismatic, handsome, and bi-lingual, Lee, who had played Kato in the short-lived US television series *The Green Hornet* proved to be box office gold.

His first major leading role in a feature film, *The Big Boss* (1971) aka, *Fists of Fury* in its US release, netted an astounding $50 million dollars on an initial production budget of only $50,000 USD. His follow-up films, *Way of the Dragon* (1972) and *Enter the Dragon* (1973), both US-Hong Kong co-productions (Warner Brothers, Golden Harvest and Bruce Lee and Raymond Chow's own studio, HK based Concord Production Inc.) were also incredibly popular. *The Way of the Dragon* (written and directed by Lee) made nearly $150 million from a budget of $130,000 and *Enter the Dragon*, which today, remains the most popular and profitable martial arts film ever, netted over $1.2 billion USD from a budget of only $850k, a staggering 400+ times its base budget in profit.[95]

Both in Hong Kong, where fans obsessively watched re-runs of *The Green Hornet*, renamed there as *The Kato Show*, and shelled out money to watch his feature films during record runs, and in China where the CCP attempted to stamp out bootleg copies of his films, Lee was nothing short of a once in a lifetime icon.

Halfway across the globe, Lee had become a western cinematic and pop icon as well. As much as Hong Kong saw him as one of their own, many in the US saw him as a kid from San Francisco, an American who went to an American university, married his school sweetheart and who had simply come back home as a huge star.

For a moment, far too brief, the cinemas of east and west seemed connected by one supernova named Bruce Lee. Tragically, just six days before the release of *Enter the Dragon*, Mr. Lee died at the tender age of only 33.

He had, however, almost singlehandedly, resurrected Hong Kong cinema.

After his passing, martial arts and Kung Fu films continued to dominate the box office, Hong Kong cinema started to make original television and film production in Cantonese and by the end of the 1970s the Hui Brothers all but ensured the continued success of martial arts films at home and abroad with the signing of action-star and in some ways, heir to the Bruce Lee throne, Jackie Chan.

Meanwhile, as the GCR was beginning its end phase, mainland China was in the throes of real-life political intrigue, mystery and behind-the-scenes maneuvering within the CCP, while its own cinema remained largely silent.

Mao desperately sought to regain full control and protect his legacy as he neared his final years, both of which had been weakened and tarnished throughout the GCR. Lin Biao, Mao's longtime confidante and designated successor died in a plane crash over Mongolia as he futilely tried to escape to Russia after his coup to seize power failed. Follow-up investigations strongly suggested that this was no accident but a deliberate assassination and was covered-up for decades.

By 1972, Mao who was recovering from a stroke and Zhou En-Lai who was battling cancer, re-installed one-time rival Deng Xiaoping as Prime Minister. This move was over the vehement opposition of the so-called "Gang of Four,"[96] a radical clique or cabal within the CCP, seen as the driving force of the GCR, and headed by Mao's own wife, Jian Qing (Qing, Zhung Chunqiao, Yao Wenyan and Wang Hongwen).

In April of 1976, just a few months after death of his number two in charge, Zhou En-lai, this "Gang" eventually persuaded Mao to purge Xiaoping once again from power (Mao had purged him before, just at the start of the GCR for suspected lack of loyalty to all things Mao). But his exile was short lived. Mao succumbed to cancer at age 82 in the fall of 1976. Hua Gofeng seized control, arrested all the members of the "Gang of Four," including "Madame Mao," (Jiang Qing) and sentenced her to death. By 1977, Deng Xiaoping officially regained power. The Great Cultural Revolution, which turned out to be anything but that, finally came to a merciful end.

In 1991, released from prison briefly for medical treatment, Jiang Qing, who once ruled all things cultural and nearly singlehandedly destroyed mainland Chinese cinema, committed suicide.

Mayhem. Murder. Mystery. And a tragic coda.

Some things you just can't make up.

And some mistakes take a long time to make right.

While China was self-immolating its cinema, Hollywood had entered a new and wildly artistically liberated decade of filmmaking. With the controlling studio system now a relic of the past, directors and actors were free to tackle any project that caught their fancy and damn the bottom-line. While this new freedom brought in some awe-inspiring box office bombs (John Travolta as *The Boy in the Plastic Bubble* anyone? Or do you prefer a pre-*Terminator* Arnold Schwarzenegger in *Hercules in New York*?), it also reflected a diversity of topic and style only hinted at in previous years. Between 1966-1976, Hollywood was experimenting with its own GCR ("great cinematic revolution,") with films like *Bonnie and Clyde*, *The Night of the Living Dead*, *Easy Rider*, *Rosemary's Baby*, *Chinatown*, *All the President's Men*, *Foxy Brown*, *The Great Gatsby*, *The Green Berets and Jaws.*

For those keeping score at home, let's see, this small smattering of films includes; ballet-like, graphic violence never before seen in a feature film, a cult horror film with a black actor as its lead, stoners crisscrossing the country on Harleys, a young newlywed who is raped by, you guessed it, the devil, a neo-noir whose lead (Jack Nicholson) uncovers corruption with a bandage firmly on his nose, Robert Redford and Dustin Hoffman uncovering presidential corruption *sans* bandages, a black female as a butt-kicking lead, a romantic yet flawed '20s couple, a neo-right wing look at the Vietnam War starring John Wayne and a butt-biting Great White Shark as its lead.

If, she hadn't been so busy censoring Chinese cinema, it's a good chance Jiang Qing may have suffered severe dizziness from the sheer artistic freedom of it all. Good, bad and everything in between (John Travolta, you know where you rank here, don't even ask).

But the former "Madame Mao," initially sentenced to death for her role in the Great Cultural Revolution and disloyalty to the party ended up serving a life sentence in prison. At her trial, Jiang Qing showed no remorse or regret. As she put it, "Everything I did, Mao told me to do. I was his dog. What and who he said to bite, I bit."[97] And though the new post-GCR official fingerprints were all over the documents, rulings and laws which carried out the GCR, Jiang along with the rest of the "Gang" were quickly seen as relics of the past. They were the scapegoats, the ones that needed to be disposed of and quickly, if the "New China" was to once and for all come of age.

Serving her life sentence in prison, Jiang was released briefly in 1991 to receive medical treatment. It was then she chose to use that brief "freedom" to take her own life. A tumultuous chapter in Chinese cinema censorship and CCP dominance and control had ended. A new one had already started to take shape in the ashes of the GCR.

CHAPTER 4
CHINA SAYS YES TO HOLLYWOOD AND NO TO DEMOCRACY:
HOLLYWOOD SAYS YES TO BIGGER BOX OFFICE

Years before she took her own life, the unchallenged control, even influence wielded by Jiang Qing over all things cultural, most notably, film, had long ceased to be. The death of Mao and the ensuing power struggle between Jiang and the so-called "Gang of Four" had resulted in a new leadership regime. Out were the architects of the politically and economically disastrous "Great Cultural Revolution." In were the "reformers," those party officials, leaders and philosophers who believed that for China to realize its vast potential, it had to embrace, at least partially, market economics and capitalism.

Despite being purged twice for clashing with Maoist policy and left for dead in political purgatory, Deng Xiaoping quickly emerged as the most powerful leader of a post-GCR China. A longtime proponent of what was called "pragmatic Marxism,"[98] Xiaoping was able to maneuver his allies and proteges in the obvious positions of power, while he retained enormous influence over domestic and foreign policy as well as the military. The result was a vastly different China than even the one that the US president Richard Nixon had visited and opened the door to renewed diplomatic relations in 1972.

Socially, Deng implemented the "One-Child Policy,"[99] to curb the growing Chinese overpopulation problem. However draconian it may have been, it was seen by many as the "lesser of two evils." The problems stemming from explosive growth and stifled means to feed and take care of that growth due to Maoism were finally being addressed. Economically, Deng endorsed several market-driven planning and management schemes, all designed to jumpstart a badly damaged economy during the GCR years. Local managers were allowed more discretion in decision-making, and private companies across many industries were "liberated" from strict CCP central planning controls, permitted to engage in at least, a limited form of capitalism growth and venture. Small farmers were once again allowed to produce yields for their own sustenance and for private sector competition and profitmaking. From a foreign policy standpoint, Deng pushed for China to be more open to the West, both to gain financing for infrastructure expansion and to secure access to new markets for Chinese goods.

This "westward push" bore fruit in just a few short years. In 1979, at a meeting in the White House between President Jimmy Carter and Deng Xiaoping, the US formally established diplomatic relations with the People's Republic of China (PRC). It also gave to China what it had long desired. The US ended its decades-long recognition of the Republic of China (ROC), the government of Taiwan. The glory of the communist revolution of 1949 was now complete, and Deng not Mao had brought the red team's banner across the finish line.

Chinese cinema was also the beneficiary of Deng's "reformist period" in the "New China."[100]

With foreign films, including Hollywood, no longer banned on the mainland, budding filmmakers had easy access to both western films and could study the industry's preferred business model of that time. In short, with public encouragement and private fiscal incentives from Deng and the CCP, Chinese cinema began to incorporate more market-driven planning and private sector investment in making, promoting, and distributing their domestic films.

And while censorship was still ever-present, under Deng's leadership, the CCP loosened those reins and allowed filmmakers to address the excesses and errors during the GCR. This resulted in a flurry of films labeled "scar dramas" by newer, bolder filmmakers. This film genre sought to capture the damage wrought by the misguided policies of the CCP between 1966-1976. Films released early in the new decade like *Evening Rain* (1980) and *Legend of Tianyun Mountain* (1980) represented a more socially honest and critical look at China under communism than was previously allowed or even imagined under the iron fist of Madame Mao. 101

The "scar dramas" weren't the only movies produced though in this "experimental" decade of filmmaking. The Shaolin Temple, a Kung Fu action film starring Jet Li would go on to be one of the all-time highest grossing Chinese films ever. It also marked the first time that Hong Kong and mainland Chinese Cinemas co-produced a film. This movie single-handedly put the Shaolin Monastery on the map for western tourists.

But, perhaps, no other Chinese film director at this time was more responsible for this newfound cinematic honesty and growing global popularity during the 1980s than Wu Tianming.

Born in 1939 in the Shanxxi Province of China, an area compared to the USA's Appalachia for its extreme poverty and despair, a young Tianming was so enamored with film, that he sold his socks for movie tickets and paid his brother to do his homework for him so he could watch movies (LA Times). Starting out as an actor at the Xi'an Film Studio, he later enrolled in the Beijing Film Academy in 1974 just as the GCR was waning to learn the craft of a director. He was taken on as an apprentice, in part secretly, by famed film director Cui Wei at the Xi'an Film Studio in 1976. He soon began to make his own mark with films like *River Without Buoys* (1983), a scathing indictment of China during the Great Cultural Revolution, *Life* (1984), which explored deep divisions and cultural differences between China's urban and rural areas, and *Old Well* (1987), which went on to win the top prize at the Tokyo International Film Festival and starred his friend and protégé, Zhang Yimou.

Yet, it was Wu Tianming's mentoring and determined support of new directors as head of the Xi'an Film Studio, like Zhang Yimou which cemented his legacy as the "Godfather"[102] of the new Chinese Cinema. Originally hired by Wu to be a cinematographer, Yimou shared his desire to direct and to adapt the *Red Sorghum* novel (1986) by Nobel Laureate Mo Yang to the big screen. Wu supported this new director and project unreservedly, raising sorely needed cash for the project, turning over the Xi'an Studio's resources for the project and fighting with Chinese censors on Yimou's behalf along the way. In fact, in a highly unusual move, Wu denounced Chinese film censorship in a 1987 interview with The New York Times. He specifically called out the head of the provincial propaganda department where X'ian Studios was located, saying "He doesn't understand films but wants to control all filmmaking...He's a simple bureaucrat...an ossified thinker."[103]

Despite living on the edge, Wu and Zhang Yimou kept moving forward. The film *Red Sorghum* (1988), about three generations of a family in the Shandong Province against the backdrop of the Chinese Civil War and the Great Cultural Revolution, went on to win the Golden Bear at the 1988 Berlin International Film Festival. This marked the first time a Chinese film from the mainland had ever won. Even other studios like the grand old Shanghai Film Studio, first established in 1949, rode this new and fresh cinematic wave of "scar dramas" with popular films like *Hibiscus Town* (1986). Here, the young, female protagonist struggles through the turmoil and pain of Mao's ill-conceived cultural revolution. *Hibiscus Town* even took home a coveted Golden Rooster, China Film's Association's answer to Hollywood's American Academy Awards. So, in part, China opened the door to the west for its own cinema and a bear and a rooster walked through!

Yet, if we have learned anything about China over the last 100 years or so, it's that with every "new" opening of its nation to the west, there is always a retrenching, a closing of this door. So, it wasn't surprising when this door to the west did slam shut in 1989. The surprise then wasn't if it would shut but when and how.

While Chinese Cinema was enjoying its nearly decade-long rebirth, the Chinese as a people were enjoying relative prosperity and economic growth. Post-cultural revolution, the CCP and its bureaucratic functionaries realized that any pure model of complete centralized planning, production and distribution was doomed to fail. Mao's earlier attempts at forced industrialization and later, at national self-criticism and transparency had also proven to both be failures.

Perhaps, some middle-of-the-road less traveled, a compromise between the promise of the great communist revolution and the realities of feeding, clothing, and growing a nation could be found. The 1980s saw a move to more capitalism, more regional discretion, and more attention to the basics of demand and supply economics.

Yet, like allowing people to enjoy partial freedom, tends to stir a desire among the masses for much more. And that could lead down a politically perilous, even suicidal path for a government more comfortable with near-absolute control than anything being shared with its own people.

By the late 1980s, protests, especially by a younger generation of students who demanded more freedoms in every facet of life, began to raise serious concerns in the CCP headquarters in Beijing. Headlines in China began to be dominated by soaring inflation, the inability of consumer products to be manufactured at a rate and price to meet the new demand and ever-growing corruption by governmental officials, all fueled this drive for change.

Hu Yaobang, the reform-minded CCP General-Secretary, a strong advocate for a mixed economy of capitalism and socialism as well as for social democratic reform, was blamed for what CCP leaders saw as growing chaos. He was forced out in early Spring of 1989. Under questionable circumstances, he died shortly thereafter in April.

To the growing number of protesters, he quickly became a martyr for reform. His death a call for action.

On the day of his funeral, April 22nd, thousands gathered at Tiananmen Square in Beijing for spirited demonstrations and demands for further reform. Similar and coordinated protests broke out in Shanghai, Nanjing, Xi'an, Changsha, and Chengdu. With the Soviet Leader at the time, Mikhail Gorbachev scheduled to visit China in mid-May, CCP leaders were greatly concerned about how best to put out this dangerous flame before it could spread. Publicly, they downplayed the protests. Privately, they were concerned. Worse, they were internally divided over how best to snuff this flame of freedom out.

Some, like Zhao Ziyang, advocated for peaceful negotiation and possibly some small measures of further reform to placate the crowds. Others, like Premier Li Ping and CCP-whisperer Deng

Xiaoping, called for suppression of the students at any cost. Divided, at least temporarily, the Chinese leadership mostly wrung its hands and waited.

By the time Mr. Gorbachev arrived, the crowds at Tiananmen Square reached well over 1 million with western press and worldwide correspondents capturing this "flame of freedom," from every conceivable angle.

Privately humiliated and having lost "face," during Gorbachev's visit, Deng Xiaoping vowed to end the flag-waving, freedom chanting madness. Swiftly and completely.

Martial law was declared. The Chinese Military surrounded the Square and blocked entrances and exits to it. Soon, photos and footage made their way across the globe of students waving American Flags, chanting for freedom while their hand-made "Goddess of Democracy," a 33-foot statue, created from foam, cardboard, and scraps of metal stood approvingly and gloriously in the center of the square.104

Deng and his cronies looked on, growing more impatient and intolerant by the minute.

With growing support globally for their courageous defiance of the communist regime, amidst calls for leaders to step down and fulfill Hu Yaobang's legacy of democratic reform, old guard Deng Xiaoping had seen and heard enough. While it was partially his own opening of the door to such reforms which led to this humiliation, for him, it was time to crush this protest and all it stood for.

In late June 3d and into the early hours of June 4th, he gave his military the order to take back the Square at all costs.

The Chinese army rapidly advanced into the unarmed civilian crowds in Tiananmen Square. They opened fire on the unarmed civilian crowds killing thousands. Tanks rolled, crushing human bodies as they advanced. Reports of soldiers stabbing students as they lay on the ground in protests only added to the horror. Alongside the military, Chinese police arrested thousands more, the majority dragged off to prison for lengthy sentences, several executed, some simply disappeared.

The budding "flower of democracy"105 had been crushed.

At a press conference on June 5th, then President George H.W. Bush condemned the Chinese actions and promised a package of sanctions. Perhaps, well intentioned, critics loudly panned Bush's "shrinking in the face of evil."106 In fairness, let's just say it wasn't as electrifying or iconic as his former boss's (President Ronald Reagan) clarion call for Mr. Gorbachev to "tear down this wall"105 (the Berlin Wall) in 1987. Which, ironically, Mr. Gorbachev did, only some 6 months after his visit to China on November 9th, 1989.

From a filmmaking perspective, the Tiananmen Square uprising had all the elements of an epic drama. A beloved figure who had a new vision or his people yet was forced from power and died shortly after under suspicious circumstances. A classic underdog fighting against what they saw as a corrupt and broken system. Powerful visuals of hope like the handmade "Goddess of Democracy" standing tall during chaos, uncertainty, and fear. And of course, an evil antagonist who will retain his own power at all costs. There's even a real-life, still image of a lone citizen standing in front of an oncoming tank. Defiance right up to the last moment. Even after all his comrades have been cleared away like human debris or scattered litter to be hauled away and discarded. He stands tall.

Kind of writes itself, doesn't it?

Yet, some 32 years later, Hollywood has refused to touch this incredible real-life, human drama. It's as if former child actor and convicted pedophile and rapist, Fatty Arbuckle himself, had come back to life and demanded to write, direct and star in this epic. Making the project simply untouchable. Or maybe, just Richard Gere, still *persona non grata* number one in China had demanded to star in any such film. His crime? Unapologetic support for the Dahli Lama and the people of Tibet. An unforgivable sin to the CCP.

Either way, China has made it clear that any such film on Tiananmen Square, a moment celebrated at the time in the west as "democracy breaking through the dark clouds of communism,"[107] was off-limits.

Clearly, Hollywood honchos listened to their Chinese masters and obediently did what they were told. If you can find any such blockbuster Hollywood movie about Tiananmen Square, please, send me the link. I'd love to screen it.

Today, China continues to ban any type of public or private commemoration of the lives lost at Tiananmen Square. Even placing a flower on the Square on June 4th is grounds for an arrest. The "courage" of the Chinese military though and their "glorious" actions that day continue to be extolled by Chinese Communist leaders. Maybe, Hollywood can make a movie depicting that type of heroism. Odds are good Chinese censors would allow that one to be screened in the mainland.

Not surprisingly, in the immediate aftermath of the Tiananmen Square tragedy, Chinese Cinema came to a screeching halt. The "Godfather" of "honest" Chinese Cinema, Wu Tianming was in Los Angeles, California as a visiting scholar when the Chinese tanks rolled in Tiananmen Square. Telling Woody Mu, a former Warner Brothers executive and friend that this was not the society he wanted for China under communism, Tianming spoke out publicly against the Tiananmen Square massacre. He also quit the CCP in protest. Clearly, returning to China at that moment was no longer an option. For the next five years he chose to stay in the USA. Among other things, he ran a video store in Monterey Park and while he no longer was making films, he confessed that, at least, he was able to watch well over 900 films during this period of self-exile.[108]

While China was imploding its short-lived "cinematic honesty," Hollywood was returning to what was labeled "formulaic blockbusters,"[109] while the West, spurred on by President Reagan's calling out Soviet leader Mikhail Gorbachev to "tear down that wall," was doing just that. Tearing down walls, artistically and literally. Just over five months after Chinese tanks crushed any flowering of democracy in the Tiananmen Square, Germany, East, and West, was reunited with the tearing down of the Berlin Wall on November 9, 1989. A relic of World War II, the Berlin Wall was erected by the Soviets to stop the massive flow of East Germans crossing from Soviet controlled Berlin to the Allied side. They were, as commentators noted, "voting with their feet, literally moving from communism to democracy."[110] By stopping people from making any such choice, the Soviets had, in large part, triggered hostilities and a thawing or "cold war" between the Soviet Union and the USA. This "cold war" would last uninterrupted for decades, continuing through today (2022). China viewed this action as a humiliation of communists everywhere and vowed that such a defeat at the hands of the west would never befall China or the CCP.

Artistically, the 1980s, in the west, at least, was the decade of bigger, bigger, best. Bigger ideas, bigger platforms, bigger budgets, bigger promotion, all leading to bigger box office. The '80s seemed to take a page from the early days of the Studio System in how stars were carefully cultivated and branded for maximum consumer appeal and profit. Except instead of a senior producer at say, MGM, assigning a junior assistant to "sit on" a star to guarantee "No scandal, no sex," stars went out and formed their own teams or "entourages" to make them "immortal." This wasn't about hiding unacceptable "truths," the way studios hid the sex lives of stars like Rock Hudson, this was about creating your own "truth" and making it as public as imaginable. And when that "truth" got stale, simply re-invent yourself" and do it again. The results of this "new-old" branding were intoxicating. Spurred on by a decade of unparalleled economic growth, American consumers spent more disposable income on art, music, and movies than ever before. And it showed.[111]

Pop stars like Madonna (Madonna Louise Ciccone) were redefining what it meant to be a "singer." With a dizzying array of her musical hit songs, books, films, concerts, marketing and merchandizing, designer fashion lines and, of course, highly stylized music videos on the recently launched Music Television Video (MTV, August 1, 1981), "singing" seemed a small part of the pop star package. Artist and mogul, Keith Haring, exemplified this bigger is always better approach with a somewhat ironic twist. Getting his start by painting images inspired by "raw" street and gang graffiti, he went on to have his own designer line of custom paintings and several stores to sell and ship his "raw" images around the world to wealthy art collectors, who apparently, wanted to keep their multi-million-dollar mansions, raw and real.[112]

Hollywood, never one to be shy in its own self- promotion, took advantage of the 1980s much like a snow-cone dealer takes advantage of a record-breaking heat wave. In short, they went bigger is always better. Budgets, star salaries, price of admission and gross receipts all went up. Way up.

In two films building on the Star Wars saga which began with his film, *Star Wars: A New Hope* (1977) George Lucas (screenwriter, producer, special effects guru) and his self-named production company, *LucasFilms*, followed up that huge hit with *The Empire Strikes Back* (1980) and *Return of the Jedi* (1983). With massive budgets for that time, of $28 and $32 million dollars respectively, these two films went on to earn $1.5 and $1.1 billion dollars in box office. Not to be outdone, in what could really be called "the decade of George Lucas," he also went on to produce the *Indiana Jones* films, Steven Spielberg's massively popular movie franchise. *Indiana Jones and the Raiders of the Lost Ark* (1981), *Indiana Jones and the Temple of Doom* (1984), and *Indiana Jones and the Last Crusade* (1989). The Indy films alone had a combined budget of just under $100 million. A staggering amount for that time as well. But in Hollywood, it's not what things cost in the 1980s, it's the profit they made. And George Lucas films made money. A ton of money. In any galaxy. All told, the Star Wars episodes and the Indiana Jones films of the 1980s went on to make a combined $4.1 billion. When you add in merchandising, Star Wars memorabilia alone, broke the $4.2 billion mark through Christmas of 2021. I'm no math whiz, but adding up box office and merchandising, $8.3 billion could set up even the most demanding inter-galactic traveler comfortably for a long time. A really, long time on an island resort far, far away.[113]

Yet, the bigger is better approach to Hollywood filmmaking of the 1980s did not rely exclusively on the Jedi or an adventurous antiquities collector to expand its own empire. Far from it. They also looked to a washed-up Vietnam Vet and a curious time-traveling kid for mega-bucks. Sylvester Stallone, who got his first break in the film industry by acting in a low-budget porn film, had hit the Hollywood Jackpot with his *Rocky* film success in the

1970s with his portrayal of a down and out punch-drunk boxer who gets a shot at the champ with *Rocky* (1976) and *Rocky II* (1979). Hollywood producers and studio moguls were awestruck when Stallone's first Rocky film was made for a paltry $1 million and went on to gross (Are you sitting down?) $225 million. His end of the 1970s sequel, still made at the low-cost of only $7 million made $200 million. Stallone followed up those *Rocky* installments with *Rocky III* (1982) and *Rocky IV* (1985). Those combined to take-in $425 million. Far from staying perched on his ringside stool, Stallone set out to create another memorable and hopefully, profitable screen character. Playing John Rambo, a military veteran struggling with Post-Traumatic Stress Disorder (PTSD) and trying to cope with his newly found civilian life, *Rambo: First Blood Part I* made in 1982 on a fairly, modest $15 million budget went on to gross over $125 million. Sly went on to make *Rambo: First Blood Part II* (1985) and *Rambo III* (1988) which combined to rake in $495 million.

And 17-year-old Marty McFly? Well, he proved himself to be no chicken when it came to making time-travel a lucrative business. *Back to the Future I* (1985) and *Back to the Future II* (1989) combined to gross over $700 million.

Clearly, Hollywood had found its formula for box-office success. Create a compelling and lovable hero which audiences won't soon, if, ever, tire of, throw in some, or a seemingly unlimited amount of dazzling special effects, a handful of snappy catchphrases (Yippee-kay-yay motherf****r, I'll be back, Whatsamatter McFly, chicken?) keep it simple, stupid (KISS method) when it came to plot and script and above all, if it worked once then it could work more than once. Scriptwriters took note and delivered the goods to their studio bosses.

Back to the Future time-traveled its way through 4 films, *Rocky* punched its way to 8 films as of 2021, *Rambo* was still creating chaos and carnage into its 5th film in 2019, *Star Wars* kept exploring a galaxy far, far away through 9 films with plans to add more and we haven't even discussed the *Die Hard* films and whether the first installment (*Die Hard*, 1984, grossing $141 million off a $25 million budget) of five never say die films, is a Christmas story that has lots of action or an action movie set around Christmas. And the 1980s wouldn't have been the 80s without Arnold "Pumping Iron" Schwarzenegger launching the first of 6 Terminator films in 1984. T1 weighed in with a very underdeveloped, even scrawny $6.5 million budget which grew to a very pumped-up $78 million in gross receipts. Overall, the Terminator did indeed come back six times on its way to grossing an astonishing $1.7 billion.[114]

No doubt about it, the 1980s marked the decade when Hollywood decided that bigger is better and more of the same is best. Behold, the birth of the formula franchise films. If, not, completely conceived in the 1980s, it sure was perfected. Hollywood, like *Rocky*, was the undisputed champ and would strengthen its grip on the champion's cinematic belt in the 1990s. But like any classic movie script, trouble was brewing on the horizon. China had eyes on the prize and a pro-China politician named Joe Biden would play a key role in helping them accomplish their dream.

But let's not get too far ahead of ourselves, too fast.

The 1980s, at least until Tiananmen Square and China's retrenchment, had proven to be boon years for its Southeast Asian neighbors as well. Deng's free market reforms and his opening up of the mainland to its southeast trading partners helped nations like Thailand, Singapore, Cambodia, and Malaysia. This opening of the door, however brief, especially helped the Hong Kong cinema thrive. If, the 1980s in Hollywood might be called the "decade of George Lucas," then that same period in Hong Kong was undoubtedly, the "decade of Woo."

John Woo, born in Guangzhou, China but raised in Hong Kong, got his first job in the film industry serving as an assistant director at the famed Shaw Bros. Film Studios in Hong Kong. Known for highly stylized action and ultra-violent sequences, often shot in slow-motion accompanied by ironic theme music, with "Mexican standoffs"112 between his hero and villain torn right out of Sergio Leone spaghetti westerns, Mr. Woo was already an admired filmmaker when he hit paydirt with his 1986 film, *A Better Tomorrow*. This film, the first of many, portraying "Triad" or Hong Kong organized gangs, their ruthless grip on society and those brave enough to try and take them down, shattered Hong Kong box office records and influenced his domestic and worldwide peers.

Mr. Woo often worked with an inner-circle of trusted actors like Chow Yun-Fat, Tony Leung Chiu Wai, Brigitte Lin, and later, Jackie Chan. But 1980s Hong Kong Cinema was even bigger than John Woo. With Chinatown arthouses in the USA, like San Francisco, as well as mainland, China, plus its close neighbors, Indonesia, Singapore, Thailand, and South Korea all showing a strong demand for its action flicks, as well as new home video technology opening up, yet, another film market, Hong Kong cinema was experiencing a strong revival. Hong Kong also implemented a ratings system in the 1980s for all films, which in part, lead to an "adult only" genre of films (soft core pornography) which by 1996 would capture over 50% of all market share for Hong Kong cinema. Unlike Hong Kong, which would grow well into the mid-1990s until several factors conspired to depress its domestic film industry, Taiwan cinema struggled to stay afloat throughout the 1980s. A surging home video industry, fueled by imports, plus shrinking consumer income combined to slow Taiwanese cinema to a crawl. The Taiwanese Government even tried to spur its film industry through targeted grants, loans, and outright investment but to no avail. Thankfully, a young Taiwanese filmmaker named Ang Lee was honing his craft and would singlehandedly save his homeland's film industry in the not-too-distant future.

As the tanks rolled into Tiananmen Square on June 4th, 1989, Deng Xiaoping was already looking for a way out. He knew that in the short run, at least, his reformist policies and encouraging China's youth to share their honest appraisal of the CCP, post-Mao, would be pointed to as the scapegoats for the "wild excesses"113 of the protesters. He would be blamed for the global humiliation and "loss of face" the incident cost all of China. And he was correct. He resigned his posts and virtually disappeared from the public eye in a blink. One of the "New Wave" of CCP leaders, Jeng Zemin, former Mayor of Shanghai and no great friend of reformism, seized control. The expected crackdown and re-tightening of control across Chinese society, especially, of its intellectual class, was applied. No surprise there. But it was the longevity of the crackdown that did surprise many, even seasoned Sino observers. It didn't last long.

In fact, several factors coincided to propel strong economic and consumerist growth across China throughout the 1990s. This, despite the decade beginning with the global reputation of China in tatters and having to suffer sanctions applied by the west, especially, the USA, as punishment for simply standing up to lawbreakers.

First, the economic reforms and trade reform measures implemented under Deng were beginning to bear fruit. The shift from China as "victim" in the region to China as "powerful leader" also was helping catapult China to preeminence throughout Asia. China under Jeng continued this normalization of relations with its neighbors, or, as Deng had touted, "Peace through development."[115] The backlash from Tiananmen Square was not as bad as expected, and aside from a terse official statement from Japan, its many neighbors seemed more than eager to work with a China which was signaling its desire to put profit over politics.

Quietly, China was unveiling the start of a long-term plan which called for Chinese participation in several international and multi-lateral organizations, with an eye on smoothing the path for an eventual World Trade Organization (WTO) membership. This was the real gold standard for world economic powerhouses. Chinese viewed entry as an all -but-guaranteed ticket to long-term economic success and membership was an absolute must.

Back home, shifting resources from state-run businesses to private sector enterprises helped further unleash economic growth throughout China. Still, even in self-imposed exile, Deng remained concerned that China could slip back into Maoism and miss fulfilling what he saw as its destiny to become not just a regional economic and political leader but a global leader. Fully equipped to unseat the USA and the EU, economically, politically, and militarily. In the early 1990s, Deng embarked on what was dubbed his "Southern Tour."[116] A several months long trek throughout the southern part of China, espousing his reformism, pointing to its success, and making the case for all of China to stay the course. In retrospect, it would seem they heeded his call.

Perhaps, most surprisingly though, was the rise of Chinese nationalism throughout the decade. There were certainly many reasons why the flame of Chinese nationalism could have been extinguished. The global humiliation of the 1989 Tiananmen Square debacle still hung-over China like thick, mid-day smog. The excitement and pride of being a finalist for the 2000 Olympics had turned to bitterness, even shame, at losing out to Australia in 1992. The "Yinhee incident"[117] of 1993 during the Clinton Administration, where Chinese ships were boarded without authorization and accused, as it turned out falsely, of carrying illegal weaponry, had caused political and social divisions. On the other hand, China was taking great pride in being, for the moment at least, the only remaining communist power in the wake of the USSR disintegration and, at long last, both Hong Kong (1997) and Macau (1999) were both formally returned to China's control and authority. Maybe, this yin and yang of shame and honor combined to reach a fevered *laobaixing* (common person) pitch during the 1990s. [118]

While the CCP contemplated ways to continue to stoke the flames of Chinese nationalism, critics feared it had crossed over into a dangerous form of xenophobia. Only time and Chinese behavior would tell.

When it came to film, Chinese cinema of the 1990s was a basket of seemingly contradictory impulses and actions.

First, some stuff never seemed to change. In the immediate aftermath of Tiananmen Square, Chinese cinema and art took a direct hit. Filming licenses were rescinded, funds for edgy projects dried up, arrests were made, censorship grew even more rigid, international travel for actors and directors forbidden. Film visionaries like Wu Tianming saw what was happening in his beloved homeland of China. He read the tea leaves even from Los Angeles and had decided not to return to China. Those that stayed made films that seemed very familiar and eminently safe, if not stale. Filmmaker Zhang Yimou directed his acting muse Gong Li in *Ju Dou* (1990). Stop me if the plot sounds familiar-A beautiful, young girl is sold into marriage to an old, wealthy but corrupt businessman. (Seeing not even a yield sign, I shall proceed). *Jiao Yulu* (1990) depicts the determined effort to modernize Hunan Province in 1962, and of course, there was a spate of state-sanctioned films glorifying the communist revolution, the struggle of the Chinese to push back the hated, Japanese invaders and a celebration of the eternal goodness of the Chinese countryside with its incorruptible morality.

Corrupt old capitalist guys. Check.

Never forget our hatred for the imperialist Japanese. Check.

Common Chinese embody all that is good, and our revolution was and remains, glorious.

Check and double-check.

Second, there was the ever-present CCP film censorship. For example, a key literary element of the novel from which the screenplay for *Ju Dou* was adapted, acts of incest, was cut by state censors. *Black Snow* (1990) which told the story of a street vendor struggling in a post Great Cultural Revolutionary China had key scenes censored and then was banned. Too much criticism targeted at the GCR, not enough glory given to communism.

*Raise the Red Lantern (*1991), directed by Zhang Yimou, starring, Gong Li (Who else?), told the story of yet, another beautiful, young concubine who is sold to a wealthy, old man in 1920s China during its warlord era. Seen as overly critical of Chinese culture with explicit sexual situations, it too, was banned. Just two years later, Gong Li, starred in yet another concubine themed film, this time in *Farewell My Concubine* (1993). Directed by Chen Kaige, the film followed the lives of two opera singers from the glory of the revolution through the GCR. CCP censors banned the film on the mainland due to perceived criticisms of the CCP, and overt homosexuality and suicide. The same year, *Blue Kite* (1993), was released. This film centered around a boy growing up in the chaotic 100 Flowers Movement, the Great Leap Forward and the GCR. Directed by Tian Zhuangzhuang, this one really hit a CCP censor's nerve. The film was banned as well as its director. It would be a crime to possess or to watch the film in China and its director was forbidden to make films or release films in China for 10 years.

Ironically, as much as CCP censors vilified these films, the years 1991-1993 marked unprecedented international critical acclaim for Chinese films. Their films which, for decades, were routinely seen as being not much more than propaganda pieces for the CCP became the toast of Paris and beyond. In a flurry, *Farewell My Concubine* took home the coveted Palme D'Or at the Cannes Film Festival, *The Blue Kite* was the Grand Prix Winner at the Tokyo International Film Festival, while *Raise the Red Lantern* won the best film award at the British Academy Awards and the National Society of Film Critics.

This "they love us, why don't you" dynamic continued throughout the 90s.

To Live (1994), Gong Li's seventh film with director Zhang Yimou (and you thought Scorsese loved Leo DiCaprio, huh?) depicted the struggle of one young couple living through the Chinese civil war and the GCR. The Chinese State Administration of Radio, Film and Television (SARFT), the official administrative body armed with censorship, though, most assuredly, executing CCP policy, banned *To Live* on the mainland. Too harshly and overtly critical of the CCP and Maoism, said SARFT. Honest and powerful said movie critics. *Shanghai Triad* (1995), directed by Zhang Yimou and starring, Gong Li, depicted the criminal underworld of Shanghai of the 1930s. "A vivid and mesmerizing portrait,"[119] which took home prizes at the Cannes Film Festival. The CCP banned Mr. Yimou from attending a screening of the film at a NY film festival in 1995. He was informed his presence would apparently, be humiliating to all Chinese as westerners watched a film about Chinese supposed flaws and excesses. He changed his flight and hotel plans as ordered.

East Palace/West Palace (1996), directed by Zhang Yuan, tells the story of how homosexuals meet and have illicit sex in two public bathrooms in parks near the Forbidden City. One of China's first-ever films on LGBTQ issues, it garnered a loyal following and critical acclaim. The film was unsurprisingly, also banned on the mainland. The same year marked a true comeback by director Wu Tianming with his *King of Masks* (1996) about an aging street performer and his young protégé.

Two films were released to help mark the historic hand-off of Hong Kong to China in 1997. *Chinese Box*, starring Gong Li and Jeremey Irons, is an ambitious film weaving multiple personal stories leading up to the transfer and *The Opium War*, an epic film telling the story of China's first war with Great Britain over the profitable drug trade. Both films were China-friendly and avoided the sharp SARFT censorship axe.

Keep Cool (1997), a vignette story of inter-personal relationships in 1990s China, was not as fortunate. The film was pulled from Cannes Film Festival consideration by the CCP. Its director, Zhang Yimou, was forbidden from allowing it to be screened there due to its apparently, unflattering, and irresponsible portrayal of modern Chinese life. Unlike say, in the US, prior restraint of a literary work, whether it be a book or a film, is a legitimate legal act which the CCP can take in its authority to "protect and preserve" the moral fiber of the Chinese people.[120] Once the book is published and read or a film is released and screened, the CCP view is irreparable damage has been done to the Chinese and their glory. You'll recall that according to Mao, art had no intrinsic purpose, it was allowed only if it served the aims and glory of the state.

Joan Chen, a Chinese-American actress, writer and director was seen as a pioneer for Asian women everywhere in the film industry when she co-wrote and directed *Xiu Xiu: The Sent Down Girl* (1998). The film depicted life in the Chinese countryside during the GCR. It was banned due to sexual content and to having done the unforgivable-some of the film's exterior scenes were shot in (gasp)Tibet. So, it could not have been surprising to Ms. Chen, frustrating no doubt, surprising, no.

Just the prior year (1997), the CCP had sent tremors through the film industry by banning Hollywood film director Martin Scorsese, screenwriter Melissa Mathison, their film *Kundun,* as well as Walt Disney Studios, which distributed the film. *Kundun*, which was nominated for 4 Academy Awards and hailed as a "breathtaking visual experience,"[121] tells the story of the 14th Dalai Lama during the Chinese invasion of Tibet in 1937. Universal Pictures had earlier rejected distributing the film for fear of upsetting the CCP and its censors. In 1998, then-CEO of Disney Michael Eisner would apologize to China, calling the film "a stupid mistake," and that "the bad news is that it was made, but the good news is that no one watched."[122] You mean besides the CCP censors, right, Mike? Maybe, it was just coincidence that shortly after the apology, Disney won the much-coveted approval of the Chinese officials to build its very own *Shanghai Disneyland*, a mega-park attraction.

The same year *Kundun* was released, another film, *Seven Years in Tibet*, starring Brad Pitt hit the movie theaters. Well, not those in China. Pitt, director Jean-Jacques Annaund and Sony Pictures were all banned for committing the same "crime." It didn't matter that Pitt played an Austrian who befriends the Dalai lama during the Chinese invasion. The fact it was based on the true story of mountain climber Heinrich Harrer was also irrelevant to the Chinese censors. Tibet was one of the completely forbidden "Three T's" which only fools, children and apparently, directors named Scorsese and Chen would challenge at their peril. Violating the other two T's, Tiananmen Square and Taiwan, would earn an outright ban just as fast.

Chinese cinema of the 1990s closed out with films like *Once Upon a Time in Shanghai* (1998), which again re-visits Shanghai of the 1940s, *The Road Home* (1999), a story of love between a country girl and a worldly teacher, *Not One Less* (1999) and an off-beat *Crazy English* (1999), a bio-pic on Chinese motivational speaker Li Yang. One of Mr. Yang's catchphrases was "Conquer English to Conquer the World."[123] Collectively, not much pushing of the envelope. The result? They were granted the privilege of being screened by a 1.1 billion audience.

So, on the one hand, the decade, in many ways, was like previous ones. Heavy censorship, strict scrutiny to ensure the glory of the CCP and its revolution, and the "Three T's" were forbidden. In fact, independent film censorship watchdogs list 6 of the top 10 all-time, most important Chinese films ever banned all happened during the 1990s. Anything that tore at, reflected poorly or even indirectly questioned the morality, wisdom, and forthrightness of the Chinese (homosexuality, drug use, promiscuity, incest) people was bound to get a film banned or, at the very least, the offending plotlines or scenes cut. And they were and it did.

Business as usual, right?

Yes and No.

As Confucius taught his students, what is most vital is often least obvious.[124] Easy to overlook. In addition to the expected heavy-handed censorship and outright banning of films, China was also laying the groundwork to dominate the worldwide film industry in the not-too-distant future.

First, what western observers often miss is the fact that despite the often-heated rhetoric that emanates from Beijing, seemingly untethered from the real world, behind closed doors they do confront reality. Even if it is less than flattering. And then they just as often take steps to change that reality more to their liking. It's just they don't feel the need to let their rivals and enemies know what they are up to. Remember, their society is a closed one. Chattiness and transparency are not considered virtuous.

As we've discussed, from the PRC victory through the early 1990s, Chinese cinema was dominated by propaganda films sanctioned by the CCP. You'll recall Madame Mao's iron grip on what stories could be told, in what form and how. Making sure art served the state and not the other way around, continued with little interruption or exception long after both she and Mao passed on. It's just that, no matter how compelling the story of Chinese courage and gallantry against the evil Japanese invaders is, or how stirring the PRC march to victory is, or even how great and morally incorruptible the common Chinese citizen is, audiences, even loyal Chinese Communist audiences, tend to get a bit restless. Even, bored. "How many times," as one writer asked during the GCR, "can we sit through yet another adaptation of *The White Haired Girl*?"[125]

Turns out even as film-crazy a nation like China is, it too, has limits.

Between 1982-1991, film audience attendance in China declined nearly 80%. At the same time, its longtime Asian cinematic rival, Hong Kong cinema, was enjoying consecutive boom years. Martial Arts, Fantasy sword play, crime action dramas, soft-core porn, HK ruled the Asian film market.

The CCP did more than just take note. They would soon act.

CHAPTER 5
THE CHINESE DRAGON REAWAKENS: HOLLYWOOD FINDS ITS LION KING

Hoping to kick-start Chinese moviegoing again, the CCP approved something which many in the film industry thought could never happen.

In 1994, the mainland officially imported its first foreign film, Hollywood's *The Fugitive*, a 1993 blockbuster, starring Harrison Ford. It grossed $3 million in domestic box office (China) and was celebrated as an "event of historic significance."[126] It also didn't hurt that the film depicts an innocent US citizen (male) running from the police and a US Federal Marshall in a desperate attempt to clear his name from false accusations that he murdered his own wife. Chinese film promoters issued statements reinforcing the notion that only a completely broken and corrupt western-style system of justice would require such behavior of anyone truly innocent.

Regardless, the door to China's previously closed theaters to the west had been opened. Even if just a crack. Based on this success, the Government approved annual imports of Hollywood films. Between 6-10 such films were shown in Chinese theaters between 1995-2000.

In 1996, China announced relaxed restrictions on other foreign film markets as well.

That same year, the Chinese sought to organize and improve the reviewing efficiency of all films.

The State Council of the PRC approved sweeping changes which gave executive authority to implement the adoption of a film examination system which would be final. Stating that "any film that has not been examined and approved by the film examination organ of the Administrative Department of Radio, Film and Television under the authority of the State Council, may under any circumstances be distributed, projected, imported or exported."[127]

Behind this bureaucratic speak, what did this move mean?

It meant that the profile of films and the industry was to be subjected to an even higher, official authority of review, unform standards would be achieved with less discretionary power of review and censorship allowed. Along with this, supplemental language made it clear that centralized control over all 29 state-run film studios, whether they be based in Shanghai, Beijing or in rural areas, would be tightened. In practice, this also meant that censorship would no longer be a production-heavy focus. Censors and staff would become heavily involved from step one in the creative idea process, scriptwriting, filming, editing and if, approved, release and distribution. The CCP also made it clear that the making of any independently made quasi and full documentary films was severely discouraged.

Films, always an important part of CCP propaganda were getting some of the same upgrade in treatment which other sectors got in China's push to be accepted in the WTO.

But it was even a deeper commitment to get it "right" on the part of Chinese leaders.

In 1997, President Jiang Zemin issued a "manifesto" of new leadership in which he called for the "construction of a reawakened spiritual civilization."[128] Chinese Communist Party officials, he said, needed to be "Soul Engineers"[129] of the Chinese citizenry. He went on to lay out a plan which called for the CCP and its cadre of "engineers" to intervene politically in every aspect of Chinese popular culture. This involved television, print media and especially, film. His CCP Propaganda Department Chief Ding Guang'en issued a statement that "politics would be and must be the driver at every level, and in everything that we do, watch, hear and say."[130] And he placed films at the top of the list to ensure that the political messaging needed to "reawaken" Chinese society and to fulfill its destiny was being maximized, now and to the future.

Even before the "manifesto" was promulgated, the Chinese knew at least, internally, that to compete and eventually, dominate, the film industry, which was their goal, some tough realities had to be acknowledged. And change had to occur.

First, the numbers simply validated what theater owners across China already knew. Audiences for movies had shrunk. A lot. People, especially, the coveted middle-class, had simply stopped going to the movies. Rival cinemas had continued to evolve and expand their storytelling, their filmmaking technique, and their audience appeal.

Second, the global film industry was continuing to change and the top-down, tightly controlled studio approach was fast becoming a dinosaur and not the profitable, awe-inspiring "Jurassic Park" type of dinosaur. Analogous to the inherently myopic centralized, communist approach to economic planning, making movies this same way just about guaranteed that no one, except those who are basically force-fed the film, would pay for the privilege.

Third, while the Chinese had always known the power of film as propaganda, the modern moviegoer also wanted to be entertained. Modern audiences had options. The concept of film as sheer escapism, sort of a guilty pleasure, always a difficult one to embrace by the Chinese, was unavoidable.

From a business perspective, the Chinese also took somber note of the success of the so-called "Hollywood business model."[131] They saw this model as a blueprint of how to create, promote and distribute films in a way that seemed to turn even average films into global blockbusters for its investors. If China was short on innovation there certainly wasn't anything stopping them from being long on replication of what others had reached through years of costly trial and error.

So, what was the "Hollywood Way" which the Chinese began to consciously emulate to best tap into both the politics and profits of film?

First, start with a small core of experienced and reliable team-members with a skeletal support staff. Then through short-term contracts, add key members who could also attract other short-term talent. This usually meant signing a reliable and proven director and at least one bankable star to the project. Add to that, core short-term talent at every phase of the film's life. Of course, either have or purchase the rights to a literary work that can be adapted to the screen and then hire a talent to make that happen as fast as possible. Continue to contract talent with very specific project-oriented needs driven by both the scope and budget. Use the power of leveraging to out-source goods and services for the film to reduce costs and time-commitment. Engage in strategic co-production and co-distribution on a regional or even, global scale. And ideally, the production and distribution teams are different, again, reducing risk exposure to any single, exclusive company or talent.

As the "model" would evolve it would encompass using the same approach at ever and ever smaller or more niche units, especially when it came to maximizing the multiple platforms that became available by the 2010s and beyond. Netflix, Amazon Prime Video, ROKU, TUBI, HULU, these were all either starting, growing, or fast-approaching on the horizon of modern entertainment.

But at this point (the 1990s), the basic model was what the Chinese began copying. In addition to subsidizing promising film talent to both study and work in foreign production, with the idea they would eventually apply their skills and knowledge for the Chinese cinema, the Chinese also began to slowly enter film co-production and collaboration. For example, in 1990 for the film Ju Dou, the China Film Corporation agreed to a co-production and distribution deal with the Tokyo, Japan based (yes, those Japanese) entertainment publishing and distribution giant, *Tokuma Shoten.* And just three years after importing its first foreign (Hollywood) film for domestic screening, China did the previously unthinkable-They co-produced, along with US, Canadian and Hong Kong studios, a martial-arts fantasy film called *Warriors of Virtue* (1997). Both the collaboration with western film studios and the film's topic, martial arts fantasy, had both been taboo for decades. Goodbye old, hello new and improved.

Of course, in true Chinese style of "favoring the home-team," any, and all film co-productions were still to be considered domestic films. This way, they could maintain their overall "cap" on allowing only a handful of foreign film imports moving forward while still benefiting from western know-how, reputation, and industry networks. Already asserting the power of their potential movie-watching audience, their western co-producers either had to accept this domestic Chinese film label or be dropped from the agreement. Guess which path they chose? You got it. Let the creative types talk art well into the wee hours. It's money that gets the movies made.

China also showed more willingness to integrate private sector corporations into their filmmaking and distribution efforts. Whether the involvement was strictly financial backing or some combination of fiscal and service, this too, was a break from purely segregated filmmaking of the past. For example, the 1997 film *Opium War*, saw the Heng Tong Film and TV Co., LTD., a subsidiary of China's number one power cable manufacturing company, Heng Tong Co., play a key role in the production and distribution of the film. Certainly, private sector investment and integration into the lucrative film industry by Chinese private sector was nowhere near the degree as in the west. For example, in 1989, while China was roiled by the Tiananmen Square protests and its own cinema all but shuttered, the Japanese electronics giant, SONY Corp., closed the deal to purchase one of the original Hollywood film studios, Columbia Pictures, for $4.3 billion. Just years later, two more original Hollywood studios, MGM, and United Artists, would be bought up as well.

But, for the Chinese, there were signs and signals that doing business as usual, when it came to domestic filmmaking and its cinema was no longer acceptable. Small signs and faint signals, maybe. But they were there. What is most vital is sometimes least obvious.

While China was simultaneously censoring and stepping into twentieth-century filmmaking, Hollywood was busy coping with soaring production costs, skyrocketing star salaries and audiences with more entertainment platforms and choices than ever before. But a jungle-loving human and a king of the jungle would combine to help make the 90s a golden decade for Hollywood.

Ace Ventura: Pet Detective (1994) and *Ace Ventura: When Nature Calls* (1995), centered around a pet detective, played by funnyman Jim Carrey. This particular detective, who often struggled with flatulence issues, said "all righty then" a lot, and had mostly bad hair days, was also armed with the ability to "talk animal." This seemingly dysfunctional detective was a big hit with lots of moviegoing humans. In fact, on the strength of these two films, which cost less than $45 million to make and grossed over $320 million combined, Mr. Carrey became the first actor in Hollywood history to break the $20 million salary per film mark. Critics savaged the films, especially the sequel, while fans, human and otherwise, squealed with delight.[132]

Meanwhile, Ms. Julia Roberts who soared to fame as everyone's prettiest woman in the 1991 smash hit *Pretty Woman,* broke the Hollywood glass ceiling for female actors, becoming the first woman to command $20 million or more per film.

And a film about a big boat which hit a little iceberg broke the mark for the biggest budget ever, dropping anchor at a little over $205 million. Of course, *Titanic* (1997) did hit the top of the world for stars Leo DiCaprio and Kate Winslet as well as director and producer James Cameron, as it pulled in over $600 million in worldwide gross. And don't feel bad for Leo who was paid a very "un-Jim Carrey" salary at just $2.5 million. He negotiated a "back-end percentage" of 1.8 points. Translation? He ended up making over $40 million in addition to his guaranteed salary for his work on this film about love and tragedy on the high seas. Kate Winslet? Well, $2.0 million is still not bad work if you can find it. But if she hasn't already done so, she may want to fire her agent who didn't get her the "Leo deal."[133]

So, with the cost of making films more expensive than ever, studios had to find ways to bring down the upfront, fixed costs. Hiring bankable stars at less than the going rate but offering "back-end" points off the gross earnings of the film quickly became standard practice. But it took savvy producers, distributors, studio executives and stars who had enough confidence in their own box-office power as well as the film's "legs," to get the deal done. Tom Cruise was one such star. He went all in on "points" with his 1996 *Mission Impossible* action film and his number came up big. He ended up banking $72.5 million on that one film alone. Five more *Mission Impossible* films later, Mr. Cruise continues to bet big on himself and the franchise film's box office future. To date, he has accomplished the previously impossible, earning an estimated $310 million on the combined $4.3 billion box-office of Missions 2-7. MI7 is slated to be released in early 2023.

Of course, Tom Cruise was not the only star to reap the fruits of their film labor throughout the 1990s and beyond. Arnold "I'll be back" Schwarzenegger reprised his 1984 *Terminator* role in the 1991 film *T2*. Long on action and short on dialogue, Arnold spoke only 700 words throughout the entire film. On the other hand, he earned $21,429 per word. Who wouldn't keep coming back at that price? By 1997 Schwarzenegger was earning $25 million salary per film. Not Tom Cruise money, but still.[134]

Called the "decade of capitalism,"[135] the 1990s started with the USSR in shambles and its former republics embracing free and mixed-market capitalism to rise-up from under the communist rubble. Across Eastern Europe, fledgling democracies began to create unprecedented wealth and life opportunities for its people. Nations like South Korea, India, Indonesia, Chile, Taiwan, South Africa, Cambodia, Laos, and Vietnam enjoyed progress through continued political liberalization. Even China, as we've seen, while stepping up the call for political purity also began to unleash the power of free markets to prep for a much-coveted seat in the World Trade Organization.

The “Cold War” may have thawed out but the 1990s saw the accelerated rise of local, regional, and global terrorism. As the Soviet’s long and failed war in Iran ended in 1989 and the US-led Gulf War against Iraq ended in 1991, multiple terrorist splinter groups sought to fill the power vacuum left in that region in the wake of the Iraqi military defeat and the withdrawal of allied forces. One such terrorist group, *Al Qaeda* (“the base or core”) founded in the late 1980s, merged with Egypt’s Islamic Jihad cells and the Islamic Group to form a swift, mobile, and determined terrorist organization aimed at bringing harm to the west and its many assets.

With advanced weapons of mass destruction cheaper, deadlier, and more portable than ever, terrorist groups like this and others posed a very real and lethal threat to its enemies around the world. The nightmare of “far-away” terror being delivered to the doorstep of western nations like the US, was something filmmakers didn’t take long to bring to the large screen.

Audiences may have learned to “stop worrying and love the bomb” (*Dr. Strangelove* 1964) but in many ways, terrorism was well, more terrifying, and worrisome. It could seemingly happen anywhere, at any time from unknown enemies.

The decade of fighting terror was ushered in by actor and notorious bad boy Charlie Sheen of all people, who, as part of an elite Navy SEALS team fought a terrorist group known as “*Al Shadadah*.” That same year (1990) Bruce Willis went from being a one-man counter-terrorist team in an upscale corporate tower (*Die Hard* 1988) to doing the same against secretive terrorists who have hijacked a plane arriving at Dulles Airport. Two years later, tough guy actor Steven Segal plays a Navy cook who, when not baking pies or simmering *bouillabaisse*, takes on terrorists attempting to take control of a navy battleship. The real world of terrorism interrupted Hollywood though. On February 26th, 1993, Islamic terrorists bombed the World Trade Center in NYC. Just over two years later, two domestic terrorists, Timothy McVeigh, and Terry Nichols, bombed the Alfred P. Murrah Federal Building in Oklahoma City, Oklahoma. Hollywood's obsession with terrorism continued unabated. In *Sudden Death* (1995), Jean Claude Van Damme kicks the puck out of terrorists who are holding the US Vice-President hostage at, of all places, a hockey arena during game seven of the NHL Stanley Cup Final.

The 1990s Hollywood war on terrorism rounded out the decade with *Broken Arrow* (1996), starring John Travolta and Christian Slater about a good guy gone bad who happens to also have nuclear missiles, and *Face/Off* (1997) an oddly unsettling film, again, with Travolta, who along with Nicholas Cage share facial transplants as an FBI Agent attempts to foil a sinister terrorist plot. Of note, the great Hong Kong action film director, John Woo, was handed the reins to this big-budget, studio driven movie. A first for him and Hong Kong directors, but not the last. Just years later, Woo would direct Tom Cruise in MI2.

The 1990s wouldn't have been the same though, if not for *Air Force One* (1997). Here, Harrison Ford sheds his Indy hat and whip and his Star Wars laser to battle East European terrorists who hijack "his plane," *aka.*, Air Force One and start killing innocents. President Ford does his best John McClane (*Die Hard*) impression and single-handedly takes down the terrorists. Word is that Islamic terrorists were discussed as being the main villains for the film, but the executives felt that it would offend less people if it were terrorists from a break-away, former Soviet Republic. And even better if the lead villain was not "foreign." Consequently, audiences see American actor Gary Oldham and get to hear him as he struggles with his on again, off again, vaguely foreign but certainly not middle eastern sounding accent.136

When not saving the free world from terrorism, 1990s Hollywood also cheers a kid who gets left behind for the Holidays but terrorizes (sort of) would-be burglars, gives birth to dinosaurs that roam the world not once, but twice, gets creeped out by another kid who sees dead people, takes us to Normandy, France for a harrowing 24 minutes of war unlike any we've ever seen on screen before, introduces us to a special boy named Gump who appreciates the variety of choices in his box of chocolates, an erudite with an appetite who enjoys eating unusual dishes with a bottle of chianti, and a group of not so-nice fellas (*Home Alone, Jurassic Park 1 and 2*, *Sixth Sense*, *Saving Private Ryan, Forrest Gump*, *Silence of the Lambs and Good Fellas)*. All box-office gold.

Hollywood of the 90s also made room for visionary directors like Quentin Tarantino, who was finding ways to make the gangster and noirish film genres seem fresh and hip with his modest, yet critically acclaimed film *Reservoir Dogs* (1992) and his hip, fresh and mega-hit, *Pulp Fiction* (1994). The latter gave us a bible reciting, potty-mouth hitman played to a perfect pitch by Samuel L. Jackson, his co-hitman who gets to dance with the mob's wife (of course he does, it's John Travolta) and a brassy, classy femme fatale embodied by Uma Thurman. She would not only become Tarantino's muse and romantic interest but an iconic action star just a few years later in his *Kill Bill* Volumes 1 and 2.

The 1990s would also witness the beginning of a Disney "renaissance." Ever since Charles Mintz stole Oswald the Lucky Bunny out from under the nose of Walt Disney, the future of animated films was forever changed. Out was the floppy-eared bunny and in was a mouse named Mortimer. The finest creation of Walt and his artist pal, Ubbe. Not yet ringing a bell?

Well, this cuddly mouse would have been named Mortimer if it had been solely Walt's choice. Thankfully, it was not. Walt's wife Lillian loved the mouse they created but hated the name.

Her suggestion?

I think you may already know it.

Led by Mickey the Mouse (later just Mickey Mouse), Walt Disney Animation studios had dominated big screens for decades with such all-time hits like the 1938 *Snow White and the Seven Dwarfs*. Still a fan favorite, this is still one of the all-time most successful film, animated or otherwise.

But for all its early dominance, the 1970s and 80s had seen a bit of a "Disney Slump."[137] Pixar Studios, founded in 1979 would begin to challenge the Mouse's empire with mega-hits like *Toy Story 1* (1995) and *Toy Story 2* (1999) and former Disney executive Jeffrey Katzenberg would team up with Hollywood icon Steven Spielberg and powerhouse music agent David Geffen to found Dreamworks SKG, which would emerge as another animation rival.

But a King emerged in the 1990s. A *Lion King* (1994), which would help spur a Disney renaissance, re-establishing it as one of the, if not the, pre-eminent animation films studio worldwide. Disney also found box office success with *Beauty and the Beast* (1991) and *Aladdin* (1992). Those films together combined for over 850 million and counting. Granted, it was no *Toy Story* 1 and 2, which grossed close to $900 million and counting, but the animated doldrums Disney had endured were fast becoming just tailwind behind *Steamboat Willie*.

A decade that began with political uncertainty and upheaval, punctuated by real terror, had proven to be nothing less than a blockbuster of a film decade for Hollywood. Tinseltown had reasserted its grip on global cinematic supremacy.

Only some unbelievable combination of incompetence, naivety, greed, and short-sightedness would allow this grip to be broken. Luckily for China, who did not hide its desire to gain equal footing with Hollywood and then, surpass it, Hollywood was not in short supply of any of the above. And, it had a double-barreled, secret weapon-Joe Biden and his longtime sidekick, Chris Dodd, just to make sure its ass(ets) would be covered.

While the 1980s in Hong Kong came to a dramatic close with over 1.5 million of a population of just 5.6 million marching to protest the atrocities taking place in Tiananmen Square, the 1990s opened with nothing but good vibes at the movie box office. Led by so-called "Second Wave" film directors like Wong Kar Wai, Stanley Kwan, and Clara Law, many of whom were Hong Kong born but studied film overseas, Hog Kong cinema enjoyed a brief, yet dynamic re-birth. Wong Kar Wai directed *Chungking Express* (1994) a film about two lovestruck cops noted for its deeply saturated and vivid colors and impressionistic style, *Happy Together* (1997) a story of a Hong Kong couple whose Argentinian vacation goes awry and *Fallen Angels* (1995) a gritty film about a disillusioned killer.

Even more prolific during the '90s, Kwan directed at least one, and frequently two films per year during the '90s with hits such as Center Stage (1991). *Too Happy For Words* (1992), and *Hold You Tight* (1997), while being named Hong Kong's Best Director for his *Full Moon in New York.*

Clara Law, born in Macau but raised in Hong Kong, also produced nearly a film a year with films like *Temptation of a Monk* (1993) and *Wonton Soup* (1994).

However talented this '90s group of directors were, and they were, the 1990s belonged to an agile and supremely gifted martial arts and former acrobatic performer named Chan Kong-sang. You may know him simply as Jackie Chan. In many ways, Mr. Chan and his friend and director Chang Cheh, were cinematic visionaries. Early on, they both saw the appeal of martial arts for the film camera as well as leading the way in developing the martial arts action genre, especially targeting it to a western audience. What Bruce Lee had started, Chan and Cheh further perfected. They helped refine the martial arts action hero formula for sustained cinematic success. More elaborate fight choreography, improved cinematography and editing and better scripts, all helped expand the house that Bruce Lee had built.

In the 1990s alone, Jackie Chan starred in over 20 films, culminating with a cross-over blockbuster called *Rush Hour* (1999). Directed by Brett Rainer and distributed by New Line Cinema, this mainstream Hollywood picture helped lift Chan, already a Hong Kong cinema legend, into the next stratosphere of global fame and fortune. The film tells the story of an uneasy Hong Kong on the eve of the official handover to China.

And he wasn't the only actor helping the Hong Kong cinema roar throughout the '90s.

Michelle Yeoh, a Malaysian born actress also starred in nearly 20 Hong Kong films during this time, Ms. Yeoh, also appearing in Hong Kong films under the name, Michelle Khan, is also a highly trained and talented martial arts expert and accomplished dancer. Starring in Hong Kong cinema films such as *Tai Chi Master* (1993) and *Wing Chun* (1994), plus her over two decades of films, as well as her martial arts training all helped her achieve the co-starring role in *Tomorrow Never Dies* (1997), the latest installment in the James Bond franchise at that time and a first for an Asian actress.

Completing this trio of acting star power, was Chow Yun Fat, a Hong Kong born and raised martial arts performer and singer. He too, starred in well over a dozen films during this period, including the popular and well-regarded *The Replacement Killers* (1998) a Columbia Pictures mega-hit.

However, the core elements which helped propel the Hong Kong cinema of the 1990s to unprecedented heights, formulaic martial arts films, star power, successful cross-over projects with Hollywood, also contributed to Hong Kong's undoing by decade's end. Stars like Jackie Chan, Chow Yun Fat and Michelle Yeoh found fame through integration into Hollywood's mainstream cinema and the Hong Kong homeland cinema suffered. Combined with a number of other factors like; a sweeping Asian financial crisis, the rise of the middle class which had and preferred other entertainment options like home video and DVDs, a martial arts action formula which had become stale and predictable, the increase of unchecked video and DVD black-market piracy in Hong Kong and mainland China, a glutted film market, along with a growing dominance of the hard and soft core porn film industry in Hong Kong (by 1995 over 50% of all films made are porn), all contributed to a dramatic slowing-down of homegrown filmmaking and distribution. The rise of the Hollywood Blockbuster of the '90s also dominated the Hong Kong market and suppressed local consumption and cut into local exports.

With lots of unease and trepidation throughout Hong Kong over what life would be like in a post-British rule as the handover in 1997 to China was completed, filmmakers also looked to the future of their own industry with uncertainty. Accompanying financial hardship didn't help the industry. As the new millennium approached, Hong Kong Cinema went from releasing well over 200 films annually to less than 100.

By 2000, Hong Kong cinema was facing increased mainland Chinese censorship and outright bans, a growing reputation for poor quality filmmaking and, despite WTO concerns, intense pressure from mainland China to not compete against its own growing cinema. Moreover, some 18 years or so before COVID-19, a lethal virus likely emanating from Yunnan, China (the SARS virus) all but shuttered Hong Kong cinema by 2003. Only 54 films were produced and released that year. While the Hong Kong government tried to set-aside artistic grants and funds to encourage domestic filmmaking, it was clear that Hong Kong studios and directors would have to make some tough creative control and co-production decisions soon or risk complete collapse of a once thriving cinema.

Meanwhile, in Taipei (Taiwan), filmmakers were facing similar challenges. Political pressure from mainland China in the form of censorship and banning films, their refusal to allow Chinese films or directors to participate in the prestigious Taiwanese annual Golden Horse Film Festival, along with rampant video piracy, all were fraying an already vulnerable industry. Still, before the Taiwanese cinema nearly completely collapsed by 1995 there were some bright spots. Taiwanese born Ang Lee who was educated in Taiwan and the USA, directed critically acclaimed and popular films such as *Pushing Hands* (1991), *The Wedding Banquet* (1993), *Eat Drink Man Woman* (1994) and *Sense and Sensibility* (1995), while Tsai Ming Liang's *Vive L'Amour* (1994) also helped define for many, what Taiwanese cinema meant during this decade. A sense of isolation, repression, rejection, and humiliation. However, Edward Yang's *A Brighter Summer Day* (1991) about the struggles of the

Taiwanese to find their identity after the Kuomintang fled mainland China and Mao's communists and occupied Taiwan by force, may have captured the essence of contemporary Taiwan the best. There was, as the film implied, a reason for hope. A people and a place in search of their own destiny. On the cusp of a new millennium under the shadow of a hostile and threatening nation.

What a sweeping epic of a film that would make, right?

Too bad it's yet another script Hollywood would never touch for fear of angering the insatiable, Chinese dragon.

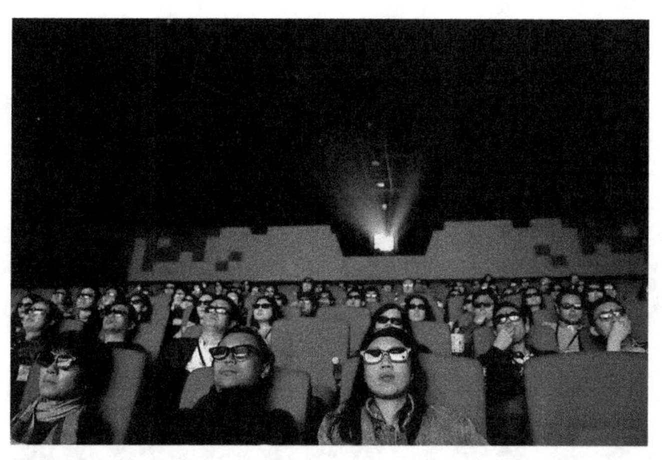

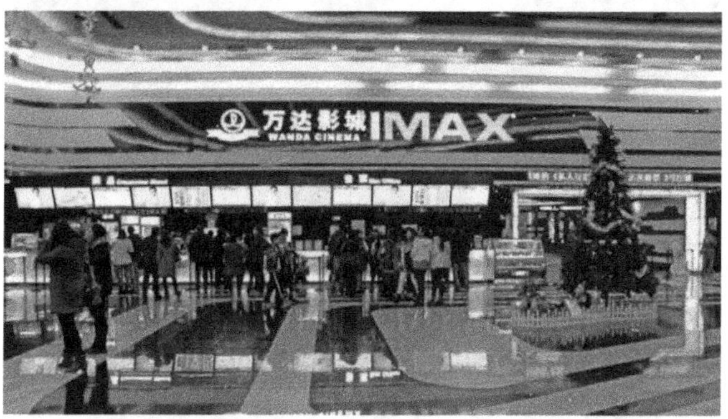
万达影城
WANDA CINEMA
IMAX

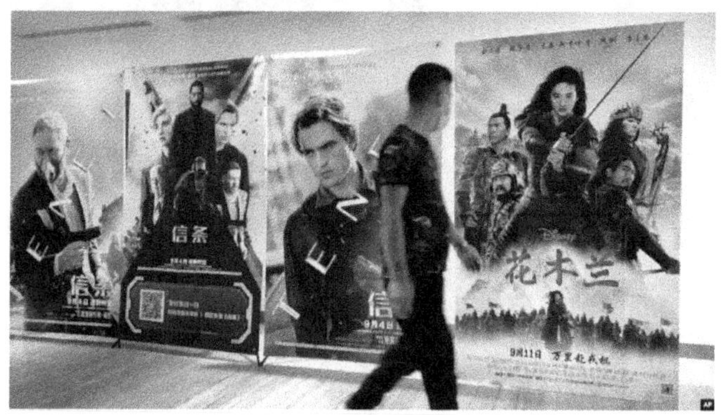
信条
DISNEY
花木兰
9月11日

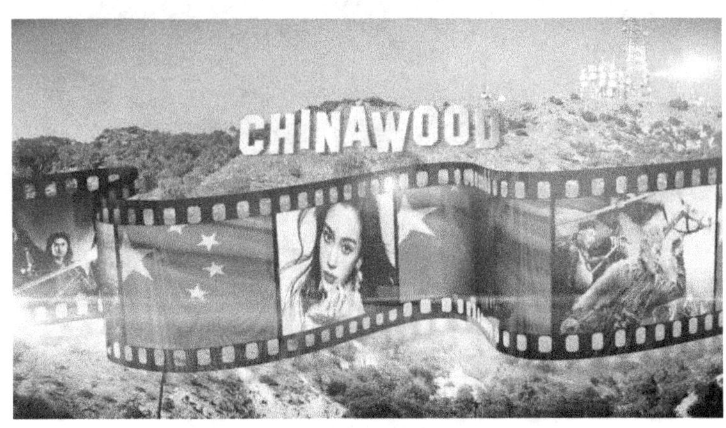
CHINAWOOD

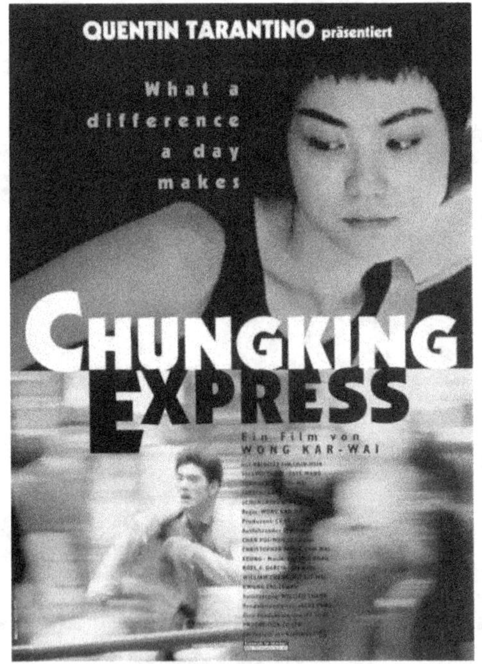
QUENTIN TARANTINO präsentiert
What a difference a day makes
CHUNGKING EXPRESS
Ein Film von WONG KAR-WAI

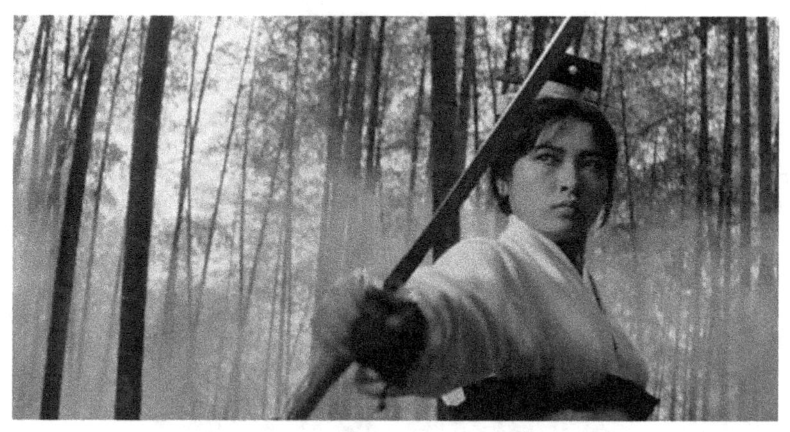

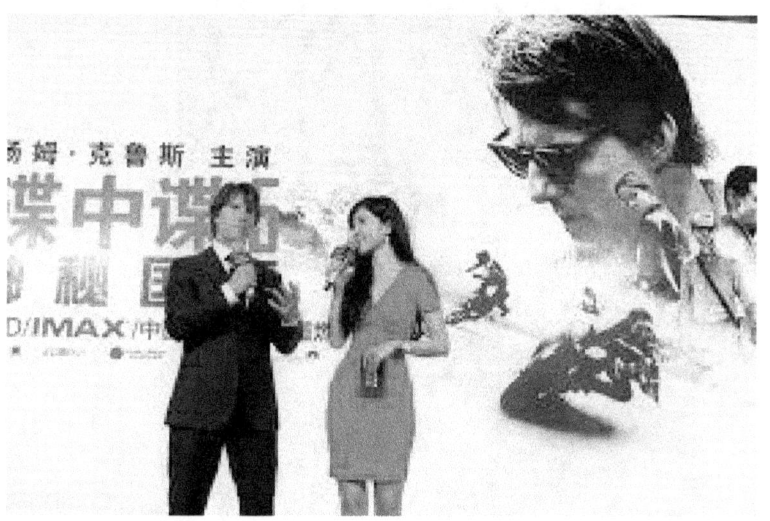
姆·克鲁斯 主演
D/IMAX

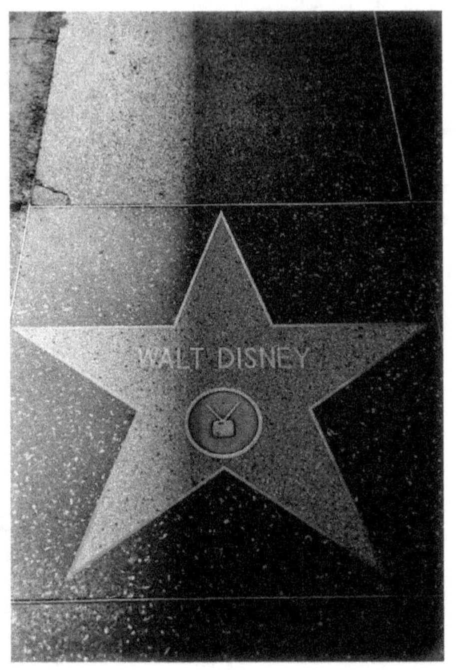
WALT DISNEY

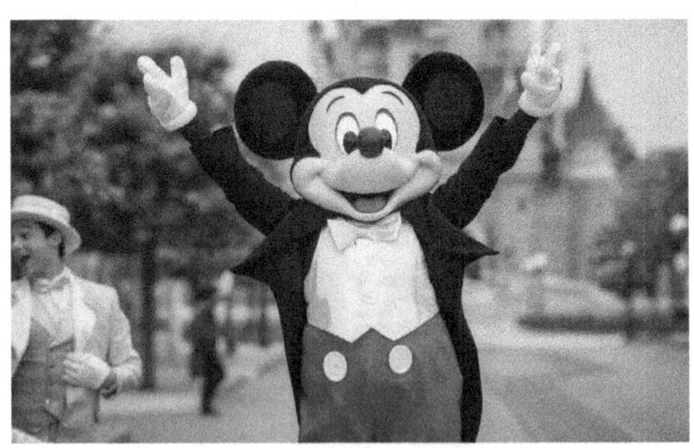

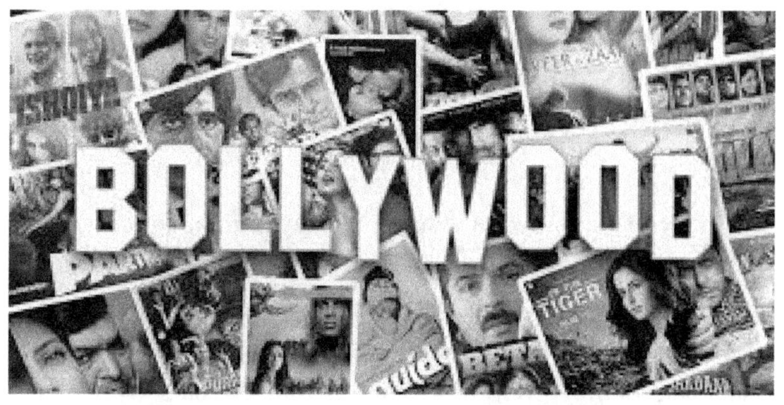
BOLLYWOOD
TIGER

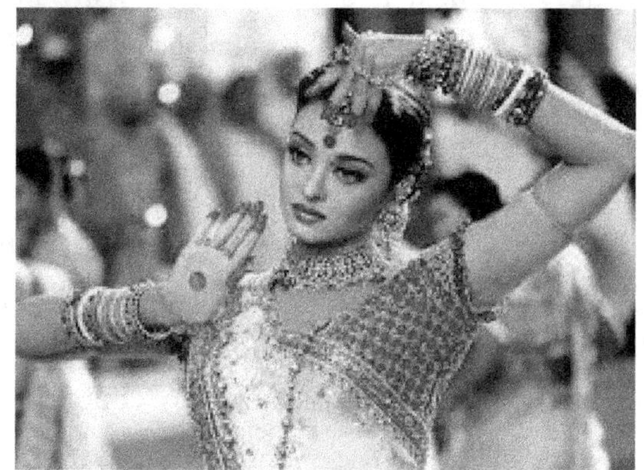

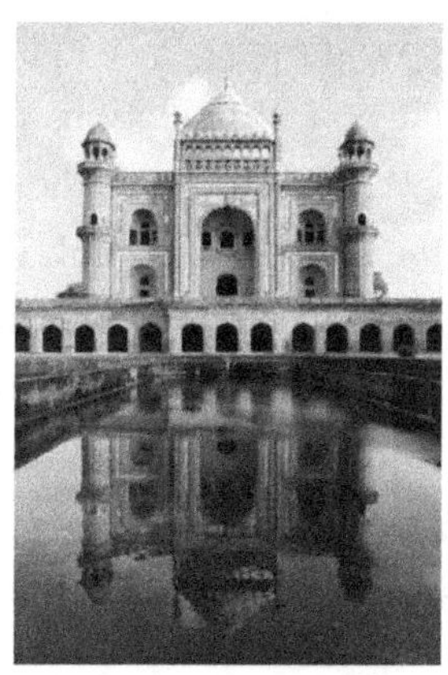

CHAPTER 6

THE CHINESE DRAGON ENTERS THE NEW MILLENNIUM: HOLLYWOOD ROLLS OUT THE RED CARPET

In some ways, China entered the new millennium much the same as it had closed out the old one. CCP censors banned critically acclaimed films like *Suzhou River* (2000) because it showed the chaos and pollution of parts of the Suzhou River in Shanghai, *Beijing Bicycle* (2000), a film directed by Chinese filmmaker Wang Xiaoshuai and produced by Taiwanese Arc Light, because it showed immoral class conflict and *Devils on the Doorstep* (2000) because it did not portray the Chinese as the "pure and passive victims"[138] they were during the Sino-Japanese war.

In other words, China still held fast to the Maoist notion that art, in and of itself, held no inherent value. It was to be controlled and manipulated for political and economic gain. It must also be constantly monitored for fear art could run contrary to state interest.

Consequently, films like the *Sino-Dutch War of 1661* (2000) which was an historical epic showing, you guessed it, the Chinese as pure victims of deceit and exploitation, passed through the censor gates. As did *I Love Beijing* (2000) though with a changed title of *Warmth of the Sun*, lest anyone think the former title was ironic due to some less than completely flattering exterior shots of Beijing. Even *Father* (2000), a partially state-studio backed project's release was blocked for four years due to CCP censorship concerns that the finished film did not show the Chinese in enough of a positive light. Finally, and secretly, the film was shown by its director Wang Shuo at the Locarno Film Festival in Switzerland.

"*La plus ca change, la plus c'est la meme chose,*" right?

(The more things change, the more they remain the same).

Well, in this case, yes and no. Let me explain.

While clearly not backing off their tight censorship grip on both domestic and foreign films, China also continued its strategic move of increased co-productions. They saw this as both a way to learn from success and increase the quality of its own domestic films (all co-productions are, by Chinese law, considered to be domestic made) all the while striving to both replicate and replace the famed "Hollywood Model" of making and selling films.

So, not surprisingly, just as they kicked off the new decade doing what they had always done (banning films and heavily censoring others), they also co-produced one of the best films of 2000 with Ang Lee's wuxia masterpiece, *Wo Hu Cang Long*, better known as *Crouching Tiger, Hidden Dragon.* With an international cast of Chow Yun-fat (Hong Kong born, a native Cantonese speaker), Michelle Yeo (a Malaysian born-English and Malay speaker), Chang Chen (Taiwanese) and Zhang Ziyi (Chinese, native Mandarin speaker), all being directed by Lee (Taiwanese born and educated in USA film schools), this was the type of project China wanted to be seen as not just being a part of, but also leading. Its own state-run and largest film studio in China, if not the world, the China Film Group Corporation along with Columbia Pictures, Sony Pictures Classic and Taiwan's own Zoom Hunt Productions called the shots.

Inspired by an ancient Chinese poem which depicts a tiger crouching behind a dark rock and a coiled, root of a large tree in the shape of a dragon residing in the forest, this film, with its cutting-edge technology, beautiful cinematography, and detailed fight choreography, went on to be nominated for 10 Academy Awards. From a very modest US $17 million budget to grossing nearly $215 million, it was the most successful foreign film import ever to the US.

And it signaled that part of the Chinese strategy was to not just compete with Hollywood in the new millennium but to overtake it.

While most of its state-sponsored and approved foreign film co-productions prior to 2000 were with Hong Kong, Taiwan, South Korea, and Macao, between 2000-2010 China would enter into over 125 film co-productions. Many of these would be with the USA (about 40%), Canada, Australia, the UK, France, India, and Russia. China saw Hollywood co-productions in particular, as a means to a better end. "We want to learn from Hollywood but to apply these lessons on our terms and for the good of all of China."[139]

Requirements of foreign films being allowed to enter China through such co-productions meant that the film would have Chinese actors, Chinese collaboration on or at least final review of script, must be at least partially shot on location in mainland China, have at least 1/3 of the film's investors be from China and all distribution power and decisions would be controlled by the state-run film company China Film Group. Additionally, any legal proceedings must have only Chinese law firms and lawyers and the film must, of course, show "China and its people in a favorable, positive light."[140]

The long-held taboos of showing or discussing the "Three T's" continued to be in effect in any co-production deal. So, with apologies to Richard Gere, Tibet, Taiwan, and Tiananmen Square were non-starters and forbidden.

Yet, despite loss of creative control, power, distribution rights and in many cases a relentless even coercive pressure to unilaterally share technology and trade secrets to its Chinese "partners," Hollywood, among others, was still eager to comply.

Why?

Well, the Chinese market of over 1.7 billion moviegoers surely had something to do with it.

Outside of Tinseltown. the US Government similarly coveted that 1.7 billion strong market as it continued with its own push to approve China's membership application to the coveted World Trade Organization (WTO).

China's dream of becoming a global economic superpower was soon to become a reality.

In 1990 as China began to reform some of its economic infrastructure and trade practices to align with WTO eligibility requirements, its annual Gross Domestic Product (GDP) was just $360.9 billion. Aided in large part by the US granting China its most favored nation status for trading purposes plus its own internal reforms, just 10 years later, in 2000 and on the cusp of WTO membership, China's GDP had grown to a little over $1 trillion.

Yet, breaking one trillion for a nation the size of China was still underwhelmingly modest.

China's leaders knew that their nation still represented vast, nearly unlimited potential for wealth and power, not just regional but unchallenged global power. Yet, ever since the glorious revolution this goal had eluded them, despite their relentless, often ruthless pursuit. What Mao had failed to accomplish during his seemingly never-ending reforms and "revolutions," what every Chinese leader since, including Deng Xiaoping's "lean toward the west"[141] policy of China had wanted, to turn China into an economic powerhouse, was now finally within its grasp.

Chinese President Hu Jintao referred to China's decision to join the WTO as a "major strategic decision based on our comprehensive analysis of our situation at home and abroad in order to push forward China's reforms and the opening up of China and aid in its socialist, modernization drive."[142]

The US and its WTO allies and trading partners saw China's membership as a "check on China's communist government and its aggressive designs and would speed up its transition to a market economy encouraging it (China) to have a greater stake in setting and following global rules and norms."[143]

Could both things be true?

On December 11th, 2001, China was granted full and unconditional membership to the WTO.

And it has never looked back.

At the time, Bill Clinton opined that by formally approving China's entry into the WTO, "The US House of Representatives has taken an historic step toward continued prosperity in America, reform in China, and peace in the world and it (the entry) will open new doors of trade for America and new hope for change in China."[144]

Chinese Premier Zhu Rongi reassured the west that, "We will abide by our pledges and earnestly fulfill all our promises."140

Wen Jiabao declared that "China will keep its doors open forever."[145]

Former President George H.W. Bush, who presided over China's initial application into the WTO, confidently proclaimed that "No nation on Earth has yet discovered a way to import the world's goods and services while stopping foreign ideas at the border."[146]

China found a way.

With the help of internet and high-tech giant, Cisco, China took what early internet pioneers called "the key to connecting the globe in a free speech platform," and weaponized it. Against their own people.[147]

And because of this collaborative "project," the vast majority of the Chinese people in 2022 continue to remain largely in the dark as far as any type of a free flow of information due to the partnership of the CCP and Cisco and their construction of the internet's version of "The Great Wall of China."[148]

The CCP's online blocking of websites, limiting access, sophisticated surveillance, monitoring and tracking methods as well as manipulation and deployment of hundreds of thousands of "*cyberbots*" to help in their state-run propaganda and information manipulation globally is just one part of its multi-faceted strategy by China's leaders to preserve and protect its own power and extend its dominance. Post the wrong thing, challenge the party line, in China standing-up to authority, even "virtually," can and does lead to the disappearance of your post and you. Posting and/or sharing of unapproved material "counter to state goals" can be punishable by incarceration, forced labor and worse.[149]

It's not that China does not know the power of foreign ideas. The real problem is that they do.

So, besides finding a way, an extremely effective and ruthless way to stop foreign ideas repugnant to the CCP dead in their tracks, China's dream of unlocking its potential became, with the help of the US and its WTO allies, became a profound reality.

From just over one trillion GDP in 2000, China, after a mere two decades of advantageous trading rules and benefits of WTO membership, now boasts of a previously unimagined 14.5 trillion annual GDP. They now spend over 900 times on their military budget alone than what they did in 2000. They have surpassed every nation on earth in terms of sheer economic power and trail only the US and that gap continues to close.

And with this new economic power continued to come increased political power and influence.

Like a film you've seen before but can't change the ending, despite knowing what comes next, it became apparent right away that China wanted a far different ending than did the US and its allies. That lovely, democratic fruit they hoped would ripen from China's entry quickly rotted.

While continuing to make promises and "solemn" pledges of reform, China largely continued its statist ways. Illegally subsidizing domestic companies, refusing to abide by WTO rules fully while insisting that foreign companies turn over sensitive high-tech secrets as a condition to market entry was just the tip of the Chinese iceberg. Rampant cyber-spying, high-tech theft, Intellectual Property and Copyright violations, unchecked black-market piracy and blatant infractions of agreed-to trade terms began in earnest seemingly before the ink even dried on the WTO agreement.

Their exploitation of WTO strategy seemed obvious if not transparent. Do everything they could possibly do to exploit the membership for their own advantage while employing stall and delay tactics, earnest apologies and calls for serious negotiations each time they were called out for their illegal practices.

In short, the WTO was built for capitalist nations who shared very basic rules of economic engagement. Its rules, its structure, its own mechanism for dealing with member states cheating was all premised on the assumption that capitalist trading partners would always have more to gain than lose by cooperation. Playing by shared rules and norms would be just a fact of life in the WTO.

But while China has allowed some capitalism in revving up its economic engine, it is also a fact that it does not and never did have any intention of playing by western, capitalist rules.

Remember, the US had "hope" that the WTO entry would check communist aggression, even lead to deep democratic reforms within China. The Chinese though looked on the entry as a "comprehensive, strategic decision"[150] for socialist modernization.

In short, warm hope versus cold calculation.

So, the answer to the earlier question?

No.

Apparently, both things could not be fully true.

Since its entry into the WTO, the US has filed nearly two dozen formal cases against China. All similarly accusing China of violating both the spirit and letter of the WTO laws. Closing off its own market, coercive practices, refusing to abide by agreed upon shared quotas, taking sensitive data and trade secrets from its partner without authorization while blocking access to its own data, all this and more.

The US film and entertainment industry was not immune from China's exploitation and one-sided approach to trade and compliance.

On April 09, 2007, after months of bi-lateral negotiations between US and China over US accusations that rampant Chinese IP, copyright, piracy, and counterfeiting violations was costing the US billions annually were leading nowhere, the US filed two major cases against China.

Both cases alleged that China had refused to address glaring and costly deficiencies in its domestic IP laws despite assurances it would and continued to place market access barriers to a wide range of US made goods including, copyright-based products like films, books, videos, and music.

As US Ambassador Susan C. Schwab made clear, "Piracy and counterfeiting levels in China remain unacceptably high. Inadequate protection of intellectual property rights in China cost US firms and workers billions of dollars each year, and in the case of many products, it also poses a serious risk of harm to consumers in China, the US and around the world."[151]

Two years later, in 2009, a WTO appeals board sided with the US, its film and entertainment industry and against China and what it ruled were its illegal and damaging trade practices, contrary to WTO law.

US Trade Representative Ron Kirk called it a "Big win for America and for film," but warned that the ruling was only effective if China "responds promptly to these findings and brings its measures into full compliance."[152]

The US Motion Picture of America Association Chairman Dan Glickman also praised the WTO decision, calling it a "major step in levelling the playing field for America's creative industries" and that if implemented, it would finally "open up the Chinese movie market."[153]

But while hope may spring eternal, the Chinese commitment to "play fair" does not.

In the immediate aftermath of the WTO decision at least, China did not appear to have any intention of implementing the compliance measures called for in the ruling.

In fact, it continued to allow less than half the number of Hollywood films into the Chinese Market than the WTO agreed upon 20 per year. Sometimes the number was more than 10, sometimes less.

But it wasn't just the sliding scale quota of imported Hollywood films which caused headaches and heartaches in US film studios. The same year the WTO ruling was handed down, China's censors abruptly yanked James Cameron's CGI/Motion capture mega-hit *Avatar* (2009) out of 1,600 Chinese theaters just two weeks into its premiere.

The film which was already setting attendance records and box-office gross ($1.27 billion) internationally and in China, was deemed to be "offensive and threatening," both to the Chinese people and to the Chinese domestic film box-office. According to one report, the CCP officials feared that the film's depiction of an indigenous people, the *Na'Vi*, rising up against its oppressors may hit to close to "home," and the film's popularity was suppressing domestic film attendance.

So, despite its WTO commitments, its pledge to "keep its doors open forever," and the ink on the WTO ruling against China still fresh, *Avatar* was halted in its tracks. In its place was shown a film about Confucius. Just in case the masses forgot that art is never just for art's sake in China here was a vivid reminder. Just a year earlier, China had banned the Hollywood superhero blockbuster *The Dark Knight* (2008) despite assurances it would be fully released. because a scene was filmed in Hong Kong.

When it comes to China, its sensitivities about what can and cannot be shown in film seem to run deeper than the Suzhou River.

James Cameron continued to publicly call upon the Chinese Government to meet and exceed its film importation numbers. He argued that the demand was there, and increasing films allowed in would only spur more movie theater and screen construction across China. A win-win for all involved.

Meanwhile, when not banning Hollywood blockbuster films and failing to fulfill its commitments to meet agreed upon number of foreign film imports, China was breaking its own domestic box office records with the sheer number of films released and screened. The same year it pulled *Avatar* from its theaters; China heavily promoted its own *The Founding of a Republic*. This was a tribute film to the glory of the Communist revolution and victory in 1949, replete with a Chinese star-studded cast. It went on to be the leading domestic box office grossing film to that point (393 million yuan or about $63 million US dollars). China also continued to aggressively pursue film co-production, releasing several films co-produced with Taiwan, Hong Kong, France, South Korea, Malaysia, and Disney Studios.

The next year (2010) was more of the same. China continued to evade its Hollywood film importation obligations while it provided subsidies and ramped up investment in its own domestic film industry. It was another full slate of Chinese made films, including a Hollywood-style disaster film, *Aftershock*, which was the big box-office winner. Co-productions continued to be a very beneficial strategy for China as this meant that any film produced was by Chinese law, a China film, so that the percentage of and profit distribution was nowhere near equal among the "equal partners" involved in making the film. And state-owned and run film companies like the China Film Group (CFG) enjoyed both vertical and horizontal integration monopolies in the film industry. Anyone else, including Hollywood, had to play ball with CFG and abide by its production and distribution decisions or risk going home empty handed. Samuel Goldwyn and Louis B. Mayer would have been jealous.

2011 marked yet another year which China continued to invest heavily in its own film industry while again, restricting, illegally, the number of Hollywood imports. *The Flowers of War* (2011) was the year's box office winner, making close to $95 million. Yet, it also had the most expensive operating budget of a domestic Chinese film ever (over $93 million).

Directed by Chinese filmmaker Zhang Zhimou, this film told the story yet again, of the Nanking Massacre during the 1937 war against the Japanese. Though, the film was told more from a woman's perspective and cast Welsh born actor Christian Bale as John Miller, who ends up being the hero of the film. It was a calculated effort to widen the film's appeal for both Chinese and English-speaking audiences. In fact, the film ended up being about 40% English and the rest mandarin Chinese. In part, the film's theme, decision to cast Bale as a "White Hero" and the cultural significance of the "Rape of Nanjing" to China, all led to protracted negotiations with Chinese censors and changes to the film over a period of several months, delaying its release.[154]

And while the film got mixed reviews from critics and it just barely broke even, it did represent a new willingness from China to invest heavily in its own studios to equal the "*Meiguo Da Pian*" (Big American Blockbusters) of Hollywood.[155]

The same year, China celebrated the 90th year anniversary of the founding of the Communist Party. It did so in part, with the screening of another heavily financed film about the CCP's founding. While this blatant sort of propaganda piece hearkened back to the early years of Chinese cinema when this was all that was officially produced and approved, this did represent a change in one significant way. *The Founding of the Party* (2011) was a high-quality, slickly produced film reflecting ever increasingly sophisticated storytelling. This was no Madame Mao's "hit them over the head" with the umpteenth rendition of *The White Haired Girl* and its lesson about the unquestioned purity, and virtue of all ordinary Chinese. No, China was continuing to learn and apply their Hollywood lessons for profit and propaganda.

And the next year, 2012, the long march toward Chinese cinematic supremacy accelerated into a sprint towards the finish line.

"Bide your time and hide your strength."[156]

For five years China had been evading addressing the WTO ruling in 2007 against them when it came to their film and entertainment practices. Not meeting their film importation obligations, employing coercive trade practices like forced proprietary trade secrets and technology transfer under the cover of co-production, continuing to be lackadaisical when it came to IP and copyright protection, piracy and black-market price dilution, even ignoring concerns that they were rigging box-office receipts and withholding revenue sharing, all this and more while they built their strength and prospered from their newly minted WTO membership. Hollywood and its advocacy arm, the Motion Picture Association of America (MPAA) led by former US Senator Chris Dodd and close friend to then US Vice-President Joe Biden, had grown tired of biding their time and watching China's strength grow. Dodd, who had earned his reputation for being one of the more, shall we say, morally flexible members of the Senate, had amassed a pile of money since leaving his office largely due to his openness to representing whomever and whatever could pay his salary. Fair enough. Why not exploit weak ethical laws for former government servants and loopholes the size of Brink trucks? The USA was not communist China, after all.

So, when he became head of the MPAA he reached out to his good buddy and someone who had already developed business ties with the Chinese Communists, Joe Biden. The Veep also had money-making on his mind. It was 2012 and a 2016 presidential run was already in his sights. The Vice-Presidential mansion was fine, but it wasn't the West Wing. And after 50 years in politics, it was long overdue. Hollywood, along with Silicon Valley, was the go-to source for gobs of campaign cash for liberal democrats, progressives, activists, consultants, really anyone without a political "R" by their name. And the longer China wouldn't loosen its grip on its film industry the longer that meant Chinese cash wouldn't flow into Hollywood and out to politicians like Biden. Though he once joked he never had time nor the interest to really watch any movies, the Vice President was, as Chris Dodd put it, "Our champion in the White House."[157] A common interest and a decades-long pre-existing friendship. Many great partnerships have been built on even less, or haven't you ever watched *Casablanca*?

Xi Jinping had been building his career within the Chinese Communist Party and burnishing his own political and leadership credentials for decades. And now, after gaining national praise for his role in managing the 2008 Summer Olympics in Beijing, a great source of Chinese pride and nationalism, Xi Jinping's own star was ascending. In September of 2012, he held the powerful title of General Secretary of the CCP in addition to being the Chairman of the Central Military Commission and the Vice-President of China. He was, like his American counterpart Joe Biden, just a heartbeat away from his nation's top-spot. Unlike Joe Biden, paying for a very expensive political campaign in a free, fair, and open election was of no concern to Xi Jinping. But making smart and strategic decisions that would ensure China's continued massive economic growth for decades to come was his top priority. This was the burden he carried as he traveled to the USA for a visit with the US Vice-President in Los Angeles in September of 2012. Respecting the past but carving out a very different future. A dilemma that calls for a balance between cold calculation and explosive action. Or haven't you seen Jackie Chan in *Rush Hour* yet?

In between nibbles over a pricey lunchtime spread at the JW Marriot, LA, Joe Biden told Xi Jinping that, "We're really close, it (the MPAA proposal) is a good deal, it would be great to get this done."[158] The Communist leader told Biden that he needed to consult with several agencies back home, including the state-run film monopoly, Chinese Film Group (CFG) before taking any action.

Finally, by the end of the day, Biden and his pal, Chris Dodd got their answer. In exchange for suspending any existing US claims against China in the WTO and all future such claims, at least "temporarily," China would agree to two key provisions. The first, that they would allow for an increase of 14 more foreign film imports per year, of which most, though not all, originate from Hollywood on the stipulation that those additional films all be in the 3d, 4D or IMAX formats as to not compete with normal domestic Chinese films and that second, the current distribution fee paid to foreign films would increase from 10-13% to 25%.154

Hollywood moguls like Disney CEO Bob Iger and DreamWorks Animation head and former Disney leader, Jeffrey Katzenberg breathed a happy sigh of relief. After 20 years of being rebuffed by the Chinese, a more equitable film importation and revenue sharing arrangement had finally been reached. Perhaps, China had felt they had bided their time enough.

The timing was also very much to former politician Dodd and current politician Biden's liking. The spigot of revenue had apparently been turned back on to Hollywood and that could only be a plus for those with the right, or more accurately, the correct politics for Hollywood. The handshake deal between the two vice-presidents, Joe Biden, and Xi Jinping, which would be codified into a Memo of Understanding (MOU) just moments before the latter would leave for China, also helped Biden's boss, President Barack Obama, save some face politically after his preferred legislation to protect US industry from Chinese against IP theft had collapsed in Congress.

American commentators like to try and find drama in events. Understandably so. The media is for-profit. Compelling, human-interest stories sell magazines, newspapers, online subscriptions, and drama, often in the form of the salacious and the scandalous, make for irresistible click-bait. So, predictably, American media covered the Hollywood-China "deal," (if you can call finally getting essentially what was owed to you after 20 years of being denied a deal, then, yes) as a victory of the personal, persuasive powers of that charming politician from Delaware. The one with the 1,000-watt, poly-grip, denture smile. Yes sir, Joe Biden had come to aid of his pal and "Sheriff of Hollywood, Chris Dodd" on a white-horse to save the good, movie-folk from that outlaw, bad guy Xi Jinping and his gang of foreign film industry outlaws like the state-run China Film Group. Or, at least, he talked them out of pillaging the town and into a deal that saved the town's women, children and moguls like Jeffrey Katzenberg who could be freed up to make hundreds of millions. Cue the music and ending credits.

Except anyone who has ever studied the Chinese and their approach to negotiations knows that the Chinese don't ever "wing it." They don't improvise. The thought that anyone, including Xi Jinping would not already know what he could or could not agree to and that the head of the CCP would ever truly take directives from a state-run company like CFG is, on its face, ludicrous. *Yue Chun*.

A more plausible explanation?

Well, setting aside the near-mystical powers of Mr. Biden's smile and his apparent ability to unlock the mysteries of the Far East for big Hollywood campaign donors over a Waldorf salad, the Chinese more probably decided that they had bided their time enough and had grown to the point that any such negotiations could now be done on their terms. They also had strategically acquired enough of a stake in the film industries on both sides of the Atlantic and Pacific oceans that they, the Chinese, were now in the middle of a win-win. Or, as Sino commentators have noted, "a win-win to the Chinese is they win twice."[159]

Let me explain.

By February the 17th of 2012, when the soon-to-be Head of China, Xi Jinping met with Biden, Dodd, and a select few Hollywood moguls like Iger and Katzenberg, the Hollywood-Chinese Cinema relationship was no longer one of master and protégé or even senior and junior partner. Over a decade of economic growth and WTO-fueled trade favoritism had helped create a very powerful China. Its GDP had skyrocketed from just over 1 trillion to well over 8 trillion. Surpassing $2.7 billion, Its domestic film industry had sped past Japan to become the world's number two box office. And with a 30% year-over-year growth, even the most pro-American business analysts now projected that China would overtake the USA film industry box office by the end of the decade.[160]

Not satisfied with simply being head-to-head rivals, China took a page out of the Hollywood playbook and began to simply target some of the tastiest film fish of the sea and then proceeded to either swallow them whole or become their boss.

The same day, February 17, that Biden had "persuaded" Xi Jinping to finally "give in" to Hollywood's demands and to abide by the 2007 WTO ruling, one of those moguls noshing with the

Chinese leader, Katzenberg, also had news to share. Katzenberg, who was head of Dreamworks Animation (DWA) at the time, which was a subsidiary of Universal Pictures and a division of NBCUniversal, announced it was joining, as a junior partner, in a venture worth roughly $350 million with Chinese investors. The investors were China Media Capital, Shanghai Media Group and Shanghai Alliance Investment. The new venture was to be called the Shanghai Oriental Dreamworks. The Chinese would be the controlling partners. The new company would be based in Shanghai and would produce animated films and other entertainment projects aimed primarily for the Asian audience. Its first major film would be the animated *Kung Fu Panda 3*.

Coincidence?

Not likely.

And just days before the two nation's vice-presidents sat down together Bruno Wu, a Chinese media mogul and founder of Sun Bedrock Investment Group (SBIG) announced the formation of a new Hollywood film investment fund based in China. With a reported $800 million to invest, the Harvest Seven Stars Media Fund, consisting of Wu's SBIG and one of China's largest equity investment firms, the Harvest Alternative Investment Group (of which Mr. Wu is also a shareholder and board member) said its mission was to target films like *Mission Impossible: Ghost Protocol* (Paramount) and the *Sherlock Holmes* franchise at Warner Bros., for direct investment. He also noted that the goal was not to just invest in finished projects but to partner with and even encourage through subsidies (investment) major Hollywood studios to create China-focused divisions that would make films aimed at China and stocked with a Chinese cast and crew. "More films will soon be made that will be more acceptable to an Asian audience."[161]

Wu also noted that this new Fund emphasized "our confidence in the strength and potential of the Chinese industry and the wealth of talent within it." HAIG's head noted that "The addition of this partnership further supports our goal of developing a leading alternative (to Hollywood) product platform in China and globally."[162]

Another coincidence?

Hollywood was also buzzing with the plans of a so-called "Chinawood" that was underway in Northeast China. A massive undertaking even for the Chinese, this $1.2 billion project between Mr. Wu's Seven Star Entertainment and the local government of Tianjin (China) was to consist of the construction of a film services base or headquarters sprawled over 800,000 square meters (8.6 million square feet) which would house a variety of Chinese film "technical, financial. And digital creative companies." All with the express goal of becoming "the world's largest film-based studios and entertainment hub."[163]

Mr. Wu said that the project would, in part, target desired film co-productions which would become Chinese domestic films but with Chinese talent, technicians and crew in the lead roles.

Was this yet another coincidence?

Hardly.

China had bided its time and hidden its strength until the moment was ripe. Unlike in years past, when it feared Hollywood and even Hong Kong films would devastate its own mainland China film industry, it was now in a position of relative strength. It could now afford, even profit from opening its doors to more foreign exporters of film like Hollywood. Twenty years of stalling Hollywood and five years after the WTO ruling, China had simply calculated that they were now poised to collaborate with and soon overtake Hollywood as the world's largest box office and film industry.

But to implement their plans they knew some concessions would have to be made so they made them. Let Joe Biden and the MPAA claim victory. China plays the long-game while the US plays the short-game.

Unlike before, when the choice seemed to be either ban all Hollywood films or be consumed by their blockbusters, China aimed this time to make it more "win-win." China would directly invest in the films Hollywood made while also encouraging co-production in China. China would essentially make money coming and going. And they could and did continue to ban outright any, and all, Hollywood films "offensive" or "not in accordance with Chinese cultural, political or social sensitivities."[164]

The same year which Xi Jinping and Biden shook hands, Chinese censors banned Hollywood hits like *Men in Black 3* (MIB3), the newest James Bond film *Skyfall* and the time-traveler film *Loope*r for a variety of reasons, some given, some not.

Remember, a "win-win" to the Chinese is that they win twice.

Of course, they had also been manipulating the movie premieres and showings, rigging ticket sales and box office receipts and underreporting Hollywood film revenue for years. But we'll get to that soon enough.

In yet another move that signaled a new show of Chinese strength and change in strategy, the Dalian Wanda Group (DWG) headquartered in Beijing and led by entertainment and real estate entrepreneur Wang Jianlin, bought the largest American movie theater operating company, the American Multi-Cinema Corporation (AMC) for a reported $2.6 billion. At that time, the largest international acquisition ever by a Chinese company.

AMC founded in 1920 in Leawood, Kansas (USA) was one of the oldest and the largest American movie theater chains operating over 347 theaters and 5,048 movie screens in US and Canada when DWG bought it. AMC had the largest share of all American movie theaters, well ahead of Regal and Cinemark theaters. Within two years, DWG reported a net profit of over $900 million.

Back home, China continued to expand its own domestic movie theater capacity. In 2005 they had 4,425 movie screens. Just 7 years later China they had well over 10,000 screens with plans to reach over 70,000 by 2020.

Two more major announcements in the Spring of 2012 cemented this year as the year when the scales tipped in China's favor in the Chinese-Hollywood "frenemy" relationship.

Disney Studios and DMG of Beijing announced their plans to jointly co-finance and distribute the third installment of the *Iron Man* superhero franchise, *Iron Man 3*. DMG chief executive promised that "Iron Man 3 was going to talk to the whole world but definitely be infused with many Chinese elements."[165] More on what that meant in practice a bit later. Meanwhile, James Cameron's Cameron Pace Group shared it was setting up headquarters in Tianjin, China at the Seven Stars Entertainment studio bases. Its stated mission was to further develop Chinese capabilities and leadership in 3-D and 4-D technologies among its filmmakers, broadcasters, and game designers. The impact of this move would be felt for decades to come.

When Xi Jinping left his counterpart Joe Biden at their February 2012 meeting in Los Angeles, he said, "I can with confidence say this this visit has indeed been successful."[166] Perhaps, more accurately, he could have said with confidence that the entire year for Chinese film would indeed be incredibly successful.

Did I say year? Decade would have been more like it.

CHAPTER 7
THE WAY OF THE CHINESE DRAGON: TRUTH HURTS, LIES KILL

The Chinese cheat. They lie. They steal. They commit fraud. They rig outcomes to avoid paying foreign partners their fair share. They engage in bad faith negotiations. They knowingly break solemn promises, breach contracts, and violate accepted rules and norms. They sponsor widespread espionage, cyberhacking, and ransomware extortion of their rivals. They engage in corporate collaboration to gain access and then leverage that access to force their new "partners" into divulging proprietary information and trade secrets to the Chinese.

They respect neither copyright nor intellectual property laws and engage in rampant academic plagiarism. They coordinate intimidation and harassment campaigns, both domestic and abroad to silence dissident voices. They forbid artists of all types from entering their nation and ban their work over everything from comments they make, dresses they wear, people they meet and even characters they choose to portray in fictional films. Domestic born artists, poets, and writers who, in any way, question the state-approved narrative are harassed, vilified, and in some cases, made to disappear. Or worse. If you happen to be a member of the LGBTQ+ community, you live a life in shadows, and silence. To do otherwise is to attract government attention which can lead to punishment and isolation. The Chinese commit unthinkable human rights violations to innocent civilians on a widespread scale.

Those unfortunate to be targeted by the Chinese Government for persecution and punishment are frequently accused of committing generic crimes against the state such as "subversion of state" or "threats to security."[167] Defending or appealing such blanket allegations is rarely, if ever, allowed.

While the Chinese extol the virtues of peace, sovereignty, and human rights at high-profile events like when hosting the Olympic Games in Beijing, they neither respect, protect nor value any of these things if it gets in the way of Chinese hegemony and imperialism. They stand shoulder-to-shoulder with and give full support to predatory, pariah nations like Russia, Belarus, Iran, and Syria to pursue immoral and unjustified killings if it serves Chinese strategic or political needs. Even at the expense of thousands of innocent lives. Back home, it doesn't necessarily get better. In the name of purification and progress, the CCP has willingly sacrificed upwards of 30-50 million of its own citizens to achieve party and state goals in past years and would not shrink from doing so again if party goals dictated it. Cogs in a machine.

They do all this and more in an integrated and what the US FBI calls, "a whole of society way."[168] All sectors and persons in China, public and private, are expected to support CCP and State goals, short and long-term. They are obsessed with becoming the most dominant and controlling nation on the planet. They are more than willing to make any sacrifice and pay any cost to fulfil their ambitions. As a citizen of China sitting on the "bench" and refusing to participate is simply not an option. Nor is questioning these plans.

If xenophobia is showing prejudice, intolerance, and dislike for people from outside your own country, then it is hard to imagine a more xenophobic nation than China.

Does all this criticism seem harsh? Unreasonable?

Well, below is compelling evidence which makes it hard, if not impossible, to argue with what I've just described. And it is this behavior and worse, and not the Chinese propaganda which we are deluged with daily, that is the real way of the Chinese dragon. Of course, don't just take my word for it. See for yourself. Feel free to raise your own questions and draw your own conclusions. As always, let the evidence lead the way.

And one more thing-Not shockingly, I do not personally know each, and every one of the 1.4 billion citizens of China. Nor do I know what is in their hearts and minds at any given moment. I'd like to think they have only the purest of intentions for their fellow humans, regardless of ideology, race, sex, or religion. But what I do know, what can be observed, measured, and judged is what their leaders and the agents chosen by these leaders do. Following is a baker's dozen or more of such things and the harm each one continues to cause to so many. After this "close-up," we'll zoom out a bit and look at the bigger picture of how all this relates to filmmaking and the movies we see.

1. *The Chinese and its Broken Solemn Promise of "One Country, Two Systems" to all of Hong Kong*

On July 1st, 2022, China's leader for life, Xi Jinping, told a relatively sparse crowd on Hong Kong's Victoria Harbor, a crowd organized by Beijing operatives, that the true democracy and birth of Hong Kong, a "New" Hong Kong, was just beginning. Just two years after oppressive, brutal, and bloody crackdowns of anti-government and pro-democracy protests had been unleashed by Beijing, somehow, according to Xi Jinping, this had all been designed to free not oppress Hong Kong. As the Chinese leader surveyed the crowd at Hong Kong's Victoria Harbor, he knew that all opposition political parties and candidates had been outlawed, thousands of pro-democracy activists were now either forced into exile, arrested, or made to disappear, and the tracking, surveilling, and monitoring of any suspected dissident was now also easier than ever. All this had been obtained and the Chinese solemn promise of “One Country, Two Systems” had only reached the halfway mark to the 50-year complete integration of Hong Kong into mainland China.[169]

The “old” Hong Kong and its devotees lay in tatters. Broken. The harsh reality, and one that Hong Kong and the British had feared, “One country, one system,” under Xi Jinping had already arrived. To say the timetable of complete integration had been accelerated would be to greatly underestimate the power, force, and brutality imposed by China to ensure all opposition voices and pro-Hong Kong activity across the island had been crushed. To many who had grown up under an independent Hong Kong their home had now become unrecognizable. This is today’s Hong Kong, remade in the vision of China’s communist leader for life, Xi Jinping.

Former Hong Kong democratic lawmaker Ted Hui who was forced into exile shared that, "I feel so strongly about Hong Kong as if I've never left. I can't let go of the place I love, and I can't let go of my comrades in prison. Hong Kong currently has more than 1,000 political prisoners, in addition to a justice system destroyed by the evil (Beijing) national security law, as well as the total annihilation of free press and democratic society.”[170]

Nathan Law, once a lawmaking colleague of Hui shared the same sentiment and remorse. Now in the UK, he believes that what is left of the true Hong Kong “exists only in struggles and in between the cracks.”[171] A journalist who has covered Hong Kong for decades acknowledges that there is now only one system-Beijing’s.

UK Prime Minister Boris Johnson has no doubt that China under Xi Jinping has both broken its promise of respecting Hong Kong’s autonomy as well as extinguishing its democracy. He stated that "On the 25th anniversary of the handover, we simply cannot avoid the fact that for some time now, Beijing has been failing to comply with its obligations. It's a state of affairs that threatens both the rights and freedoms of Hong Kongers and the continued progress and prosperity of their home."[172]

The Biden Administration's Secretary of State Anthony Blinken, a man not known for tough rhetoric or hyperbole called China's actions towards Hong Kong nothing short of a "dismantling of freedoms in Hong Kong." He went on to further denounce China's treatment of Hong Kong as evidence "That Beijing authorities no longer view democratic participation, fundamental freedoms, and an independent media as part of this vision."[173]

As for China, Xi Jinping made it clear that only "patriots," meaning those loyal to Beijing, should be allowed to lead, fill administrative positions, and govern in Hong Kong. With that, he officially swore in John Lee as the new leader of Hong Kong. Lee had become the face of Chinese brutality for Hong Kongers as he oversaw the arrests, beatings and imprisonment of student protesters and pro-democracy activists with an iron fist. He also ordered the early morning raids and crackdowns of independent newsrooms and media outlets across Hong Kong who were not seen as sufficiently loyal to Beijing. Clearly, he had earned Beijing's trust through his own unquestioned obedience to Beijing and willingness to intimidate and punish student activists with force. Now he stood beaming up at his benefactor as the Chinese Communist Flag was unfurled behind the two leaders.

Xi Jinping punctuated his comments to the crowd by asserting that "True democracy is only now beginning for Hong Kong."[174] Coming from an authoritarian, communist dictator for life, even

Xi Jinping had to appreciate the irony in that statement. But I doubt he even noticed.

Happy 25th Anniversary Hong Kong. Not sure I want to see how you've aged at your 50th.

2. *Persecution and Abuse of the Uyghurs*

When not rushing to dismantle Hong Kong's tradition and culture of democracy and open participation, the Chinese engage in the systematic persecution, internment, torture, forced castration and "re-education" of an entire race of people, the Uyghurs. Why? Because their chosen religious beliefs apparently offend and threaten the "real" Chinese and their preferred way of life.

A cache of recently leaked Chinese files containing documents, profiles, images, and footage directly from the Xianjiang (China) Police Department leave no doubt as to the horrific human rights violations being perpetrated by the Chinese against the roughly million Muslim Uyghurs of the Northwestern region of China. Widely validated by digital forensic experts, this most recent evidence confirms what the intel community- through informants, documents, drone, satellite footage, families of captives and survivors who managed to escape, have asserted all along-that the persecution is real, widespread, and undeniable.[175]

Many international leaders immediately condemned the images and footage, including the foreign minister for Germany, Annalena Baerbock, who immediately contacted China's foreign minister Wang Yi telling him that the leaked files were "shocking reports and new evidence of very serious human rights violations in China."[176] US State Department spokesperson Ned Price told the press that "We (State Department) are appalled at the reports and the jarring images."[177]

What had been only rumored up to this point, now also appears undeniable. That the Chinese official policy is "shoot to kill"[178] any Uyghur who attempts to escape the internment camps. This, despite Chinese CCP officials continued claim that the Uyghurs are voluntarily coming to the camps to engage in re-education and to disavow their Muslim religion. They are, according to the CCP, doing this to happily become a part of the Chinese Communist system.

Not so, says Human Rights Watch Executive Director Kenneth Roth. "They (the leaked files) certainly correspond with the many, many testimonies that Human Rights Watch have received." Roth called the continuing abuse of the Uygur race at the hands of the Chinese "a brutal crime against humanity, the likes of which really do not exist anyplace else in the world today."[179]

Chinese foreign ministry spokesperson Wang Wenbin rejected the entire massive number of leaked files, calling it all just attempts by "anti-China forces at smearing Xinjiang," and said that the media are just "spreading lies and rumors."[180]

Tell that to the dozens of Uyghurs who testified at a public tribunal hearing in London recently. Risking their own safety and the well-being of their families still in China, these survivors described brutal conditions at these so-called "camps." One such survivor, Qelbinur Sidik, shared her experience and what she saw which included Uyghurs of all ages being forced to wear iron shackles and chains during hours long classes of "re-education."

She testified that "Chinese guards in the camp did not treat their prisoners as human beings. They were treated less than dogs, they enjoyed watching them being humiliated and their suffering was for them (the Guards) pure joy."[181]

Many of those who testified at the Tribunal spoke of physical and sexual abuse during interrogation sessions. “They were not only tortured but also raped, often gang-raped, the things I witnessed and experienced, I cannot forget,” Sidik added. “I too, was subject to forced sterilization.”[182]

Rozi, another Uyghur who testified, said that “I was forced into an abortion when I was six and a half months pregnant.” Her youngest son was taken prisoner when he was just 13 and she prays now for his freedom. “I want my son to be freed as soon as possible. I just want to see him be set free.”[183]

Kayrat Samarkand, an ethnic Kazakh, who grew up in the mountainous region in Xianjiang, recalled his own time at the Chinese “re-education” camps. He says that a typical day would start at 6:00 am where everyone would have to sing songs in praise of Xi Jinping and profess their love for him and hatred of religion. Each would have to memorize and recite the “126 lies about religion.”[184] Each prisoner was then forced to state that “only the Communist Party can lead you to a bright future, and that all religion is a lie.” The guards would beat those who sang praises or declared “truths” with insufficient energy or enthusiasm. Only after being shackled into a body-fitting and constricting “iron-suit” for hours on end, did Kayrat decide he too, needed to join in singing and heaping praise on his Chinese captors.[185]

A recent report published by Amnesty International (2021) also detailed the systematic mass incarceration and torturing of the Uyghurs and Kazakhs in Xianjiang, China. It also describes the extensive cover-up by the Chinese to hide and deny what is actually going on there. One section of the report details the use of so-called “Tiger Chairs” by the Chinese. These are steel chairs which completely “cage” and immobilize victims as they are systematically tortured and beaten by their Chinese captors.[186]

Who knew that lies and rumors could cause so much real pain and suffering, right, Wang Wenbin?

And while most of the media seemed to believe that Dinigeer Yilamujiang, a Chinese Uyghur cross-country skier enthusiastically "volunteered" to carry a Chinese flag at the 2022 Chinese Winter Olympics, no one in their right mind should. Maybe, they just didn't care or didn't want to offend their Chinese hosts or upset the TV revenue "apple cart." Perhaps, someday they can take the time to explain their reasoning to the Uyghurs who didn't get to wave a flag and who didn't get to watch the games as they were too busy in shackles and chains getting "re-educated."

3. Persecution and Torture of the Falun Gong People

Of course, the Chinese Government doesn't solely persecute the Muslim Uyghurs and Kazakhs. They forcibly harvest the human organs of living people, many of which practice the banned Falun Gong faith, and then sell these organs and human tissue to more "appropriate" and preferred Chinese citizens and high-paying foreign clients.

When not taking their human organs from them, the Chinese Government tracks, detains and persecutes the 30-50 million Chinese practitioners of the Falun Gong religion and their chosen way of life. Why? Well, despite initially embracing the Falun Gong religion early on, even praising the Buddhist and Confucius roots of this religion, they became a threat to the CCP's exclusive stranglehold on power and loyalty as the number of followers grew. So, then-leader Jiang Zemin in 1999, responded by issuing decrees banning their faith and making illegal all those who chose to continue to worship. Falun Gong went from being a popular religion one day to an evil cult which threatened state power the next. That is also when the Chinese government stepped up its harassment, incarceration, and torture of Falun Gong devotees.

Consequently, today, they and their religion are outlawed. Officially branded as subversives and illegal activists.

As stated above and explicitly shown in the documentary *Human Harvest* and in *The Bleeding Edge*, a film based on that documentary, thousands of Falun Gong faithful, some dead, many living, have had their organs involuntarily harvested. The Chinese then sell or even give these organs to more "worthy" and "non-subversive" Chinese or foreign clients and tourists in what has become a very profitable business for China.[187]

Critics and independent investigations like The China Tribunal, organized by The International Coalition to End Transplant Abuse in China and chaired by UK's Sir Geoffrey Nice, a former prosecutor at the Yugoslavia Criminal Tribunal, confirmed the unthinkable. Yes, China had been and continued to forcibly harvest organs from both deceased and living humans for profit. Its report indicated that it (The Tribunal) was "certain that Falun Gong was a source, probably the principal source of organs through forced organ harvesting."[188]

Sir Geoffrey added that "Our conclusion shows that very many people have died indescribably hideous deaths for no reason, that more may suffer in similar ways and that all of us live on a planet where extreme wickedness may be found in the power of those, for the time being, running a country (China) with one of the oldest civilizations known to modern man."[189]

Unfortunately, the UK Tribunal also found no evidence that the practice of organ harvesting in China, especially being forced upon Falun Gong, Uyghurs, Kazakhs, and Christians, had stopped nor that the Chinese had any intention of stopping this horrific practice.

Both the Tribunal as well as other independent sources and human rights experts estimate that China carries out over 100,000 forced organ harvesting procedures annually. This makes China easily the world's worst offender. The UK has proposed legislation to ban anyone from the UK travelling to China to purchase human organs. Italy, Spain, and Taiwan have already passed such proposals into law with many other nations vowing to follow suit. You may not want to hold your breath waiting for Xi Jinping and the CCP to crack-down on this barbaric, immoral practice though. It seems to serve current Chinese political and profit-making goals all too well to halt anytime soon.

4. Chinese Manufacturing and Distribution of Fentanyl

That is why it is also difficult if not impossible to accept Xi Jinping's indifference or outright ignorance of the fact that China has now become the world's largest manufacturer of fentanyl and fentanyl precursor components. Once this lethal drug is manufactured, the Chinese then actively collaborate with known Mexican drug cartels to facilitate its illegal smuggling and distribution into the United States through its own southern border. Yet, another example of China's political and profit-making goals dovetailing nicely, regardless of ethics or morality. Commentators have called the massive smuggling and distribution of fentanyl into the US an "undeclared war" on the America, particularly its youth.[190]

By 2022 fentanyl had become the #1 cause of death among US citizens aged 18-45. Deaths due to fentanyl overdoses in the USA among this age group now surpass suicide, car accidents and COVID-19. Between 2020-2021, nearly 80,000 died from fentanyl. US Drug Enforcement Agency (DEA) officials have warned the Biden Administration that the lacing or mixing of fentanyl with marijuana, heroin, meth, or even prescription pills like Adderall, used to treat attention deficit disorder, even in tiny amounts like a slight surface dusting, will cause immediate death.

In the Spring of 2022, five West Point Army Cadet football players on Spring Break in Ft. Lauderdale, Florida overdosed from cocaine that had been dusted with fentanyl. In the summer of 2022, Arizona border patrol police confiscated enough fentanyl, to kill over half of the entire state's population. And recently, Virginia State Police and DEA officials busted up a multi-state drug ring which was distributing Chinese fentanyl from a Shanghai vendor which, according to reports, was operating openly and without regulation or police interference in China. The amount seized was enough to kill 14 million people.[191]

On July 15th, 2022, the US DEA seized over 1 million fentanyl pills in Inglewood, California. The US DEA Administrator Anne Milgram said that "Fentanyl is killing Americans at an unprecedented rate" and that too many Americans "realize too late that what they have ingested contains fentanyl."[192] She cited dozens of lethal overdoses across the US in places like Wilton manors, Florida, Austin, Texas, Cortez, Colorado, Commerce City, Colorado, Omaha, Nebraska, and Washington DC, just to name a few.

The wave of illegal fentanyl drugs being manufactured, smuggled, and distributed throughout the USA is in no way stemming or slowing down. Officials warn that it is getting worse not better.

China's response, both to the Trump Administration and now, to the Biden Administration has been rather anemic. Then-President Trump complained in 2019 that "My friend President Xi said to me that he would stop the sale of fentanyl to the United States, this never happened, and many Americans continue to die."[193] In November of 2021 President Biden publicly mourned the deaths of 100,000 Americans due to fentanyl overdoses but chose to not mention China's ongoing role in those deaths.

However, the US DOJ did bring charges the next month (December of 2021) against Chuen Fat Yip, a Wuhan-based drug manufacturer for producing and selling fentanyl. The DOJ alleges that Yip has produced and sold hundreds of millions of dollars of fentanyl and anabolic steroids out of Shanghai and Hong Kong and has conspired with Mexican drug cartels to smuggle fentanyl and opioids into the US.

But aside from what critics called a "highly staged and mostly symbolic" arrest of some online fentanyl chemists, China has not made shutting down or even disrupting the flow of fentanyl from China to Mexico for delivery to the US a priority. And why would they? Robbing your chief rival of some of its most valuable assets, its youth, its future generation, because of their own demand for drugs and addiction doesn't seem to chafe any moral codes for China. If the addict wants to feed his or her addiction it's not their problem, right? A Chinese official made this clear when saying that "US has only itself to blame not China" (for the fentanyl overdose deaths).194

Recent pleas in 2022 from the Biden Administration to the Chinese Government to do more to shut down Chinese fentanyl makers and rampant drug money laundering from its sale in China seems to have fallen on tin ears. So far, it's mostly status quo between Chinese fentanyl manufacturers and Mexican drug cartel distributors. Both are getting richer and more powerful at the expense of America's youth. And its future. And this too, seems to serve China's goals all too well for them to halt.

5. *The Unleashing of Covid-19 on the World*

Through its own recklessness, negligence, lackadaisical health regulations or even possible genetic laboratory sabotage, an incredibly lethal virus (COVID-19 and later, its mutated variants) was released on the world in December of 2019. It quickly spread and caused upwards of 6,400,000 deaths and 548 million infected patients and counting as of the Fall of 2022. Whether it was caused by bats or pangolins in a wet-market in Wuhan (China) or from a genetics laboratory conducting incredibly dangerous pathogen experimentation in Wuhan (China), one thing seems certain-this human-killing machine of a virus originated in Wuhan, China.[195]

So, how do the Chinese, the nation of origin of this catastrophic virus respond? First, they deny the existence of any such virus. After satellite images and video surface of China locking down Wuhan and medical teams in Hazmat protective gear surface, they ignore requests for medical information and updates. Then, after several months pass without any data or information as to the nature of the virus and its lethality, resulting in a precious loss of time for the rest of the world to prepare and react, Chinese officials then pressure the World Health Organization (WHO) to announce the lack of lethality of such a virus.

Next, through their integrated propaganda machine and ownership and influence in multiple media outlets, including several in the USA, the virus is downplayed (commentators and news articles comparing it to a common flu early on) and audiences are admonished to not engage in any "anti-Asian" behavior. Meanwhile, Chinese officials accused the USA of secretly planting such a virus in Wuhan and attempted to "spin" the global spread of the virus and their own response as "heroic," "exemplary" and "to be admired." An official CCP video was made to celebrate and salute the "bravery" of its leader, Xi Jinping, in "destroying" this "foreign virus."[196]

Part of China's "brave response" in 2019 and through 2020 involved first hoarding, stockpiling and then selling life-saving equipment to foreign nations at marked-up prices to ensure maximum profit for themselves even as thousands of such units were found to be defective, useless, and of course, non-refundable. The result was that even more infected patients died worldwide as they were denied the ability to fight this COVID agent of death. This may be why official state-run Chinese media referred to Covid-19 as "the Italian virus," no doubt reflecting their displeasure at the Italians for having the audacity to complain of overpriced and defective health-gear sold to them by, you guessed it, the Chinese.

6. Brutal Covid Lockdown, Admirable and Noble?

Through the spring and summer of 2022, China was forced to admit the obvious-that a second wave of COVID had spread through both Wuhan and major metropolitan areas. They responded by implementing its "Zero Covid Tolerance"[197] policy. From reports, formal and informal, along with leaked online videos, this policy appears to be utterly ruthless and futile, given what we now know about how the virus spreads and mutates. At best, this policy is an obsessive desire to have no COVID illnesses whatsoever in a nation of over 1.4 billion people. At worse, painful memories of China's Great Cultural Revolution came flooding back to those who survived that time. China literally forced its citizens to stay locked inside their homes, with uniformed teams announcing curfews and checking that doors to homes were locked and bolted. Reportedly, residents were arrested, beaten, and even tortured for daring to go outside for a breath of fresh air. Leaked online messages by citizens in lock-down indicate their fear of being taken to a "hospital" for non-compliance where lights are on 24/7 and violators are placed in solitary confinement.

Shanghai, a city of 26 million, endured a lockdown which was so relentless and unyielding that food supplies dwindled, needed medicines failed to get delivered, and citizenry mental health suffered to the point that many took to screaming and venting their frustration at night through windows of their locked apartments. Large steel mesh fences were set-up by Government Hazmat officials in gated communities across the city to ensure residents were both "locked-down" and "locked-in." A city-wide lockdown which was to last one week turned into several months. All this while official CCP drones hovered over the city with verbal warnings that "all must curb their soul's desire for freedom and to comply with all COVID-19 restrictions."[198] Suicides, not surprisingly, have sharply increased recently in Shanghai.

This so-called "Citizen-Management" is nothing new to China, home to such a large population.

7. *24/7 Citizen Surveillance, Monitoring and Social "Credit" Scores and Ranking*

As part of this "management," the Government tracks, monitors, surveils and "flags" their own citizenry of 1.4 billion people for the "good of the whole." What and whom else they find threatening they censor, ban, defame or forcibly detain. Thousands of interconnected surveillance cameras help support a monitoring and "social credit" system which China uses to rate or score its citizens on how they act, behave, and do or say in public. For example, "debits" or behaviors that can lower one's social score include jaywalking, smoking in a non-smoking zone, failing to pay back a loan on time, perceived lack of enthusiasm at CCP rallies or anniversaries, posting "fake news" of which anti-governmental or anti-Xi Jinping posts are considered to be "fake" (Why would anyone ever disagree with the Government or Xi Jinping?), purchasing too many video games, falling asleep at a film celebrating the PRC Revolution, even being late for a meeting. Low scores can get you blocked from entering public places or can even affect your financial standing, career status or ability to get a future loan. You may be bumped from airline flights, blocked from staying at top hotels, placed on a "No loan" list, even have your dog taken away from you for a low social credit score.

Anyone at any time can be stopped by a Chinese official and for any reason, or no reason, be made to answer questions as to their plans, activities, or intentions. The need to first obtain a warrant to search and possibly seize is not a right which exists in China for its citizens. Daily "citizen surveillance" can also involve being forced to hand over one's cellphone for inspection, private data being downloaded to a government database or even having one's contacts and history of activities in their cell phone or laptop copied then deleted. No due process, no lawyer, no formal charges. You know what you did, say Chinese officials. Or, in some cases, what you were thinking about or planning on doing. If you thought Tom Cruise's *Minority Report* (2002) was some sci-fi future fantasy, well, the future is now in today's China.

8. *Great Firewall of China, Then and Now: It's Not Just What You Do but also What You Post and Read*

Back in the day, when dinosaurs roamed the Earth and the internet was still developing, circa 1998, many politicians, entrepreneurs and artists were rightly extolling the incredible power and potential of the internet. They, like so many regular folks, saw this new technology as a near miracle for connecting people from all backgrounds across the globe and providing worldwide forums of instantaneous expressions and reactions. China, however, saw the internet, as they frequently see everything, through the prism of CCP control and power. And they feared a future of open and free internet communication, expression, and citizen access.

So, as others rushed to expand this new tool of human expression, China took calculated steps to restrict it. By 1999 China had developed a sweeping plan of monitoring, controlling, and surveilling the internet and its users. Sounding like something more befitting an Austin Powers spy spoof and not a real governmental project, and certainly not something to be taken seriously, the plan was named "The Golden Shield Project."33 Today it is better known as "The Great Firewall of China."199 And the plan, the stakes, and the punishment for violators turned out to be, sadly, anything but a spoof.

Collaborating with the California based high-tech company CISCO, an elaborate system of internet control was developed over 8 years at a cost of $700 million. The mission of the project was to "purify" the internet for Chinese netizens and to "monitor, block and filter" all "sensitive" material, especially from foreign sources.35 Some of the highly advanced tech tactics used for this purpose include IP blocking, packet filtering, credit records examination, website winnowing, social media profiling, flagging problematic phrases, words, names, and organizations as well as using speech and facial recognition software.

According to *OpenNet Initiative*, a leading advocate for worldwide internet freedom, China deploys the "most advanced content-filtering and blocking internet policy in the world."200 The Chinese Government also enlists private companies such as Baidu, China's most popular search engine, to implement state policies and administer severe search restrictions in its own search algorithms in support of "The Golden Shield." Ditto when it comes to Weibo, China's popular social media giant.201

At its onset, then Chinese President Hu Jintao (2002-2012) emphasized the importance of controlling the internet, remarking, "Whether we (China) can cope with the internet is a matter that affects the development of socialist culture, the security of information, and the stability of the state."[202] Today, the entire system of controls, filters, monitoring, surveillance, and punishment, overseen by China's Ministry of Public Security (MPS) has been called simply, a "modern marvel."[203]

But to some the technological "marvel" is simply a tool to suppress dissent, repress freedom of thought, and chill any sort of free exchange of ideas. A recent PEN (Poets, Essayists and Novelists-a non-profit dedicated to protecting freedom of expression worldwide), report found, that under Xi Jinping, tools of repression continue to expand and the use of high-tech to control his people is one of many ways the CCP leader has tightened his grip of power. According to the report, "With an increasing array of technological, legal, and ideological tools at the government's disposal, Beijing is ever more able and willing to *systematically erase expressions of dissent* and calls for social change, silencing internet users who dare cross ever-shifting red lines and shutting off channels of circumvention under the banner of "cyber sovereignty."[204]

In addition to exerting control over what its people say, search for, access and see, the Chinese Government also has proven insidiously adept at controlling what its people can post, share, and create. No doubt, other totalitarian governments are taking notes and dreaming of the day when they too, can enjoy a near-complete control of information flow in their nation.

9. *The Banning of Celebrities (foreign and domestic) and their Art*

As part of the many tools China deploys to protect itself against perceived "threats," both domestic and foreign, the CCP in conjunction with the SAPPFRT bans celebrities from entering China and forbids their artistic "product" (books, films, music, artwork) from being exhibited or distributed. Even a partial list of recently banned Hollywood celebrities and famous rock stars includes; Selena Gomez (once took a photo with the Dalai Lama), Miley Cyrus (once squinted her eyes in a photo pretending to be Asian), Sharon Stone (ok, she was pretty evil in *Diabolical* and a spoiled brat in *Casino* but her real sin to the CCP was when she met the Dalai Lama), Harrison Ford (testified at a US Senate Foreign Relations Committee on behalf of an independent Tibet in 1995), Brad Pitt (acted in the film *Seven Years in Tibet*), Katy Perry (wore a Sunflower Dress, no, really) Bjork (yelled Free Tibet at a concert), Jon Bon Jovi (Dalai Lama support), Justin Bieber (skateboarded in Beijing), Gigi Hadad (took a photo of herself with a cookie in the shape of a Buddha), Martin Scorsese (directed *Kundun* in 1997 about the 14th Dalai Lama, had a subplot about Chinese mobsters stealing microchips in *The Departed*, and used Taiwanese crew in his 2016 film *Silence*), Keanu Reeves (attended a concert China disapproved of) and of course, the most notorious of all banned Chinese celebrities, that Tibetan-Dalai Lama-Lovin' Kingpin, actor Richard Gere.[205]

Being a Chinese celebrity or star athlete is also no shield against being banned or enduring worse treatment for some real or perceived offense. Just ask female professional tennis player Peng Shui who publicly accused a CCP official of sexual abuse and she soon disappeared. No social media updates, no press conference from her or her agent, not even a good-bye emoji text. Reports of her well-being have been mixed and she has yet to return to the WTA to play matches. Demands from tournament officials from Wimbledon (London) and Roland Garros (Paris) to China to be assured of her safety get ignored. That'll teach her never to "humiliate" a sexually abusive (alleged) CCP official in public again.[206]

And while PEN is understandably, most concerned with writers and artists, it also raised the point that the Chinese Government under CCP leader Xi Jinping wields its power to also ensure no one becomes so popular on social media or that no one posts anything "goes viral" without prior CCP approval. The objective, PEN asserts, is so that nothing or no one manages to slip beyond state control and eclipse its leaders. This last part seems to ring eerily true in the case of beloved, fan favorite, Chinese actress Fan Bing-Bing.

FBB's social media and celebrity star at one point threatened to eclipse even Xi Jinping (aka, Pooh-Bear). She was young, famous, extremely popular and millions of her followers seemed to hang on her every word and action, even "begging" to know her "fave" dress, current crush, even what she had for breakfast on any given day. CCP officials became wary and threatened. She suddenly vanished from social media, abandoning her millions of fans without so much as a farewell post or selfie for them to savor and re-post. She simply disappeared from the public eye. Months went by without so much as an update. There was rampant speculation among her followers about her whereabouts and even her physical well-being. Finally, she briefly resurfaced to make a public apology for her "transgressions," and thanked the CCP for "teaching her the true way."[207] Uh-huh.

And as discussed earlier, international award-winning Chinese film director Chole Zao and her films remain banned from China because several years ago she shared her belief that China is a land of many lies. That'll teach her for telling her truth.

Privacy, independent thought and action, even basic human rights, things many in the West take for granted are simply not viewed there as human necessities. Protecting, preserving, and perpetuating the Chinese Communist Party is, ultimately, the only thing that matters. Challenge this basic premise at your own peril and that of your family.

10. China's Ruthless Oppression of Writers, Thinkers, Poets, and Teachers

This ongoing indictment of China when it comes to human rights, freedom of expression and the respect for basic human dignity isn't mere polemics or me engaging in exaggerated rhetoric. I have no axe to grind nor apple to polish. As a writer and filmmaker, I am of course, especially concerned about the freedom of my colleagues around the world to do what I am doing this very moment-expressing my opinion and raising questions which, as a free citizen and fellow artists, is my inherent right. Not so in China. Groups like Human Rights Watch, Amnesty International, The United Nations High Commission on Refugees (UNHCR) and The Borgen Project, all raise deep concerns about China's repression of its citizens. The NYC based PEN, cites China as one of the, if not the, worst offender worldwide in repressing freedom of expression and systematically silencing dissent. In their words, "China's extensive censorship apparatus limits speech both within and outside its borders. Although new digital platforms have expanded the means of expression, they have also provided more opportunities for repression. In China, even a simple Tweet can land its author in jail. Since President Xi Jinping took office in early 2013, he has overseen an extensive crackdown on free speech, implementing additional laws and censorship controls on the Internet, media, and publishers."42

In PEN's recent and exhaustive report on Censorship and Suppression of Freedom in China (*Forbidden Feeds*) they conclude that under Xi Jinping, China has increased its social media control and online censorship all under the guise of "countering online rumors" but what they are really after of course, is complete and utter control of the "truth." The only "truth" is what the Chinese Government says it is, everything else is a lie and must be suppressed.

In addition, PEN investigative journalists point out that "individual Chinese writers, journalists, and creative artists have been censored, harassed, imprisoned, and even disappeared after they speak out about sensitive topics such as the rights of ethnic and religious minorities, corruption, and the lack of democratic reform."[208] Evidence compiled by PEN and Amnesty International suggests that dozens of Chinese writers are currently in prison because of their works and creative expression.

One such artist was 2010 Nobel Peace Prize Winner Li Xiabo. Li Xiabo was a well-known and highly respected literary critic, writer, and reformist. He taught at Beijing Normal University and was a visiting scholar at several institutions outside of China, including The University of Hawaii, University of Oslo, and Columbia University in NYC.

Shortly after the announcement that he had won the Nobel Peace Prize for his works, which the CCP saw as a humiliation, he was arrested, accused of "inciting subversion of Chinese state power"[209] and sentenced to 11 years in prison. He was refused legal defense, forbidden to see his wife and family, and later, when he was suffering from a progressive form of liver cancer, he was denied medical care until his health was so badly deteriorated that he died in custody shortly thereafter. His wife, Lu Xia, remains imprisoned as a signal to other possible "Liu Xiabos" and what will happen to them and their own family if they dare question or refute the party line.

Far from being an isolated case, Li Xiabo is one of many similar instances of ruthless suppression by the Chinese Government. They are particularly ruthless and intolerant with writers, poets and academicians who are seen as dangerous to the monopoly of power the CCP enjoys. PEN cites nearly 100 ongoing cases of individuals being harassed, intimidated, or simply made to disappear due to their writings, speeches, posts or even tweets.

11. It's Not just What you Write or Think, It's also your Sexuality that troubles the CCP

China's record on LGBTQ+ rights is also at the very least, troubling. China only decriminalized homosexuality in 1997 and didn't remove being gay as a mental disorder in 2001, same-sex marriage remains illegal and so-called "abnormal sexual behavior" remains banned from public media. As an LGBTQ+ Chinese advocate shared recently, "Our goal is to simply survive, to continue to be able to serve LGBT students and provide them with warmth. We basically don't engage in any radical advocating anymore,"210 she said. Why? Well, widespread fear of CCP ordered Government crackdowns and reprisals drive many within the LGBTQ+ community deep into the shadows and silence.

The recent "lesson" of Li Ying, a Chinese female soccer star may be instructive here. On June 22, 2021, Li celebrated her "coming out" publicly as gay by posting several pics of herself and her female partner on WEIBO, China's heavily censored version of Twitter. While the posts soon went viral, they were also deleted and taken down just as quick without any explanation. The community may have been provided with an explanation just days later when dozens of LGBT accounts on the popular Chinese WeChat messaging app. were also taken down without explanation. While no explanation was forthcoming despite social media unrest, CCP member and editor of the State owned and operated Global Times, Hu Xijin, did dismiss speculation as unwarranted, saying that there was "no restriction on lifestyle choices of sexual minorities or discrimination and suppression."[211]

Yet, just weeks later, as part of leader for life, Xi Jinping's "National Rejuvenation" (sound familiar? Remember Mao's Great Cultural Revolution?) citizens were reminded that same-sex was illegal and that all "abnormal sexual behaviors" (Xi Jinping apparently interprets all homosexual behavior as abnormal) were banned from public media. Xi Jinping also decreed that all "effeminate men" deemed "not masculine enough"[212] would be banned from television and other entertainment outlets. He also emphasized that through this "National Rejuvenation," the Party (the CCP) would tighten its control over all aspects of Chinese life like business, culture, entertainment, education, and religion to ensure the masculinity and purity of China. Several media outlets also amplified the "concern" that homosexuality was purely a western export into China meant to weaken it and that the LGBTQ movement was infiltrated by foreign gay rights operatives with agendas poisonous to China.

As part of this national rejuvenation initiative, it was announced by China's National Radio and Television Administration that all television broadcasters must "resolutely put an end to sissy men and other abnormal esthetics," and must ban all "*niang pao*" men (a vulgar Chinese slang term for any man deemed effeminate) from all programming. Further, the NRTA stated that, "Broadcasters should avoid spotlighting or hiring any performers who 'violate public order' or have 'lost morality.'"47 In the past, the term "lost morality" in China has included personal sexual proclivity and any overtly gay behavior.

And in what we might as well call the Fan Bing-Bing effect, dozens of popular and highly viewed Chinese celebrity sites and accounts were taken down including that of Zhao Wei, a highly popular Chinese actress and film director (*Shaolin Soccer*, *Mulan: The Rise of a Warrior*) with no explanation.

As a CCP member stated what now seems rather obvious, "LGBT people in China should not at this stage seek to become a high-profile ideology."[213]

Shadows and silence.

12. *Beware the Pagoda: Chinese Corporate Espionage, Coercion, Cyberhacking and Extortion*

On July 7, 2022, the head of United Kingdom's MI5 Ken McCallum and the Director of the USA's FBI Chris Wray held an historic, unprecedented joint press conference at Thames House in London. The reason? China and its widespread state-sponsored espionage and cyberhacking, of course.

Director Wray called China the "biggest long-term threat" to both the US and UK. He went on to explain that "The Chinese government is set on stealing your technology…whatever it is that makes your industry tick…and using it to undercut your business and dominate your market. And they're set on using every tool at their disposal to do it."[214]

When not banning or making subversives disappear, China engages in massive espionage and widespread, government sponsored cyber-hacking of sovereign nations and private entities. Their targets are many and diffuse but certain sectors like aerospace technology, military manufacturing and Artificial Intelligence research and development are especially coveted. While no nation is technically off-limits from their spying, the United States has and continues to be the PRC's most valued asset to acquire by any means necessary.

Any foreign proprietary trade and manufacturing secrets they are unable to obtain through covert spying and illegal hacking they simply obtain through covert coercion and bullying. Forcing companies into compliance and obedience is seen by China as simply the price and privilege of doing business with it. Either open your books, reveal your secrets and "share" with the Chinese government and its agents or take your business elsewhere. And with laws which force foreign companies to use Chinese law firms whose loyalties to their foreign clients are at best tepid, American companies complain that they do not fully understand the scope of what they are agreeing to until it is too late. The Chinese though, conduct business with eyes wide open. They are well aware of the leverage their massive 1.4 billion market represents and they ruthlessly exploit it at every opportunity.

The FBI director warned that China uses every possible asset it has, professionals and civilians to support its espionage mission. "We've even caught people affiliated with Chinese companies out in the U.S. heartland, sneaking into fields to dig up proprietary, genetically modified seeds, which would have cost them nearly a decade and billions in research to develop themselves," Wray said. "And those efforts pale in comparison to their lavishly-resourced hacking program that's bigger than that of every other major country combined."215

Wray warned that all businesses need to be very wary of working with the Chinese. They don't respect or adhere to the accepted norms and protocols of doing business internationally. Their aim as always, is to advance the CCP agenda.

McCallum, the MI5 boss, made public that just a few weeks before, in May, China had launched a sophisticated cyberattack on key UK aerospace firms and classified military technology sites. A similar sophisticated cyberespionage campaign of targeted attacks against US Companies and its Government, including Verizon, state and local waterworks agencies, high-tech security firms, and the NYC subway system, have all been linked back to China.

But apparently, that's just the tip of the Chinese iceberg when it comes to the depth and scope of ongoing hacking and espionage initiatives the Chinese are launching against the US. In late July of 2022, a US Senate Homeland Security Affairs Committee public detailed several troubling allegations against the Chinese and their operatives. The Report outlined a series of espionage attempts from China targeting the US Federal Reserve and Central Bank dating back to 2013 to undermine US Monetary Policy. The Report alleges that at least one key Federal Reserve employee was detained on a trip to Shanghai by CCP operatives and was threatened along with his family, if he did not provide them with classified economic information and assistance. Another employee allegedly had been "turned" by the Chinese and was transferring large volumes of data from the US Federal Reserve to Beijing, while yet another Chinese operative within the US Federal reserve had been transferring sensitive "modeling codes" from the Central Bank to Beijing over a period of months. US Representative Kat Cammack (FL) responded to this Report by warning that "China will stop at nothing to infiltrate America."[216]

US Government Agencies and employees have been for years now, targets of Chinese espionage and extortion but US Intel sees an uptick in predatory behavior in recent years. For example, recently, Chinese hackers stole millions of US federal employee personnel files from the US Office of Personnel Management (OPM) and in 2021 the US Department of Justice (DOJ) formally charged 2 Chinese hackers working for the CCP with cyberespionage and hacking. They were allegedly targeting US medical firms which were developing vaccines for COVID-19 and its mutated variants. Chinese hackers also allegedly stole at least

$300 million worth of proprietary data and protected intellectual property from dozens of US corporations. Don't look for these cowardly acts to be part of any CCP video celebrating its "brave response" to COVID anytime soon.217

Chinese Communist Party officials dismissed all such claims by both the UK and the USA as lies, distractions and irresponsible claims.

The same day in which MI5 and the FBI were warning of the threat of widespread Chinese espionage and online hacking of vulnerable and highly sensitive sites, the US DHS formally charged two more (making it 5 so far) individuals with aiding Chinese espionage efforts. Specifically, the FBI alleges that these individuals were working with the Chinese Government to engage in, what the FBI referred to as "transnational repression schemes."53 In other words, they were part of a coordinated, state-sponsored effort by the Chinese to harass, intimidate and silence Chinese dissidents in America. Speak out against China, challenge the CCP narrative and apparently, no matter where you call home, you are not safe from the tentacles of the Chinese Communist Government.

Just ask Mr. Arthur Liu, father of US Olympian figure skater Alyssa Liu, who was the target of Chinese state-sponsored spying and harassment as he and his daughter prepared for her participation at the 2022 Winter Olympics in Beijing. Mr. Liu had spoken out against the Chinese Communists in the past and escaped China during the 1989 Tiananmen Square protests and violence. The FBI figures that China wanted to discredit or at least embarrass both father and daughter to negate any success Ms. Liu might have had on the ice representing the US and not China.

But it's not just high-profile Olympic figure skaters and their families who are monitored or surveilled for possible "dissident" thinking or behavior. Just ask Shawn Zhang a teen who lives in Vancouver, Canada. Hours after Shawn re-tweeted a post from his Weibo social media account, a post that was not pro-Xi Jinping, his mother, who lives in Wuyi, China, was contacted by the Chinese police and a CCP official. She was informed that such behavior, engaging in anti-Chinese, anti-Xi Jinping behavior (they are the same under leader for life, Xi Jinping) was unacceptable and that she had better tell her son to take down the post…or else.

Besides the chilling demand and swiftness of response by Beijing, the Zhangs also don't know exactly how the Chinese police were able to identify Shawn's posts and trace them to his mother in China. But they have some ideas. Virtual and physical monitoring and outreach probably were involved. As Shawn said, "My social media account is probably under their close monitoring. They will read everything I say, I am probably on their watch list."[218] The message, even unspoken is clear, speak your mind, post your thoughts, so long as they glorify China and its leader. If not, vulnerable family members back "home" in China may pay the price for your dissidence.

By mid-2022 the FBI announced it had already arrested a dozen individuals spying in the US who were seeking to similarly discredit or intimidate American citizens who had in some way spoken out against China or Xi Jinping. An FBI spokesperson said that there were many open file cases or investigations of similar harassment of US citizens or visitors within the US it was pursuing. Canadian officials have also expressed concern about Chinese violating Canadian citizen rights and freedoms and have been pursuing similar cases.

But this too, is the way of the Chinese dragon. They conduct brazen and widespread espionage, theft, hacking, ransomware extortion and now, bullying and intimidation of all who dare speak out against them. And when they or their agents are caught, they simply issue blanket denials and deflect culpability. Frequently added for good measure in the denial is a not-so-subtle suggestion as to the potential damage such "outlandish" claims will do to future trade opportunities between China and her accuser. And you so desperately want a crack at that 1.4 billion consumer market, don't you?

Brilliant, isn't it?

In its most recent report, the US Director of National Intelligence also reiterated the long history of Chinese espionage, corporate theft and hacking it has engaged in to exploit and cripple its competitors like the US and Europe. In his words, China represents a "prolific and effective cyberespionage threat."[219] Indeed.

The FBI estimates that the annual cost to the U.S. economy of counterfeit goods, pirated software, and theft of trade secrets is between $225 billion and $600 billion. They also identify China as the world's worst violator of international and US domestic intellectual property and copyright laws. Its continuing mission is clear-Put foreign companies at a huge competitive disadvantage and its own Chinese companies at an advantage. And state-sponsored espionage, hacking and ransomware extortion appear to be seen and deployed by China as merely effective means to a desired end.

Smart companies may just start wondering if doing business with the Chinese is ultimately, worth the price.

On that note, everyone should beware the Trojan Horse that comes shaped like a Chinese Pagoda. A really big Chinese Pagoda.

In 2017, the Chinese made an unsolicited offer to finance a $100 million tourist attraction in the US capitol of Washington

DC. This new attraction would be a rather elaborate Chinese garden located within the National Arboretum. It would have authentic looking temples, pavilions, rock gardens, exotic fish and the centerpiece, the showstopper would be a huge 70-foot-high white pagoda. Local tourism officials began to salivate a bit, dreaming of the thousands of tourists that would visit each year and the extra revenue this Chinese "wonder" would bring.

Some US counterintelligence and security officials also began to daydream a bit. But in their dreams, it wasn't the additional revenue that captured their imagination it was the word "why?" Why the offer, why now (US-China relations were strained) and, why this specific location which the Chinese had apparently, been very insistent upon. So, they did what any intel officers worth their G-level pay would do-they dug into the project details. Seems this spot which the Chinese coveted had a very high intel value. It would be built upon one of the highest spots in all of Washington DC (the 70-foot-high pagoda) just two miles from the US Capitol and would have been the perfect spot for foreign intel collection of cell phone and landline signals from within and around the US capitol and lawmaker offices. Another project feature that set off US intel alarms-Chinese officials insisted upon shipping classified materials for the project into the US through diplomatic pouches which are beyond US Customs officials inspection and review. For the pagoda to have a new home in the US several sensitive questions would first need answering, and the Chinese weren't forthcoming.

The pagoda project was quietly scrapped. Chinese efforts to infiltrate the US continue.

13. *Increasing Chinese Soft Power Influence and Spreading CCP Propaganda*

When not attempting to steal US and other developed nations' trade secrets, corporate proprietary information and classified technology and military secrets, or disable its rivals' infrastructure through hacking or through ransomware attacks and extortion, or even gift your rival a pagoda, China has, since 2004, funded what the FBI calls a "soft power" initiative on college and university campuses worldwide. Through the CCP United Front Work Department, whose mission it is to spread communism and gain new recruits, China funds its so-called Confucius Institutes. The stated purpose of funding these Institutes and setting them up on foreign campuses is to share China's culture, traditions, and language with students to foster better understanding and international relations. Tough to argue against that right? Seems innocuous enough.

Critics though, like the US based National Association of Scholars have argued that the real mission of these Confucius Institutes is to cultivate a propaganda "beachhead" on American campuses. The true aim of the Chinese they argue, is to deploy these Institutes to help promulgate the CCP narrative and propaganda. The Chinese, the say, are especially focused on targeting impressionable students at classical liberal arts schools where there is already a natural willingness to embrace or at least be sympathetic to communism.

The NAS says that China also uses the Institutes to monitor, track and surveil Chinese students studying abroad and Chinese American students and faculty, as well as others who express sentiments or behave in ways that do not support China or its goals. Critics like the NAS and Representative Jim Banks (R-IN) point to recent arrests of Chinese faculty like at the University of California at Los Angeles (UCLA). There, a visiting Chinese faculty member was caught stealing sensitive missile technology and sending it back to his CCP handler in China.

Under the Trump Administration these Institutes came under closer scrutiny from the State Department and the FBI and concerning patterns of funding and behaviors were uncovered. These included actions by many Institutes in defending China's Covid-19 response, countering any, and all, who suggested China take responsibility for and disclose its role in the spread of this deadly virus and allegedly, helping coordinate the dissemination of CCP propaganda negative to the US. Allegations of Chinese students and Chinese-American students being harassed online for any postings or texts they may have made not in line with the CCP messaging as being in part, coordinated through or with the Institutes and its data bases.

To counter these propaganda operations, the Trump Administration through the Department of Homeland Security (DHS), ordered universities to fully disclose its relationships, including funding, with these campus-based Confucius Institutes. By early 2022, 104 of the 118 Confucius Institutes across the US had closed due to such scrutiny and disclosure requirements along with the negative media attention this brought. However, the Biden Administration rescinded this disclosure order and as of the summer of 2022 several Institutes were back in operation, though being rebranded simply as "Centers for Language and Cooperation" or similarly generic sounding titles. Given their history and funding purpose though, it is hard to believe their core CCP driven mission has changed.

NAS Research Associate Ian Oxnevad is one who does not believe the mission has changed at all, he refers to these new centers as "Confucius Institutes 2.0," and continues to be concerned that any such Institutes are merely "vehicles for China to shape perceptions of China among American students." Speaking on behalf of the NAS, he continued by stating that, "It's a propaganda outlet. At the same time, it also offers basically a location that China could conduct basically economic espionage out in the open, in the sense of stealing secrets that are developed in academia and then sending those back to China."55 He and other scholars at the NAS also feel that the Confucius Institutes or similar such agreements between China and the US "allows for the spying on dissidents. If you have critics of China, whether they're from China or not, in a specific institution, having faculty there who are picked by the Chinese government obviously allows them a way to monitor them."220

Certainly, not all see the same threat of having a CCP sponsored institution on American campuses. Western Michigan University and Georgia State University are among several American campuses that have chosen to re-configure their educational and cultural agreements with China. Each now partner with The Beijing Language and Culture University and share cost and oversight of exchange scholars from China and development of curriculum on Chinese culture and language courses.

What hasn't changed is China continues to maintain a "One-Way" policy when it comes to permanent, on-campus cultural cooperation and exchange. For example, when the US has in the past approached China about establishing and funding American Institutes in China to ostensibly serve the same purpose as the Confucius Institutes they were immediately rebuffed. If, the purpose was to truly foster better understanding and learning between the two nations then why should it be only one-way traffic when it comes to establishing permanent missions, perhaps, like say, US subsidized "Lincoln Institutions," in China?

Does this mean I am against all cultural exchanges and academic cooperation between China and the US? Of course not. My own home university (CCU) is engaged in a US-Sino student exchange which by all accounts seems wonderfully successful. But, where there is allegedly a lot of smoke, as with allegations against several Confucius Institutes of Chinese propagandizing, espionage, and harassment of those with opposing views, there is far too frequently, a fire. At the very least, a call the fire station to check things out seems justified.

But allegedly supporting their predatory goals through Confucius Institutes is only one of a myriad of ways China seeks to penetrate and exploit US academia. A recent 2019/2020 FBI Risk Report on China reminds us that of the roughly 1.5 million international students and faculty who visit US campuses annually, the vast majority pose no threat. They come with only the best intentions-to learn, share, grow and cultivate positive connections with their American hosts.

However, the FBI also makes clear that China systematically seeks to exploit this openness of academia on US campuses and classrooms to further their own nationalist goals. They do this through the training and placement of hundreds if not thousands of Chinese visiting students and faculty who are, in reality, "non-traditional collectors"[221] of proprietary research, data, cutting edge technology and confidential information. They work on behalf of the Chinese Government, are supervised by and report to the CCP and their mission is to save the Chinese from having to spend time and resources on doing their own domestic research and development. In other words, steal rather than innovate.

The FBI also warns all US campuses that China does not value nor protect academic freedom or integrity of research and publication. They point out that the Chinese engage in rampant plagiarism and knowingly ignore academic standards and copy and steal original work. The mission is what takes priority. And that is to become the dominant economic and political nation of the world. A new world order or more precisely, according to Professor Fei-Ling Wang of Georgia Tech, a world run by "China Order." He argues that modern China with Xi Jinping at the helm is a "tenacious dictatorial state of 'controlocracy' and sophisticated totalitarianism." The irony, he claims, is that this "China Order," this need to be excessively insular and hostile to everything foreign, weakens China and sets it up for failure not success.[222] We shall see.

14. *The Chinese Weaponize Neurological AI Software to Ensure Loyalty to the CCP*

Director John Frankenheimer's masterpiece, *The Manchurian Candidate* (1962), is a classic neo-noir psychological thriller. The film was deservedly nominated for two Academy Awards (Best Editing and Best Supporting Actress-Angela Lansbury) and was credited with giving Frank Sinatra's career a much-needed shot in the arm. Releasing the film during the peak of US-Soviet tension during the October 1962 Cuban Missile Crisis was a savvy marketing move. Its promotional strategy included a near-hypnotic trailer and a warning to audience members not to miss the first five minutes of a film "like no other."[223] Frankenheimer's direction of Richard Condon's 1959 novel (*The Manchurian Candidate*) pulled no punches in its dystopian view of Chinese and Russia brain-control weaponry. Here, the unknowing dupe is a US military POW during the Korean War who then becomes a lethal weapon in the hands of his Communist captors and masters. They brainwash him and then send him to the US to assassinate the President.

Fast forward to 2004. Under the direction of Jonathan Demme, the Hollywood reboot of *The Manchurian Candidate*, starring Denzel Washington is released. The film updates but tries hard not to upset the Chinese, so, this time, the plot centers around the Gulf War and an evil, sinister global mind-control corporation. Early on, when reports about a reboot surfaced, Chinese officials condemned the original film and dismissed the idea of any brain-control nonsense and suggested it was a western fantasy and obsession.

Fast forward to 2021. The US announces it has imposed sanctions on The Beijing Academy of Military Medical Sciences and 11 other Chinese research firms. Why? Well, despite condemnation by many in the science community over purported Chinese unethical research and strong Chinese denials, reports surface that the Chinese are indeed testing humans in their development of so-called "Brain-Control Weaponry."59 One such report asserted that China was developing sophisticated neurological weapons that could paralyze and control both its enemies and its own people. A source close to the research became convinced that the CCP was "trying to develop and perfect genetic editing, human performance enhancement and brain machine interfaces."224 In short, brain control.

Then US Secretary of Commerce, Ms. Gina Raimondo, expressed strong concerns that Beijing would deploy such research to control and impose forced "re-education" over its own citizens, targeting the Uyghurs, of which more than a million are being held in guarded camps in Northern China. Secretary Raimondo stated that "Unfortunately, the People's Republic of China is choosing to use these technologies to pursue control over its people and its repression of members of ethnic and religious minority groups." Further, she added, "We cannot allow US commodities, technologies and software that support medical science and biotechnical innovation to be diverted toward uses contrary to US national security."[225]

Slightly fast forward to 2022. Chinese biotechnical researchers employed at the China Comprehensive National Science Center in Hefei (Anhi, China), based on their own online posting, claim that they have successfully developed "mind reading and brain control"[226] artificial intelligence (AI). The purpose of which they note would be to "measure citizen loyalty to the Chinese Communist Party (CCP) through analysis and reading of brain waves and associated physiological outputs." The researchers went on to note that the AI results "can then be used to further solidify their confidence and determination to be grateful to the party, listen to the party, and follow the party."[227]

CCP officials were reportedly so pleased with this breakthrough in mind control technology that funding for further research and experiments was increased. Of course, they were. So much for western fantasy and obsession. Just don't expect to see this storyline in the next reboot of the reboot of *The Manchurian Candidate.* Unless of course, the Chinese researchers were transformed into say, North Koreans through the magic of Hollywood. Less offensive to the Chinese, more profitable for all involved.

15. *China Supports Russia's Horrific War on Ukraine*

When not engaging in unethical, cutting-edge neurological weaponry, China proudly stands shoulder-to-shoulder and arm-in arm with the world's predatory and pariah nations to better advance its own expansionist agenda. That's right, old-fashioned bullying through sheer force and ruthlessness.

As Russian leader Vladimir Putin continued to order massive bombing attacks on Ukrainian civilians, including hospitals, maternity wards, pre-schools, and a shopping mall resulting in thousands of deaths of women, children, and infants during the summer of 2022, Xi Jinping proudly stood by his side. And while the rest of the civilized world strongly condemned Putin's unprovoked invasion and slaughtering of a sovereign nation and its people, China defended Russia's aggression, offered encouragement, and financial and military aid. Xi Jinping seemed more than happy to uphold China's end of its recent "Friendship for Life" agreement and alliance with Russia. Why? Well, if you immediately yelled out "Taiwan," then you get to move to the next level for proving at least a basic understanding of the way of the Chinese dragon.

As the Russian invasion of Ukraine dragged into its 275th day, an invasion which Putin declared would last a paltry 3 days when launched and end in Russian glory, the Chinese continued to breach Taiwanese airspace with Chinese jetfighters and bombers while holding combat exercises directly across from that island. Friends for life, Putin, and Xi Jinping. The gift that keeps on giving.

All this and more, is indeed the way of the Chinese dragon.

Now, certainly, many nation-states do some of these things. And some bad-acting nation-states do many of these things. But China is, arguably, the only nation in the world today that does all these things. China stands alone in its systematic suppression, censorship and surveillance of its own people, its ruthless persecution of other races, and its denial of even basic human rights to its citizenry. Let alone the human rights violations of foreigners it deems subversive, threatening, or who have in some way, offended its seemingly unlimited list of national sensitivities. When Kim Jong-un dreams of the nation he wishes he could rule and the vast power he so desperately covets, China and Xi Jinping spring to his mind.

So, to revisit the questions posed at the start of this chapter-Harsh? Yes.

The unvarnished truth often is.

Unfair? No.

Unreasonable? Hardly.

Impressive? Sure. Obsession always is, in its own way.

CHAPTER 8

CHINA TAKES CONTROL: HOLLYWOOD LEARNS MANDARIN. MAVERICK GETS A NEW BOSS.

When one looks at China the way they look at themselves in a "whole of society" way, as a vast nation of interchangeable parts, all aimed (ideally) in one direction, relentlessly marching towards one goal with a near-obsessive willingness to pay any cost and bear any sacrifice to reach it, then it is hard not to be impressed. Also, fearful, wary, and alarmed, but impressed all the same. Just as a Chinese Dragon in a New Year's Day parade must have all its parts (people) connected and coordinated to move seamlessly and powerfully as one, so too, must China, a nation of 1.4 billion parts move in the same way. Allow even one misstep, one "dissident" to get out of line and the dragon veers from being this highly complex, coordinated creature and quickly dissolves into utter chaos. And when dragons go into a tailspin, beware. At least, this appears to be the Chinese thinking when it comes to controlling their population and what seems to be their absolute fear of free-will, diversity of thought and freedom of expression. Where democracies like the US hold these concepts to be sacred and the inherent right of all people, Chinese leaders seem to view them as a three-headed monster that must be vanquished, at all costs.

But to take pains to better understand the how and even the why of China's behavior, does not mean we must give China a free pass as it marches in lockstep towards its global ambitions. We know why China continues to make movies about how the courageous Chinese fought back against the bloodthirsty Japanese "wolves" but still, doesn't mean we have to plop down $12 bucks for the privilege of watching it. Again.

China may operate in a China-centric world, but the rest of us are not obligated to do so. We still have freedom of thought, expression and will. At least for the moment.

And to be fair, when I say, "the Chinese" or "China," again, I do not know what is in the hearts and minds of every 1.4 billion Chinese citizens of that nation. Just as clearly, evidence suggests that certainly, not every single citizen fully supports or welcomes every action taken by its leaders and agents chosen by those leaders.

But this is true of every nation, isn't it? Fair or unfair, the whole is judged by those parts which govern, lead, dictate or command the rest of those making up the whole. No nation is one perfectly seamless, monolithic mass of humanity. But China, through its rigorous indoctrination of its people, unyielding enforcement of its unyielding codes of acceptable and unacceptable behavior, and its ruthless punishment for all who dare to challenge or question its actions, may be the closest thing we have to one united, obedient nation of people on the planet today.

Compared to its closest rivals, like the USA, which by design, is a divided Federalist system with separate branches or units of governments which check and balance each other, often creating inertia, gridlock and conflict, China endures no such obstacles, by design and unity of purpose. There is also a great divide between public and private entities in the US. For example, Founder and Chair of Tesla, Elon Musk, took to Twitter, a company he was seeking to purchase (as of July 2022) to publicly criticize the Biden Administration and specifically, President Joe Biden. Musk asserted that Mr. Biden didn't seem to know or even understand basic economics and as a result, many of his policies were making inflation worse not better. Such a public spat between a corporate leader and the nation's leader in the USA is commonplace. Democracy is messy but the theory is that only through a marketplace of ideas exchanged through open and unfettered forums will the best policies be identified. No one person or entity does or should have a monopoly on ideas and vision. To lead in a democracy, is, by definition, to invite scrutiny and criticism. Fair or unfair, founded, or unfounded, leading in a democracy is not for the timid, thin-skinned, or faint of heart.

In China, such a messy, open, and honest exchange between private and public leaders like Musk and Biden is virtually unthinkable. But then again, private companies ultimately operate only at the behest of and for the glory of the CCP in China. According to revised National Security Laws, every company and all its parts must serve the greater good and that greater good is defined by and then enforced by the CCP. Whether it is Jack Ma of Alibaba, Robin Li Yanhong of Baidu, Ma Huateng of Tencent, or any of the corporate giants of China, publicly questioning or challenging CCP policies or aghast, Xi Jinping personally, as Musk did to Biden, would certainly bring professional and personal devastation to the crosser and to his or her family.

No Chinese business sector or industry is "safe" from CCP control or somehow neutral in its operations. The FBI, as noted, refers to this Chinese approach toward business as a "whole of society approach." Everyone is expected to do his or her part. And if that means, as it frequently does, that you and your company engage in espionage, coercion, theft, infringement or worse, then so be it. You, your company, its employees, are all merely interchangeable cogs in a machine. The notion that a corporation in China would be granted the legal status of a "person" with many inherent and unalienable rights that continue "*in perpetuum*" like those which corporations enjoy in America, is also, unthinkable to the Chinese.

In part, this is why who really controls Tik-Tok and has or can gain access to its user profiles and data in China continues to be controversial and significant.

Astonishingly, though, these core differences between American and Chinese companies-their outlook, their approach, their legal standing, their values and norms, their loyalties, their endgame-still seems to elude so many Americans and westerners, who continue to believe, despite a mountain of evidence to the contrary, that for some reason, they and their business will be the exception.

Why would the Chinese treat a foreigner different or even better than they do their own people? Answer: They would not and don't.

For example, in response to Chinese police clubbing and beating peaceful protesters outside a bank in Zhengzhou (China) in mid-summer of 2022, Xi Van Fleet, who survived Mao's revolution and fled China years ago, shook her head in knowing disgust. The protesters, whose bank accounts had been frozen for months as part of the official Chinese Covid lockdown policy, begged to be allowed to access their own funds. Many in the crowd said they needed their money simply to pay bills, buy food for their children, pay their rent. Some were being threatened with eviction. The police told them it was an unlawful gathering, sprayed them with tear gas and physically beat several until the crowd dispersed. Funds stayed frozen. How dare they demand access to their own money?

This in no way shocked Xi. "China," she said, "is not a normal country. It is a communist country through and through. Ever since its founding in 1949, communists do not respect private property. They do not respect human rights and human lives."64 As Mao once noted, "Communism is not love. Communism is a hammer which we use to crush all enemies."228

Fair enough. At least no one can say they didn't see it coming.

Consequently, three questions seem to be most compelling now to address:

1. How does the fact that China is, in so many ways a bad actor on the world stage, relate to the films we now see, if, at all?
2. Has Hollywood been complicit in enabling China to supplant it (Hollywood) as the world's number one cinema?
3. And thirdly, so what if China is now the world's number one cinema? Does it really matter who or what nation calls the shots with the movies we see?

As to the first question posed, here's how.

You may recall that the Chinese Communists do not view art in any of its forms, especially films, as having any inherent or abstract value. Their perspective, immortalized in the words of their former leader, Mao Zedong, "There is no such thing as art for art's sake,"66 is that the only value of any art stems from what it can do to support the cause of furthering the glory of the People's Republic of China. So, as we have seen, when it comes to film, the CCP used film to reach the masses and to tell, as current leader for life Xi Jinping has vowed, "the story of China in a good way."229

In other words, without any of the bad or even questionable bits. If the CCP had published the book you are now reading for example, you'd have read maybe most of Part I, and Part II would have been blank pages or possibly CCP approved poetry or songs in praise of Xi Jinping and the CCP. This isn't speculation or demagoguery from some extremist, art-hating ideologue, this is taken right from the CCP speeches and laws since 1949. This includes the recent expansion of CCP power and decrees about the role of art in current-day China and its obligation to help keep China "strong and pure."[230]

Consequently, the Hollywood-American view of movies as escapism or entertainment is just that-a very Hollywood idea. It is no coincidence that the so-called "Golden Age of Hollywood" when the number of moviegoers proportionate to population reached its peak was during a post-World War II era. American audiences wanted a reprieve from the horror of war, it was a time to be enthralled, to be swept away by bigger than life stars draped in dazzling wardrobes, doing wonderful things in even more wonderful and exotic locations. Cutting-edge technology, developed during the urgency of the war was now being applied to film and movie theater sound in ever more creative and convincing ways in studios like Disney, Paramount, MGM and Universal. And while there were "Buy Bonds" films crafted by Disney and others to help the war effort and patriotic recruitment shorts made during the war, Hollywood was back doing what it was founded to do in the first place-entertain and make money to make more films to entertain more and make more money. The circle of moviemaking life.

The Chinese Communist Party, much like the Kuomintang Nationalists before them, though, have always viewed this artform (film) much differently. They see it as a powerful weapon in its overall propaganda and messaging network. For decades, many immigrants dreamt of an America as a land of golden opportunity, freedom, a place where the only limits were those you placed on yourself. They saw an America of riches, of romance, of adventure, a place where dreams really could come true. And where did they get such a notion? From Hollywood, and the magic of movies, of course. While audiences in America were chomping on popcorn nervously watching Anthony Perkins in a hair-net holding a butcher's knife slowly approach Janet Leigh in the shower in Hitchcock's *Psycho*, being wowed by Gene Kelly's fancy footwork in *An American in Paris,* soaking in the music of *Singing in the Rain*, or hoping Dorothy made it back to Kansas (*The Wizard of Oz*), Chinese audiences were watching inspirational films about the glorious revolution led by Mao, the courage of Chinese soldiers against the imperialist Japanese invaders and later, the courageous Chinese staring down the mighty American military, chasing them back to where they started during the Korean War.

Have I simplified things a bit? Sure. But the overall point remains valid. Hollywood attracted audiences into theaters by promising entertainment and thrills. China demanded its people attend showings to learn about and be inspired from the glorious people's revolution. Same medium, two very different approaches and objectives.

When not conducting state-sponsored espionage, intimidating, and harassing possible dissidents no matter where they call home, and persecuting citizens because of their ethnicity and religious beliefs, China engages in a relentless campaign of highly sophisticated propaganda to convince the world that it in fact, does none of these things. China has a preferred CCP message and narrative it wants the world to see, read and hear about. As Xi Jinping has said in the context of film, China does want the world's filmmakers to tell the story of China. Just so long as it is told in a good way. By now, we should all know which parts of that story off-limits, and which parts are to be glorified and immortalized on film. The preferred CCP narrative goes something like this, "Don't think of China as a menacing, heavily armed and autocratic predator, think of China as a giant, cuddly panda of a nation. And who doesn't like pandas? Nothing to fear here. Besides, as one of the world's oldest civilizations, we are wise and benevolent."

And what is one of the best and most persuasive mediums to deliver this narrative to the rest of the world? Through movies, silly. Whether you sit in a comfy movie theater, perhaps, one of the thousands of Chinese owned AMC theaters or live-stream your favorite shows at home on your *ipad* or laptop, it is the story, the message, the CCP approved message, that counts. It has always been this way. At least to the Chinese.

As a Chinese filmmaker who was tortured during Mao's cultural revolution once sardonically noted, "If they didn't think that what I do and the stories I tell were important I wouldn't have been tortured."[231] Talk about bittersweet solace.

Using a whole-of-society approach to achieve their political, military, and economic goals, China takes advantage of every opportunity—from joint ventures to economic espionage—to develop and maintain a strategic economic edge. This much we have already discussed and detailed.

China also practices what is called "technology nationalism."[232] The Chinese government restricts the ability of certain types of foreign companies to participate in its market, requiring them to instead form joint ventures with Chinese companies before they can gain access to the domestic Chinese consumer market. Once formed, Chinese companies then use some of these collaborations as opportunities to gain access to foreign proprietary and trade information. To help accelerate this advantage, the Chinese government is also pursuing the creation of a group of "national champions" consisting of state-owned companies, favored with generous, often illegal subsidies (based on international agreements China has signed), many recipients of sophisticated hacking and espionage to bolster their individual business and sector advantage. The overarching goal here, and one which China has been publicly adamant about, is to become completely self-sufficient and with no need to trade or interact with foreigners. A China completely walled-off from the rest of the world. Still think China is not xenophobic.

But is this the aim of the Chinese Cinema as well? Certainly, we have seen it go from initially importing Hollywood films to help develop its own fledgling cinema, to banning all Hollywood movies while filling its own theaters with CCP propaganda films and Maoist bio-pic "puff pieces," to aggressive, even predatory investment in Hollywood to control how China is portrayed and to develop cross-over blockbusters, to its current posture, restricting Hollywood films while controlling its showings, revenue, and timeslots as it heavily promotes its own homegrown films. Today's Chinese moviegoer sees a higher percentage (about 85%) of only domestic made films than ever before. Complete insularity when it comes to film in China may be closer than we think.

With all of this in mind, what role has Hollywood played in helping China get to this point? Should the Academy give Hollywood a special best supporting Oscar for China's rise to the top?

Well, by way of answering both questions, let's ask a related one. Are all artists sell-outs? Is some selling-out, some compromising one's art for commercial purposes inevitable, even necessary? Mozart didn't like giving piano lessons, but he did. Picasso allegedly didn't like grand gallery openings of his art, but he went along with them. Hitchcock apparently hated doing "press junkets" but he did them. And maybe the director of Red Dawn really didn't want to digitally alter his film at an additional cost of $1 million, changing the villains from the Chinese military to the North Koreans. But he did.

Why? Because they all knew that without some compromising, some "selling-out" to those that control the purse-strings they couldn't keep on doing what they loved, their art wouldn't get seen, their films wouldn't get distributed. They'd all cease to be performing artists. And how many artists do you know who truly, absolutely cannot stand the thought of performing, or having someone, maybe even many "someones" viewing or enjoying their art? Yeah, me neither.

"The greatest trick the devil ever did was to convince good people that he did not exist."[233]

"The greatest skill is to get the west to censor itself before even presenting its work for our review."[234]

But are there any lines that shouldn't be crossed, even when "selling out?"

Does compromise ever morph right into complicity?

Let's take a closer look at how Hollywood has responded to the growing influence and power of China. I mean, is it true that Beijing now calls the shots in Hollywood?

Well, let's see how Disney conducts its business when dealing with China. If ever there was a true iconic American success story it is Walt Disney. Not just in the film industry, animated and otherwise, but across all sectors of business. And it's not like this is a company running on nostalgic fumes. In 2019 alone, Disney cast its movie magic in owning the top 6 box office blockbusters which raked in a combined $3.2 billion. That is a lot of cheese for one mouse. This wasn't about just getting lucky one year at the box office either. Disney holds the record for most individual Oscar wins (22) and nominations (59) in movie history. It is a $130 billion conglomerate which owns the American Broadcasting Company (ABC), the Entertainment and Sports Programming Network (ESPN), Pixar Studios, Marvel Studios and Lucas Film Studios and Productions.

So, if anyone or any studio in Hollywood could give China the proverbial finger and do things the way it wants to then it seems like it would be Mickey and his playhouse pals.

Of course, this is also the Hollywood stalwart and corporate giant which when it apologized profusely to China for its release of the 1997 Martin Scorsese film *Kundun* which was critical of the CCP and its suppression of human rights in Tibet. But since actions speak louder than words, Disney also agreed to several conditions to be allowed to open its Disney theme park in Shanghai. These included; allowing several hundred CCP members to display the CCP hammer & sickle flag and CCP insignia at Disney offices in China, permitting CCP meetings at corporate facilities, allowing CCP training and propaganda teaching at Disney corporate sites in China during and after regular work hours, allowing CCP leaders to attend Disney Board Meetings and allowing CCP leaders to provide verbal and written "insight" and guidance to Disney executives and managers prior to any major corporate decisions affecting China. These were all seemingly done for two reasons, 1) Avoid any further offense, intended or unintended, to the Chinese people and the CCP and 2) Allow for the successful and highly profitable Disney-China partnership in the opening of Disney-Shanghai Amusement Park.

Ironically, just about two months after Disney unveiled its Shanghai theme park, a competing theme park with very similarly Disney-themed rides, characters, shows, events, and merchandise opened up not far from Disney's new park. Disney quickly moved to halt this new park based on quite obvious copyright infringement and trademark violations. Disney's legal lawsuits and complaints were even more quickly dismissed by Chinese Government Judges with little to no explanation.

So, it seemed strange when Disney found itself in the middle of a nasty controversy again with China years later, when it released its surefire 2020 blockbuster movie "Mulan." The film, a live action reboot of the popular animated films boasted a mostly Chinese and Asian cast and a big budget. And yet, for reasons we discussed earlier in this book, it bombed at the box office. But that wasn't the controversial part. It was where Disney chose to film and whom they chose to thank in the film's credits that had lots of folks, including members of the British Parliament riled up. Some of the scenes were filmed in the Xianjiang region and Disney thanked the Chinese Government and people of Xianjiang for their cooperation in the making of the film. Now, if you are thinking to yourself, "Gee, I've heard that name before," good for you. You have. This is the area where, we now know, for a fact, that thousands of Uyghurs and Kazakhs are being brought to against their will, imprisoned and re-educated under threat of and with actual force, human rights violations, rape, castration, and torture. There is also growing evidence that children in these camps are being sex-trafficked and sold as slaves by China.

Now Disney didn't come out and say, "Hey, we are for the ethnic cleansing going on here and so choosing to film part of this movie there is more like a celebration than a condemnation." But getting a big "Thank You" on screen for a major blockbuster film from one of the original Hollywood studios with no mention or hint about what goes on in that region, sponsored by the folks Disney is thanking, are exactly the type of propaganda coups

China covets. And Disney gifted the CCP a tidy little victory. Not sure what, if anything, was given in return as the on-location filming sure didn't transform this Mulan mess into a winner.

As for Disney's side of things, well, studio film president Sean Bailey discussed how you must partner with organizations, you know, even ones engaged in ethnic cleansing, and Disney "had no other options but to film part of the movies in Xianjiang to be authentic."235

Really? Let me see if I understand Disney's position here. Making a film based on a fictional character from a 1500-year-old Chinese poem, in part, depends on how authentic the locations are and Xianjiang "had to" be used? Because even though nearly all the film was shot in New Zealand, audiences are so keen and aware that if Xianjiang wasn't used, then the entire project would collapse under the weight of this inauthentic 78 seconds of screen time? Gee, if only there was some sort of CGI that could simulate that scenery without actually going there and thumbing your nose at the thousands of Uyghurs and Kazakhs who are locked up just yards away from where you are filming your "authentic" fantasy sword play. Sigh.

So, are we supposed to believe that during negotiations in this co-production between China and Disney that this issue about filming on location in Xianjiang and the Uyghurs never came up? Or, if it did, Disney executives and film producers were simply blissfully ignorant of what was going on in that region and had no idea how thanking the Xianjiang officials would be perceived by the CCP, Chinese audiences and the victims of this state-sponsored ethnic cleansing? Hard to believe that Mickey got where he got by being this much of a blind mouse.

Back home in the USA, Disney's eyesight seems to be pretty keen. It spots what it sees is unjust treatment towards the transgender community when it comes to bathroom restrictions in states like Georgia and boycotts filming there and it takes consummate care to change what it hears is offensive language like “Fairy Godmothers’ Apprentices” to “Fairy Godmothers in Training.”75 Disney is also considering eliminating the “Fairy Godmother” term altogether to appease gay activists who find it offensive It has done away with their traditional welcome of “Ladies and Gentlemen and Boys and Girls”[236] so as to not be exclusive to those visiting the park who don’t identify with either of those terms and has a transgender character on its Disney produced *Baymax* TV show who declares that “Men have periods too”[237] as a nod to their LGBTQ+ viewership. Disney spokespersons say they do all this and more in the name of diversity, equity, and inclusion. Ok. Fair enough. Never a good strategy to make your guests at the Magic Kingdom or elsewhere feel excluded or somehow devalued. Now, how about a bit of worldwide consistency when it comes to arguably, even more harmful, offensive things like rape, forced sterilization, and torture? Or should Disney simply ignore what the Chinese are doing to the Uyghurs, Kazakhs and the Falun Gong population but insist Chinese officials start calling them “real Chinese citizens in training”[238] from now on?

In fairness, Disney may be the most scrutinized major player in Hollywood, but it is far from the only one with either blinders on when it comes to China or embracing a “let’s look the other way” attitude, all in the name of making box office bucks.

And it’s not just what studios, producers and filmmakers decide to cut from their movies that matters. It’s also about what they decide to add into their films to appease Chinese censors. Let’s take a closer look at both.

During the 2011 rebooting of the 1984 film *Red Dawn*, MGM studios along with the film's director Dan Bradley were well on their way to what they hoped would be a blockbuster hit. While the original had Patrick Swayze in the lead along with Jennifer Grey (both would reunite in 1987 for the monster hit Dirty Dancing) this reboot boasted new Hollywood hunk Chris Hemsworth along with Adrianne Palicki of TV's Supernatural fame. The story had been updated from having the Russians as the villain to a post-NATO world where now the Chinese are the world's predator. So, in this stylish reboot, with the western economy in shambles, a weakened NATO and the US military spread far too thin abroad, the Chinese, because of the US defaulting on the huge debt owed to them, are "repossessing" the US, beginning by a strategic invasion. With no military to fend off these invaders, teens form a militia named "Wolverines" to fight back the enemy and defend their homeland.

Lights. Camera and hold on.

The Red Dawn production and release hit a snag. A major snag. The script was leaked, and the Chinese censors were outraged. Apologies were made, vague promises of landing a release in China shared and MGM ended up spending over $1 million and halted production to digitally erase all images of the Chinese military in the film. The script was changed, scenes were re-shot, Chinese symbols erased, dialogue edited into Korean, and the Chinese were replaced by the film's new villain, the North Korean military. Yes, in the new version the North Koreans make their way to Spokane, Washington and invade the US with their paratrooper force.

The film's producer Trip Vinson claimed that "We were very reluctant to make any changes, but after careful consideration we constructed a way to make an even scarier, smarter and more dangerous Red Dawn that we believe improves the movie."[239] In Hollywood film producer double-speak this can be translated roughly by the following, "We never should have upset the Chinese. What were we thinking? Let's just all pray they forgive us, distribute, and promote the film in China, and we all make a huge bundle of cash just like we envisioned when we greenlit this reboot."

In the end, the film earned $50.9 million against a $65 million budget and never did get approval from the CCP censors for distribution in China. Not sure if they ever approached the North Koreans.

Go Wolverines. Go.

Skyfall (2012) boasted a talented cast led by Daniel Craig as Bond, James Bond, Judi Dench, Javier Bardem and Ralph Fiennes. And with superstar Adele writing and performing the film's theme song of the same name, MGM and Columbia Pictures knew what it had. And after pressure and heated discussions, what it wouldn't have. In the original version superspy Bond kills a Chinese security guard while rescuing a female character. You may recall though, that portraying Chinese as villains or killing any Chinese characters on screen are both taboo to CCP censors. So, to ensure their approval, the studios ordered changes which eliminated the scene with the death of the Chinese security guard, cut all references to Chinese prostitution and to any suspected torture by Chinese police and added Chinese extras and shot additional scenes in Shanghai and Macau all in the hopes of appeasing Chinese censors. James Bond may fear no man, but the CCP and all that potential box office is an altogether different thing.

Of course, even when filming in Shanghai, Macau, or Hong Kong, filmmakers need to be wary. In *Mission Impossible 3*

(2006), a chase scene across the rooftops of Shanghai featuring its star, Tom Cruise, was a crowd-pleasing moment. Except when his character, Ethan Hunt, ran past clothes on a clothesline. Apparently, showing anyone doing their laundry outside is also taboo. The scene was cut to avoid offending the Chinese.

About the same time MI3 producers were removing Shanghai laundry, the *Pirates of the Caribbean: At World's End* starring Johnny Depp were busy removing Chinese cast member Chun Yow-Fent. Why? It is unacceptable to Chinese censors for any film to depict Chinese as pirates. Now we know.

With Brad Pitt leading the way, Paramount was confident it had a hit on its hands with 2013's *World War Z*. Depicting an apocalyptic world decimated by a mysterious virus which early on is speculated that it originated from China, humans are now hunted dominated by infected zombies. Of course, since we all know that mysterious, lethal viruses could never originate from China (!), and more importantly, such speculation could peril distribution in China, Paramount studio executives ordered all plot references to China be scrubbed. Apparently, the plot about viruses struck a nerve as Chinese censors and distributors refused to allow the film to infect the domestic Chinese audience. Well, that and the film did star Brad Pitt. I guess "Seven Years" is a long time.

X-Men Days of Future Past (2014) decided to really go all in.

First, its plot, about a dystopian future where wars have ravaged the world and Central Park in New York City is a prison camp run where mutants are under guard by Sentinels appealed to focus groups in China. So far, so good. Its producers though made sure to add 3o minutes if scenes shot exclusively in Hong Kong, inserted cameos and cast with Chinese stars like Fan Bing Bing (this was prior to her mysterious disappearance) and a popular

Chinese boy band at the time. The result was a very nice (for China) box office opening of over $39 million.

Michael Bay (Director and Producer), and Steven Spielberg (Producer), also went all in with the *Transformers* franchise fourth installment (*Age of Extinction*) this time starring Mark Wahlberg. With millions of dollars invested in heavily marketed Transformer toys already on shelves across China, the film was shot in Hong Kong and mainland China, with stars like Li Bingbing, Zou Shiming and Han Geng rounding out the cast and a plot that Variety described as "splendidly patriotic if you are Chinese," T4 was off and well, transforming the Chinese box office with an estimated $42 million opening. Though one film critic described the film as "boiling a putrid film that is long overdue for extinction,"[240] he no doubt missed the finer point of the merchandising money magic cast in China by this putrid bit of entertainment.

While *Looper* (2014) didn't fill Chinese stores with merchandise pre-distribution, that doesn't mean it didn't go out of its way to woo Chinese viewers. In the original, a scene set in Paris of the future has a time traveler encouraging another to return home. After some consideration though, the studio changed that scene to be set in Shanghai and has the time traveler discouraging anyone from returning to Paris but instead inserted the line, "I'm from the future, you should go to China."[241] They also added Chinese actress Xu Qing to also bolster their chances in China.

Interestingly, Chris Fenton, who was President of DMG Entertainment Motion Picture Group at the time and one of the distributors of the film *Looper*, has since publicly lamented the power and influence of China over Hollywood and calling for it to stop.[242] In the 2015 science fiction-comedy, *Pixels*, starring Adam Sandler and his good pal, Kevin James, Pac-Man is an animated video-game hero who must try and save the world from aliens. Or something like that. This film in no way could ever be mistaken for a serious thriller. Yet, it too ran afoul of the Chinese. Early on, the Pixel plot showed aliens blasting the world and in one scene they shot a laser-beamed hole in the Great Wall of China. Now we all know that in the 1996 film *Independence Day,* the White House gets blown up. But not so when it comes to Chinese monuments. Through leaked emails, we now also know that Sony executives feared Chinese anger and so insisted that instead of the Great Wall of China the aliens should decide to blow up, say, the Taj Mahal in India. Which they did. In the end, the real bomb was Pixels, the movie, though I believe Adam and Kevin took it like grown-ups and went on to make more films together.

Even in outer space, the basic principles of Chinese censors and audience appeasement still apply. In *Gravity* (2013) starring George Clooney and Sandra Bullock, and *Martian* (2015) starring Clooney's good buddy Matt Damon, heroic astronauts, and life-saving international space stations both become Chinese. This, even though the Chinese space program is still largely a nascent dream. No matter. Xi Jinping believed that Hollywood blockbuster films could help this dream of space exploration by the Chinese become a reality quicker if positive propaganda were shown in films of today. *Voila*, or whatever the comparable phrase is in Chinese and China's answer to NASA is shown prominently on movie screens worldwide.

In 1963 Stan Lee and Steve Ditko created a comic book character referred to as the "Ancient One." Born some 500 years earlier in "Kamar-Taj," a hidden, magical land high in the Himalayas, the "Ancient One" eventually becomes Sorcerer Supreme and then mentors his younger protégé, Dr. Stephen

Strange, in the art of manipulating ancient Tibetan powers of magic for good. In short, the "Ancient One" is a Tibetan monk high priest who embodies pure intentions. You see where this is going right?

In 2016 the blockbuster film *Dr. Strange* based on the 1960s comic book hero was being produced by Marvel Studios and distributed by Disney Motion Pictures. In this Hollywood version, the Ancient One was changed to being a white, female Celtic mystic portrayed by actress Tilda Swinton. When questioned as to why the radical change, one of the film's screenwriters simply stated the obvious. "If we acknowledge that Tibet is a real place, and that the Ancient One character is Tibetan then you risk alienating one billion Chinese. We cannot do that."[243]

Neither could the Iron Man. In that case (*Iron Man 3*), the studio pushed for and got subtractions and additions. First, the subtraction. In the original comic book stories, the evil villain, "The Mandarin," was a Chinese mastermind. In the film, his character was changed to a western actor who was hired by the real villain, a Caucasian genius who was rejected once by Tony Stark, aka, the Iron Man in a business proposal to portray an evil villain. The additions? Well, when the film was first released, China was dealing with a consumer health issue in real life. Apparently, many batches of Chinese milk were contaminated with unsafe levels of mercury due to poorly regulated manufacturing and quality control. To offset worries and avoid loss of money, Chinese censors insisted that scenes with one of the character sin the film be inserted, showing him drinking the contaminated product, China's Gu Li Duo milk, and suffering no ill-effects. The benefit of Chinese medicine was also added, along with two Chinese actors not in the original version and finally, instead of the original shot, a new shot of cheering Chinese school children was added towards the end of the film.

And the *Fight Club* (1999) gave up without much of a fight when it came to landing distribution in China. Its controversial, yet powerful ending where the unnamed narrator and Marla witness explosions signifying change to the world's corporate structure was cut. It was replaced with a "happy" ending for Chinese audiences. In this version, bureaucratic officials were able to arrest the narrator and prevent any vandalism or damage to property thus signaling the world was not going to be destroyed.

But perhaps, no Hollywood blockbuster reflects the evolution of China's cinematic power and the flexing of its censorship muscles more than Tom Cruise's *Top Gun* and its 2022 sequel, *Top Gun: Maverick.* As the Atlantic deftly points out in its review, the original, directed by Tony Scott and produced by Jerry Bruckheimer and Don Simpson in association with Paramount Pictures was a testosterone infused testament to Ronald Reagan's America circa 1986. Seeing itself as celebrating American military might, hardbodies and hardware, the producers approached the US Navy to gain its cooperation and promotional powers. Early on, script changes eliminated a crash involving Maverick to avoid showing the failure of Navy planes or its pilots. Tom Cruise's love interest was changed from being a Navy personnel to a private consultant lest anyone see a member of the US Navy breaking and flouting rules on relations between enlistees. While the enemy in the original Top Gun was murky and unknown, it didn't matter. It grossed nearly $180 million in North America alone and recruiting for the Navy and sales of Ray-Ban glasses both shot up. Military recruiters set-up desks in movie theater lobbies to convert testosterone induced feelings of pride and patriotism into five-year commitments. Paramount had found its partner in the packaging and promotion of jingoism.

After saving the world at least five times as a member of the IMF Team (*Mission Impossible* 1-5), Tom Cruise, aka, Ethan Hunt, took a quick break so he could cozy into the cockpit of a Navy fighter jet circa 2022 as a test pilot and save, well, if not the world, at least a batch of hit-headed newbie pilots from their own poor judgment. Maverick was back for another heavy dose of American military might and pride.

Not quite.

As we've seen much has changed in the world of cinema, inside and outside the theater since Maverick first put on his brown leather bomber jacket. For one, the pure, unadulterated, and unashamed love of country and flag so powerfully crafted by Tony Scott in the original had given way to a sort of self-loathing shame and hatred by at least half the nation in Trump's America. No one would even dare think about setting up recruiting posters and tables in movie lobbies in the Biden-Harris America of 2022. And honestly, it wasn't the US military which the producers of the sequel sought desperately for its cooperation and promotion. It was China.

Of the top 100 box office grossing films worldwide between 1997-2013, China co-financed only a dozen. But between 2014-2022 that number shot-up to 45, nearly half of all the top 100 grossing films have a clear and indelible imprint-Made in China.

So, it shouldn't shock or even outrage anyone (even though it did) that when pictures of Maverick's brown leather bomber which had patches of Taiwan and Japan on its back were leaked during filming changes were made. Japan and Taiwan, longtime allies of the US, are not seen as friendly allies to China. You'll recall that China does not recognize the autonomy of Taiwan and considers it part of a “One China” policy. So, besides possible alienating China and losing a portion, maybe even all, of that huge moviegoing market, there was another consideration to be made. Skydance Media, a Los Angeles based television and film company financed in part by Beijing-based TenCent, a Chinese high tech media firm, was a major investor in this newest ode to American might, Top Gun: Maverick. And whenever a Chinese based company is involved there simply is no running away from the fact that China and the CCP is involved.

US Navy Captain Pete “Maverick” Mitchell would now be taking orders from a new commander and the patches had better be removed. Copy that.

So, any early discussions about having Top Gun: Maverick reflect real world politics, any thought of Maverick getting involved in a high-stakes showdown of chicken with real-world rival China over say, the airspace of a certain island called Taiwan was shot down before it could even taxi onto a draft script.

Maverick may be in the cockpit, but China now calls the shots.

CHAPTER 9

MOVIES, MONEY, AND ARTISTIC FREEDOM: DOES IT REALLY MATTER WHO CALLS THE SHOTS?

The argument to downplay or even dismiss Chinese command and control over film goes something like this:

"So what if a few minor scenes or lines are deleted or if a few minor characters or dialogue is added? If the changes either don't offend the Chinese or make the film more attractive to a Chinese audience, then what's the harm? It's a win-win right?"

First, recall that to the Chinese a win-win is that China wins twice. Second, what happens when it's not just over whether to be authentic to the original storyline or script like when Marvel Studios ditched the original "Ancient One" a Tibetan Monk male for a Celtic female to appease the Chinese? Or when studios switch out a future Paris for a future Shanghai? What happens when the stakes are literally life and death?

For example, *The Bleeding Edge*, a feature film based on real events and exhaustive research, and *Human Harvest*, a documentary film, are both considered by critics and film festival audiences to be powerful, significant, and shocking. Both films are directed by Leon Lee and tell the true story of how the Chinese are promoting and profiting from "Transplant Tourism."83 As discussed earlier though, many of the organ donors are not willing, still alive on the operating table even without the benefit of anesthesia. Many involuntary human donors end up dead. As the documentary makes clear, these victims are simply being tortured and exploited for their religious beliefs. Tibetans, Uighurs, Christians, and Falun Gong followers have all been targeted for these horrific human rights violations at the hands of Chinese doctors. *The Bleeding Edge* is a gripping film starring Chinese-Canadian actress and former Miss World Canada, Anastasia Lin. Both films have villains, victims, and heroines. They have jet-set style and back-alley grit. Stories of humans struggling against an oppressive, corrupt regime while much of the world watches, seemingly indifferent to their plight, mesmerized by the money markets of China. In short, both have in large supply what makes a film a blockbuster.

Yet, *The Bleeding Edge* never got a theatrical release or wide distribution deal. Nor did *Human Harvest.*

Why? Well, it doesn't take too much dogged sleuthing to conclude that China used its leverage, its power, and its Hollywood insider status to simply make sure these films, critical of China, never found the audiences they deserved, destined for arthouse obscurity.

It may start with a patch on a brown leather, Navy bomber jacket but where does it end? Has groveling compliance and door-mat appeasement ever proven to be a wise and effective long-term strategy for success in business? In politics? In life?

Well, American businesses seem to think so.

Several major US airlines, including American Airlines, Delta and United Airlines deleted any reference to Taiwan as its own country in their maps, flight plans and routing to comply with China's demand. Of course, they first issued an apology.

The giant retail store, The Gap, also apologized to China for their egregious sin of selling T-shirts with China on their front but without also including Tibet or Taiwan. A spokesperson informed China that these shirts were indeed "incorrect" and more appropriate t-shirts would be made and sold per China's wishes.[243]

Retail and travel certainly don't enjoy a monopoly when it comes to acceding to the wishes and demands of China. Google, Yahoo, Microsoft, and Apple have all contorted themselves into corporate pretzels at times to please China. Recently, Apple removed its news app "Quartz" from its stores across China after CCP officials complained that the news was too positive about the Hong Kong democracy street protests. Apple also took apps designed for Virtual Private Networks or VPNs off its shelves to appease China. This, even though these VPNs are one of the only means which many Chinese netizens have to circumvent the Great Firewall and enjoy some modicum of freedom of expression and escape oppressive censorship. Proving that at its core only profit and pleasing big market users like China matter, Apple also scrubbed all pro-democracy songs from its Chinese stores and announced that it was transferring iCloud data to Chinese servers. This, despite concerns from freedom advocates that such a move would allow CCP censors even easier access to emails, texts, and other network information of anyone deemed to be a dissident or a threat to China.

Whatever happened to "Don't be evil?"

The sports world offers no respite from such blatant appeasement either.

The NBA, the place where its top stars routinely demand and get contracts worth billions of dollars, must, out of necessity, constantly generate mountains of cash to keep its overpaid stars happy or at least content until the next round of salary negotiations. So, not surprisingly, the NBA and its commissioner Adam Silver, has long coveted penetrating the Chinese market. So, when one of his league's General Managers, Daryl Morey of the Houston Rockets had the audacity to tweet a brief message of support for students who were protesting and dying in the streets of Hong Kong for democracy, the NBA quickly united to protect its billion-and-a-half live streaming deal with China. Commissioner Silver apologized to China for any offense and mumbled something about the tightrope he walks between freedom and being faithful to consumers and LeBron James who has made well over $1 billion playing hoops in the NBA immediately defended China and chastised Mr. Morey, tweeting that Morey "was not educated on the situation" or had been "misinformed."[244]

As TV host Bill Maher quipped, the translation of LeBron's tweets is "There's a lot of shoes to be sold"85 as he criticized James and the NBA for being spineless in their pursuit of Chinese treasure.

And not to pick on Lebron James, I do appreciate his on-court ferocity and other-worldly talent as much as the next fan, but off-court, perhaps he is the one who needs to be educated on the price, the real price of appeasing a communist-totalitarian regime. Believe it or not, the only thing that matters in this world is not how many signature sneakers you sell. Free speech, freedom of expression and human liberty do still matter, don't they?

I guess the NBA truly is "Where amazing happens."[245]

So, while the NBA needs to explain what its brand truly stands for both on and off the court, Hollywood, as Desi of Lucy fame might say, also has some explaining to do too.

And the first thing it should explain is what is its price? Is there any line it would not cross for profit? Is there any line leading into the swamp of moral ambiguity that it would stop at and reflect before proceeding? Even just a bit?

Of course, let's be clear here-The "It" I am referring to in this instance is not that really creepy clown character in Stephen King's "It" novel and subsequent film. No. It in this context refers to Hollywood. And while there are many movers and shakers in Hollywood and powerful movie "players," let's take a closer look at how three preeminent filmmakers have dealt with China over the years. Because in many instances, these three modern legends have set the tone and example for all of Hollywood when it comes to dealing with Communist China.

Steven Spielberg is the most decorated filmmaker in history. Collectively, his films have garnered the most awards, he has been nominated eight times for Best Director Oscars, winning twice and once for Best Producer, an American Film Institute (AFI) Lifetime Award, a Cecil B. DeMille award for directing achievement and has been cited by Time Magazine as the Top 100 Most Influential Persons in the World. If ever there was someone who represented modern Hollywood and enjoyed the power and prestige that came with such a lofty perch, it is Mr. Spielberg. If ever there was anyone who could take a stand and tell China off and live to see another day (with apologies to James Bond), it is Spielberg.

And he did. But as it turns out, his relationship with China is well, "complicated."

He enjoyed the full collaboration of Chinese officials when he and his crew spent 8 weeks filming in the Forbidden City of China. For nearly 500 years this was the site of the Ming and Qing Dynastic rulers, home to 24 Chinese Emperors. So, fittingly, Spielberg filmed a portion of his 1987 movie "The Last Emperor" in the Forbidden City. It was a collaborative effort with China about the boy Emperor Pu Yi. Reportedly, China had a good deal of input into the final cinematic project and seemingly, both sides were satisfied with the cooperation.

Fast forward to February of 2008. Steven Spielberg, the artistic advisor to China as it prepares to host the Summer

Olympics quits. He announces that his ongoing efforts to persuade China to not trade with the Sudanese Government for its role in the systematic ethnic cleansing (Genocide) of its own people had failed. His pleas had apparently fallen on deaf ears in China which had a robust oil trade with Khartoum (Capital of Sudan). Spielberg was among several in Hollywood who believed that because of China's strong economic ties to the Sudanese region it (China) could wield great influence in ending the conflict there and putting a halt to the human rights atrocities. China adamantly disagreed. Spielberg was skewered in the Chinese media. Actress Mia Farrow (Rosemary's Baby) was instrumental in leading Darfur activists to pressure Spielberg and called his decision to quit "his Lilian Hellman moment." This is a reference to Ms. Hellman (a playwright) who finally said her own conscience dictated that she speak out against then-Senator Joe McCarthy and his communist "witch hunts."[246]

Ms. Farrow may as well have been speaking about the plight of the Uyghurs in 2022 when, in 2008, she publicly wished that more Hollywood heavyweights would speak out against China and human rights violations wherever and whenever they occur. I would imagine she wishes the very same thing today.

Just eight years later in 2016, Spielberg made another, vastly different announcement. His company, Amblin Entertainment, comprised of DreamWorks Studios, Participant Media, Reliance Entertainment and Entertainment One was forming a new venture with China based multi-media giant, Alibaba, headed up by Chinese entrepreneur and its richest individual, Jack Ma. Alibaba would become the largest investor/owner of Amblin after Mr. Spielberg.

But the story to Spielberg's relationship with China had at least one more plot twist.

In 2020, Jack Ma was ready to launch the largest Initial Public Offering (IPO) of another venture, a finance technology company called the Ant Group. The IPO was estimated to be a $34 billion revenue generator. All that was left was a perfunctory legal approval by the CCP. Specifically, a "No Objection" certificate. Yet, if our reading of the CCP has told us anything it is that nothing is ever "perfunctory." Especially when just a few weeks prior Mr. Ma had referred to the Chinese banking system as having a "strong pawnshop mentality…and a model that will fail to fuel future growth."[247] In the west such comments would be seen as a tame criticism. Hardly worthy of discussion. Not so in China.

The CCP ordered the certificate be withheld, began secret surveillance of Jack Ma, professionally and personally, and began a campaign to discredit him and pressure his ouster from his own company. CCP officials right up to and including its leader, Xi Jinping, openly became suddenly very concerned about Jack Ma's popularity, his rising Hollywood profile, and his power. The result was that for two years Jack Ma was in hiding. Reportedly shook by CCP private demands and threats, he all but removed himself from Alibaba and no longer even had a set on its corporate Board.

If, Steven Spielberg, Mr. Ma's Hollywood friend and partner, had an opinion on the matter one way or the other or felt the urge to show support for his friend, he remained silent. Perhaps, his Lilian Hellman moment had passed.

By 2022, Mr. Spielberg's principled stand against China's passivity towards Sudanese atrocities seemed like ancient history. As China was preparing to host the Olympics again, this time the Winter Games, Spielberg's very own Amblin Entertainment worked closely with China to promote the event. Commercials prominently featured Spielberg's new release, Jurassic: World

Dominion's dinosaurs hyping the upcoming competition. It was a win-win. Director and Hollywood mega-mogul Spielberg provided China credibility amidst calls to boycott the Games over China's human rights violations. China heavily promoted his new project with the vast Chinese moviegoing market.

And comments like those of Uyghur Munevver Ozuygur who claimed that "China does not have the right to host the Olympics while committing all the torture, cruelty and genocide against Uyghurs,"248 seemed to not have been heard at all. Maybe it was the roar of the dinosaurs.

Like I said, it's a complicated relationship.

And not just for Hollywood royalty like Steven Spielberg. In fact, it's hard to imagine enjoying anyone becoming successful in Hollywood and somehow avoiding dealing with China and the complexity which that regime brings with it.

Spielberg's good friend and fellow Hollywood legend, Martin Scorsese, also knows this complexity all too well.

In 1998, his sweeping historical epic*, Kundun,* was released to much critical fanfare and acclaim. The film represented both a career milestone and a dramatic departure for the filmmaker. A career achievement as he had always wanted to tell the story of the 14th Dalai Lama and in an authentic and powerful way. Mission accomplished. A dramatic departure from the gangster/crime genre which he had made his mark with already by this time with films like *Taxi Driver* (1976), *Raging Bull* (1980), *Goodfellas* (1990) and *Casino* (1995) and would return to with more recent films like *The Departed* (2006) and *The Irishman* (2019).

The backlash from China for this Disney/Scorsese collaboration was as sweeping and epic as *Kundun*. The film was banned, the CCP expressed outrage over the audacity of Disney to ever allow such a film to be released about the Dalai Lama and Tibet and its creative force, filmmaker Martin Scorsese received a lifetime ban from China for his efforts. We've discussed earlier in this book how the CEO of Disney at the time, Michael Eisner, threw himself at the mercy of the Chinese and promised they would never again have to endure such an affront from Disney.

So, a line was drawn. Not a line which stopped censorship at the water's edge but rather a line which no creative, artistic type dare cross in the name of not offending China.

Years later, in 2007, while basking in the glory of winning a Best Director and Best Picture for *The Departed*, ironically, a remake of a 2002 Hong Kong film called *Infernal Affairs*, Mr. Scorsese had a worldwide platform to say what he really thought of the ongoing atrocities and human rights violations in China. Perhaps he had learned his lesson with *Kundun*, perhaps he just didn't want to unnecessarily politicize the ceremony. Either way, he chose silence over speech when it came to the topic of China.

Quentin Tarantino, one of modern Hollywood's authentic "film auteurs,"90 maybe also its last, has refused to kowtow to China's censorship demands. And of course, he and his investors, which ironically includes the Chinese-based Bona Film Group, have paid a steep price for Mr. Tarantino's creative stance.

Some backstory is needed here.

In 2012 *Django Unchained* was about to become the first Tarantino film to be released and screened in China. Zhang Miao, President of Sony Pictures-Chinese Branch, had shared with the media already that the director Tarantino had been part of an editing process of the film to prepare the film to meet the Chinese censorship demands. He downplayed the process and its effect on the film's content. "What we call bloodshed and violence is just a means of serving the purpose of the film, and these slight adjustments will not affect the basic quality of the film – such as tuning the blood to a darker color, or lowering the height of the splatter of blood," Miao continued, "Quentin knew how to adjust that, and it's necessary that he is the one to do it. You can give him suggestions, but it must be him."[249]

Whether it was really him who made the edits or not, the result was that just as *Django Unchained* starring Leo DiCaprio and Jamie Foxx was about to hit the Chinese theaters, the word came down from the Chinese censorship bureau-pull the film.

Even the editor-in-chief of China's state-run Global Times publication, Hu Xijn, thought China had gone too far. In the aftermath of pulling the film, he posted, that "The harm that this action itself brings to politics far exceeds the harm that would have been caused by not censoring the offensive scene."[250]

In 2019 Tarantino was again on the verge of cracking the Chinese market with his newest film *Once Upon a Time in Hollywood.* And, just as before, the film ran into issues with Chinese censors. This time martial arts legend Bruce Lee's daughter, Shannon, complained to the Chinese National Film Administration about how her famous father was depicted in the film. Shortly afterwards, Tarantino was told to choose-Either edit the offensive Bruce Lee scenes which the Chinese officials also did not approve of, or risk having the entire film banned in China. Did he really want to suffer another *Django Unchained* power play by Chinese officials? It wasn't long before Tarantino made his stance clear. "They can take it or leave it the way it is,"[251] he noted in public. He would not edit the scene nor cut it out completely.

Not surprisingly, *Once Upon a Time in Hollywood* was indeed banned. Pirated copies filled the void of the real thing in China and Tarantino as well as his investors, which ironically, included the China-based Bona Film Group lost millions. Ridiculed by some, vilified by others for, first, his depiction of Bruce Lee, then, second, his refusal to recut or change the film to appease Chinese censors. For Tarantino, this was a line he drew creatively, that he refused to cross. His line, his film, his rules.

Fast forward to 2022 and his films have yet to premiere in China. It seems even less probable now after this latest rift. On the other hand, they can get bent, right? It's not a price if it is never paid.

Spielberg. Scorsese. Tarantino. Three Hollywood legends with elite status, impeccable filmmaking pedigree and power and influence to burn. Yet, individually, and collectively, they reflect just how intertwined modern Hollywood is with China. It is impossible in some ways to draw any line between us and them when "they" have become such an integral part of "your" side. Spielberg's Amblin Entertainment has deep financial and creative ties now with China. Even Jack Ma the richest man in China at one time and who founded Alibaba saw his fortune shrink from $45 billion to $22 billion after he angered the CCP could not escape their tentacles. How could Mr. Spielberg, even if he wanted to?

Mr. Scorsese learned what happens when you dare to make films on one of China's "T" taboos-Tiananmen Square, Taiwan and of course, Tibet. Don't bet on seeing any *Kundun* sequels anytime soon. Instead, his most critically successful film to date, *The Departed*, as noted, comes from Chinese filmmaking.

And in Mr. Tarantino's case, whether you like or dislike, agree or disagree with how Bruce Lee is portrayed in his film you can't dispute the fact that the filmmaker chose creative freedom or coercive censorship. How many others making films today would have made the same decision?

But while Hollywood and its glamorous denizens are often accused of working and living in a bubble, insulated from the real world, the industry is in no way alone in its mixed messaging towards China, its skin close relationship with this totalitarian regime nor its hypocritical posture.

Talk about wanting to have it both ways.

The Biden Administration came out against "China's ongoing genocide and crimes against humanity"[252] by deciding to not send an official US Diplomatic delegation to attend the 2022 Winter Olympics held in Beijing. Was this an echo of President Carter's principled stand against the Russian invasion of Afghanistan and its own human rights abuses when he boycotted completely the 1980 Games in Moscow?

Not quite.

Despite claiming that the White House "sent a clear message and that the human rights abuses in China mean that there cannot be business there as usual with the Olympics,"[253] that is exactly what happened. Business as usual took place.

All qualifying US athletes could and did fully participate. All sponsors did fully pay China for the privilege of being able to advertise during the Olympics and NBC, the US television network did fully pay China for the broadcasting rights of these same Games with limitations imposed by the CCP of what they could and could not show back home, of course. Despite grandiose and high-profile efforts of companies like Nike, Intel, and the NBA to demonstrate their commitment to human rights, civil rights, and progressive causes around the globe, when it came to China perhaps, they were blinded by visions of Chinese lucre dancing in their heads.

And the Speaker of the US House of Representatives Nancy Pelosi, who to her credit did initially call for a diplomatic boycott, ended up warning all US athletes to essentially "zip it"[254] and avoid saying or doing anything that might anger their Chinese hosts. The Olympic Games weren't the time for making such political statements. Really? If not then and there, when, and where?

Well, according to at least two powerful US corporate executives, the time may never be right to speak out.

Recently, Ray Dalio, the founder of Bridgewater, a multi-billion-dollar hedge fund, simply likened Chinese oppression, and genocide to them (the CCP) being like a parent. "As a top-down country, what they are doing is they just behave like a strict parent."[254]

Right, Ray. Only if that strict parent is a serial abuser, torturer, killer, and dictator who does not respect nor recognize any human rights.

US based (Santa Clara, CA) Intel Corporation certainly knows which side its semiconductor chip is buttered and it's not on the side of human misery.

CEO Patrick Gelsinger recently publicly apologized to China for US laws which prohibit Intel or others from ordering products originating from the Xianjiang region of China. This is where China has set-up its forced "re-education and labor internment camps."

Employing that tried and true, yet morally bankrupt excuse of "everyone is doing it," Gelsinger asserted that "We found there was no reason for us to call out one region in particular anywhere in the world, because there's many regions in the world having issues of such a matter."[255]

Really? No reason in the world to call out such "issues?"

How about 1.2 million reasons which is the estimated number of Uyghur humans being kept in internment camps against their will in Xianjiang region and as recently as October of 2022, another 300 or more Uyghur and Turkic Muslim intellectuals being imprisoned solely for their beliefs.

Seems the NBA's Houston Rockets and the Corporate world's Intel have something in common-They both don't exist to offend anyone. And by offending someone they mean not stating the truth about what China is doing to its own citizens every single day. Got it.

How about a different NBA owner? One with the defending champions, the Golden State Warriors? Surely, someone who lives and breathes the NBA air of progressive ideals and equity in the heart of California must have strong feelings about the ongoing genocide in China. Turns out, he does.

It's just that he could care less.

On a recent podcast, Mr. Chamath Palihapitiya, of the Warriors, in response to a question on this topic said, "Nobody cares about what is happening to the Uyghurs, okay? I'm telling you a hard, ugly truth…but of all the things I care and worry about, yes it (the genocide) is below my line."[256]

At least he drew a line of things he cares about and things he does not, right?

Unlike when Houston Rockets GM Daryl Morey tweeted support for those protesting for freedom in Hong Kong, and star James Harden felt compelled to tweet "We Love China,"[257] LeBron James called for Mr. Morey to be "properly educated"[258] or the NBA posted "regret for seriously hurting the feelings of the Chinese,"[259] there would be no profuse apologies this time on behalf of the NBA to the Uyghurs.

The NBA where amazing seems to happen often.

But maybe Mr. P. was right, after all, who cares?

As the owner of the Houston Rockets put it, "We are here to just play basketball and not offend anyone."[260] "Just shut-up and play," as political pundit Laura Ingraham once famously demanded *The Dixie Chicks* do after they publicly criticized the Bush Administration at a London concert.[261]

So, what about Hollywood circa 2022? Should they just "shut-up and make movies?"

Or, in their case, more accurately, should they start to "speak up and make movies?"

Would they be willing to do both? Could they? As we've made clear, it's a complicated relationship they're now in with China.

CHAPTER 10

DRAWING A LINE AND PAYING THE PRICE: INSULT THE CHINESE DRAGON AT YOUR OWN PERIL

Complicated is one thing, compliance is another.

According to the most recent report on Hollywood and China (*Made in Hollywood, Censored in Beijing*) published by PEN (NYC), it may not be changing anytime soon.

"Beijing has sent a clear message to the filmmaking world, that filmmakers who criticize China will be punished, but that those who play ball with its censorship strictures will be rewarded," and that while some may deny it, the authors of this report concluded that "The Chinese Communist Party, in fact, holds major sway over whether a Hollywood movie will be profitable or not—and studio executives know it."[262]

James Tager, the lead author of the report and deputy director of free expression research and policy at PEN also refuted those who claim that altering films to appease Chinese censors is trivial and not worth resisting. "While some of these alterations may seem minor—the cutting of a Taiwanese flag here or the removal of a minor plot point there—cumulatively such censoriousness cuts against artistic and cultural freedom, silences dissenting voices and can skew the global perceptions that are shaped by powerful films."[263]

Just ask the creators of *The Bleeding Edge* about powerful films that have been all but silenced by Chinese influence and power. And how many filmmakers out there are not even trying to make films like *The Bleeding Edge* or other stories worthy of our attention because of fear of Chinese reprisal. As the PEN report makes clear, it's not just the edits or re-cuts made to appease the Chinese it's the films that are simply never made because no one wants to anger Beijing. As the authors state, "It's Hollywood that now regularly censors its own movies to appease the Chinese Communist Party—the world's most powerful violator of human rights."[264]

And even non-studio, low-budget, well-meaning Indie films are not immune from the reach of China and the CCP censors. As noted film authority Stanley Rosen at USC put it, "Don't think that if you're doing something that's not intended for China, that's an indie film meant for a small market, that China won't notice and that it won't hurt your blockbuster film. It will."[265] As one Hollywood producer, who remained anonymous for fear of angering China said, "Most people in this industry do not burn China because there's an expectation of 'I'll never work again."[266] The PEN authors noted that many Hollywood insiders spoke to them but only on the condition of anonymity because all conveyed the sense that Chinese power and influence is everywhere. As one filmmaker said, "If what's happening now with China isn't having a chilling effect on what we make or don't in Hollywood then I don't know what that phrase means. And I do."[267]

Frequently, it the "pre-textual" censorship imposed by China that essentially does its work for the actual censors well before the film is even made. In practice this means that many filmmakers, screenwriters, and producers "self-censor" to avoid the wrath of China. They realize that the more they "self-censor" the greater the chance their film is one of the few that China allows into its theaters each year. While other nations like the US do not impose a quota system, relying on market demand and theatrical success to guide such decisions, China allows only some 25-35 films from outside of China each year. And as discussed earlier, they often rig the timing of cinematic release of imported films to not reduce their own domestic box office. While this violates both the WTO rules of trade and longstanding agreements struck between China and the MPAA of Hollywood, such is the reality of western industries trying to do business with China. Remember, win-win means China wins twice. Their view is simple-You need them more than they need you. And while it wasn't always that way when it came to Hollywood, it sure is now.

If Hollywood versus China was a heavyweight bout it would have been stopped a while ago on a TKO by China.

So, if this is indeed the present, what will the future of film look like with China calling the shots?

Honestly, a lot like it does now. Only more so.

China will continue to be the preeminent force in world cinema, exerting their influence and advancing their message through film. As Xi Jinping calls it "the story of China" will continue to be told but in a "good" way. In this story truth and positive don't ever have to collide or share the same screen space.

China's shrewd, aggressive, even predatory strategic investment and outright purchasing of major Hollywood studios, theaters, movie themed amusement parks, distribution networks and monopolies on domestic livestreaming with corporate giants like Beijing-based Tencent, will continue to pay dividends. The market share of world cinema which China now enjoys will continue to grow as part of their "Made in China" vision.

China will continue to reap huge profits and CCP approved propaganda from imported films they co-produce. As PEN also makes clear, it is not just that China wields leverage over what films are or are not made for the world to see, the films that hit screens are pro-China and quite frequently, anti-US and anti-capitalism. Since the comic-book blockbuster is now largely what Hollywood makes and is allowed to distribute in China, look for these to continue to be pro-communist and pro pan-Asia. In other words, American super-heroes conceived in the pre-and post-war climates when the American brand reigned supreme will now continue to openly question the morality, culture, and basic assumptions about America, what is stands for and its future. This will continue to be contrasted even more sharply with films and Chinese-driven heroes who are openly patriotic, suffer no moral ambiguity nor crisis of conscious and who once again, embody all that is good, pure, and wholesome about communist China. Their story, their money, increasingly their actors and in many cases, their movie screens.

As the CCP brutally accelerates the integration of Hong Kong into communist-run China, the Hong Kong cinema, long known for being fiercely independent and innovative, will increasingly become a mouthpiece for the CCP and mainland China. Look for films that will tell the story of a harmonious, happy, and now, even more powerful China. Taiwan and its own cinema will soon follow.

As the CCP continues to pursue its ambitious plans to further enhance its own superpower status globally, like its Digital Silk Road Initiative and its "Belt and Road" modern-day fiscal colonialism in the SE Asian region and beyond, their films will continue to glorify both where China has been and where it is headed. Let Captain America and others speak of official corruption back home, Chinese heroes will do what they are created to do, advance the Chinese narrative. And make gobs of money along the way.

Anyone who dares to speak out against China will be targeted, harassed, and vilified. If it is a Chinese celebrity or corporate mogul then she or he will be made to disappear for a while and then reappear with shall we kindly say, an attitude "readjustment." They'll have millions fewer social media followers and billions less dollars to connect with and spend but so be it. That is the way of the Chinese dragon. It will not be changing anytime soon.

And in those few instances when Hollywood stars like Angelina Jolie "insulted all of China"[268] by implying that Taiwan was an independent nation then studios like Disney will quickly fix the problem. In her case, she and her family shared a very public birthday cake in Shanghai with fans and then learned how to make Chinese Dim Sum. How utterly heartwarming. Her film *Maleficent* which stood to lose millions if it was denied Chinese distribution over the insult was then allowed safe passage to thousands of domestic screens in China. Ms. Jolie could afford to make even more Dim Sum, and Disney could breathe a sigh of relief. The film made millions as planned.

And when stars, even those that shine less bright than Angelina do, like faux wrestler and Dwayne "the Rock" wannabe actor John Cena, manage to insult China, they will quickly grovel to China and beg for forgiveness. Recently, Cena, who joined his idol The Rock" in the newest *Fast and Furious* film, did the unthinkable. He called Taiwan an outright country. No Angelina styled implication. For this sin against China, he quickly uploaded a video apology for the whole world to see. In it he spoke Mandarin and said he was very sorry, he'll never do it again and that he "loves and respects China."[269] His film, no longer "slow and injurious," was allowed through the gates of China. Forgiven and his film got distributed. Whew. That was too close for comfort. Actors, they do say the darndest things, don't they?

When not coercing apologies for various real and imagined affronts to their nationhood and communist self-esteem, their profit-taking from film will continue to soar, especially as COVID depressed box office numbers bounce back. And it will be the Chinese narrative that will be infused in as many films as possible. Its preferred brand, one where no Chinese villains exist, no weakness is allowed and no dissenting views accepted, will continue to be delivered wherever films are watched around the world. No matter the size of the screen or the type of device, the CCP will continue to have full access to tell its story the way it wants without fear of anyone daring to tell a story of any of the taboo "Ts."

And if anyone does dare to try to tell stories which reflect poorly on China then securing financing, sponsorship and Chinese distribution, even worldwide distribution, becomes a whole lot harder. Friends with deep pockets start to become scarce. Not to mention the harsh reprisals that will flow from Beijing as Spielberg, Scorsese and Tarantino found out. Like the fish in the aquarium who stopped trying to swim to the other side long after the wall blocking its path was removed, Hollywood, as we have seen, seems to know its place and to have accepted it. Part of that price to enjoy the privilege of making movies which almost everyone has willingly chosen to pay.

US Senator (R-TX) Ted Cruz apparently wants to make that price even higher to pay but with a domestic twist. Recently, he proposed a piece of legislation entitled "Stopping Censorship, Restoring Integrity, and Protecting Talkies Act," aka, the SCRIPTS Bill. The bill, if passed, would force the Hollywood studios and producers to choose between accepting federal funding from any US Department of Defense units or altering the film's content to satisfy Chinese censor demands. He later expanded the bill to include any funding from the US Government. As the Senator asked, "What message does it send that 'Maverick' an American icon, is apparently afraid of the

Chinese Communists?"[270] Referencing the editing out of the Taiwanese and Japanese patches on 'Maverick's' famed leather bomber jacket to appease the Chinese, Senator Cruz went on to state that "For too long, Hollywood has been complicit in China's censorship and propaganda in the name of bigger profits. The SCRIPTS Act will serve as a wake-up call by forcing Hollywood studios to choose between the assistance they need from the American Government and the dollars they want from China."[271]

The Act also called for Hollywood studios to provide the Congress with a list of all film titles sent to China for their approval for review. As one film executive responded, "Good luck with that."[272] However, one of the more significant changes of this Act would be to prohibit film studios engaged in co-productions with China from securing US Government assets like jetfighters, tanks, armored vehicles or access to US military bases and personnel if the final product (the film) is conditioned upon final approval by China censors.

Cruz referred to the battle over films with American heroes like that other Cruise as an "information warfare"[273] with China and implored Hollywood and corporate American to take a "whole of society" approach in telling our story.

On the heels of the Senator's proposed legislation, former US Attorney General William Barr addressed the growing dominance of China in many industries, not least of which is film. "Sadly, examples of American business bowing to Beijing are legion. Take Hollywood. Hollywood's actors, producers and directors pride themselves on celebrating freedom and the human spirit. And every year at the Academy Awards Americans are lectured about how our country falls short of Hollywood's ideals of social justice. But Hollywood now regularly censors its own movies to appease the Chinese Communist Party, the world's most powerful violator of human rights. This censorship infects not only versions of movies that are released in China but also many that are shown in American theaters to American audiences.274

Mr. Barr went on to note that Hollywood was far from being the only industry in America to kowtow to China and the PRC, asserting that America's big tech companies have also become pawns of Chinese influence. I think that's what screenwriters might call "cold solace."

But even if the SCRIPTS Act was passed and signed into law which is highly unlikely, would that really change the film industry all that much? And is it really that simple as Hollywood kowtowing to Chinese demands as Attorney General Barr asserts?

Well, No and No.

Of the roughly 100 films released for worldwide distribution by the "Big Six" of Hollywood each year (Warner Bros., Paramount, Disney, Fox, Universal and Sony) very few are either movies about the US military where DOD assets and facilities would even come into play or would need to rely on some form of US Governmental funding or other asset. Besides, as we've discussed at length, Hollywood just does not have any real motivation to make the type of "gung-ho, military recruitment style" movie anymore. *Top Gun: Maverick* may have marked the end of an era there. Tom "Maverick" Cruise just turned 60, I think his time in active duty will need to end soon. And long gone are the days when Disney gladly cooperated with the US to help in its armed services recruitment and wartime bonds buying campaigns.

More importantly, the "Big Six" certainly know that China would never approve of any film which depicts American military might or core values in a positive light. So, will they even make such a film to begin with, knowing that it (the film) would then fall under SCRIPTS regulations? Highly unlikely. I guess that's where the kowtowing Barr spoke of shows up on the radar.

What about the rest of the roughly 7-800 indie films released each year? They are overwhelmingly small budget films, not normally using military or US Government assets and even a smaller percentage of these indie films will end up in Chinese theaters. This is opposed to the "Big Six" film studio blockbusters marked for Chinese distribution, and even then, that number is relatively, very small as well.

But if nothing else, legislative proposals like SCRIPTS do draw attention to the plight of Hollywood. While much of it has been self-inflicted, they now find themselves boxed-in when it comes to which scripts get greenlighted and the often creatively distasteful compromises that must be made for their films to do big box-office. In the US and increasingly, worldwide. And a huge portion of any worldwide gross is, you guessed it, done in China.

Judd Apatow, longtime Hollywood film writer, director, and producer, has joined a very small handful of industry professionals who have publicly tried to sound the alarm over Chinese control. He sees it at both a macro and micro level in his business. "What I perceive as more chilling is a corporate type of censorship that people don't notice, which is a lot of these giant corporate entities around the world, Saudi Arabia or China, and they're just not going to criticize them, and they're not going to let their shows criticize them, or they're not going to air documentaries that go deep into truthful areas because they make so much money."[275]

Mr. Apatow has spoken publicly what many have thought or only shared anonymously to organizations like PEN about what really goes on every day at the operational level in Hollywood. The truth? China's influence is vast, inside and outside of Hollywood. The choices made about what to make or what to not touch has China's fingerprints all over it. Apatow uses the example of himself or other writers who may want to make a film about the Uyghur detention centers in China and say, a brave prisoner who manages to escape to tell the world of the horrors really going on behind those gates. Apatow has no doubt about such a story, such a film. It simply would not be made today. "No one would buy the pitch," if a filmmaker went to a studio now and said, "Hey, I want to write a movie about the concentration camps in China and Muslims in concentration camps, make a movie about someone who escapes."[276] The situation, Apatow asserts, is worse than many want to admit. "Instead of us (Hollywood) doing business with China, and that leading to China becoming more free, what has happened is a place like China has bought our silence with their money. They have just completely shut down critical content about human rights abuses in China, and I think that's much scarier."[277]

Chris Fenton, a former president of DMG Entertainment Motion Picture Group with headquarters in Beverly Hills, California and Beijing, China, is also concerned with the vast control China asserts over Hollywood and the real life consequences.

"What I didn't expect was the American public to react in a way that was completely stupefied and completely unaware of what kind of kowtowing and placating of the Chinese Government had been ongoing, not just with the NBA, but with Hollywood and various other businesses, for as long as it had been going on. So, that was a wake-up call to me because it was a wake-up call to the American public about how companies were engaging with China that wasn't really part of being a patriotic American."[278]

The consequence of all of this, Fenton believes, is damaging and only getting worse. "It's not just the Hollywood issue, it's not just the tech issue, it's not just the basketball or the sports issue, or even various other industries, it's all across the board. To get products and services into the market, there are certain rules you have to play by in order to get past the CCP, so they allow you access to their consumers. But those processes, those regulations, those things that we need to live by to do it have gotten worse and worse and more amplified over time. And the encroachment on what's true to Americans has got to the point where we need to stop it now and fight back, or we are going to lose because it's going to the point of no return."[279]

As Sam Spade might have said, "Doll, clearly, Hollywood ain't even Hollywood anymore."

CONCLUSION
FLIPPING THE SCRIPT

"When it is obvious that the goals cannot be reached, don't adjust the goals, adjust the action steps." — Confucius

It took over 100 years. Over one-hundred years of Hollywood movie-making magic. Over one hundred years of dazzling the paying customer. Over one hundred years of the world being inspired by, competing with, and motivated to replace Hollywood as the world's number one cinema. The global storytelling leader. The most powerful visual narrator ever invented and perfected. It took more than a century, but China has finally climbed over Hollywood and reached the top of the filmmaking mountain.

Even before audiences were captivated by movies that could both move and talk or, as in *The Jazz Singer* (1927) even sing, there was Charlie Chaplin touching hearts and tickling the funny bones of fans everywhere as *The Tramp* (1915). In what seemed like the blink of an eye or the quick switch of a film reel, audiences around the world were mesmerized by the star power and glamor of Hollywood.

From the dancing of Fred Astaire and Ginger Rogers, who, as we now appreciate, did everything he did but backwards and in pearls, to the dazzling technicolor quest of Judy Garland and her Yellowbrick friends trying to make their way back home in *The Wizard of Oz*, to the poetic beauty of Gene Kelly and Leslie Caron in *An American in Paris*, or the rough and tumble heroics of John Ford's John Wayne in *The Stagecoach* or *The Searchers*, Hollywood ruled all it surveyed.

And that world was never more elegant than when Grace Kelly played a dangerous game of cat and mouse with retired cat burglar Cary Grant along the French Riviera in Alfred Hitchcock's *To Catch a Thief.* Never more dangerous and poignant than when Ingrid Bergman bid a sad farewell in *Casablanca*, never more playfully seductive than when Bogie met Bacall in films like *The Big Sleep*. Never more, well creepy and spellbinding than when Anthony Perkins as Norman Bates declared that there was no stronger love than a boy for his mother in *Psycho*. No matter the story or the setting, the early decades of Hollywood seemed magical, bigger than life, giants with no equal.

The sprawling studios of Hollywood had plenty of room for all types of stories to be told and all types of audiences to enjoy them. Just so long as they were the paying type as Sam Warner used to say. Whether it was the wordsmithing genius of Preston Sturgis, the dizzying speed of the Howard Hawks' banter, the sweeping epics of Cecil B. DeMille, the psychologically probing film noirs of Ida Lupino, the masterful suspense of Hitchcock films, the grittiness of a John Huston film or the sheer genius of Billy Wilder, the global appeal of Hollywood had no rival.

As the order, dominance and stability of the Hollywood studio system toppled, it seemed to coincide with the rest of the world being engulfed in chao and change. Just a few short decades after World War II a much different Hollywood was emerging. More introspective, self-critical, violent, and dark, less sumptuous, elegant, innocent, and bright.

The very American film noir with its disillusionment, violence and betrayal dominated the box office for years. Hollywood further questioned the priorities, prejudices, and morals of American society in films like *The Graduate*, *Midnight Cowboy*, *Easy Rider* and *Guess Who's Coming to Dinner*.

Visually stunning science fiction films like Stanley Kubrick's *2001: A Space Odyssey* predicted technological betrayal of humans in deep, dark space. Even superficially silly and whimsical films starring the adoring Audrey Hepburn and the "new" Cary Grant (George Pepard) in *Breakfast at Tiffany's* had dark, even troubling undercurrents about narcissism, abandonment, and amorality. Where once glamor and stardom was the currency of Hollywood and by default, the American calling card to the rest of the world, its own films seemed to be a metaphor for what Hollywood had itself become. Maybe even all of America in a post-war world.

Still, Hollywood as an industry continued to sit atop the global cinematic tower like a growling yet vulnerable King Kong. Its closest cinematic rivals still seemed like small planes pestering the great giant as he swatted them out of the sky.

But like Kong, its days atop the tower were also numbered and the number of planes trying to bring the beast down were multiplying. Even as Marty McFly was experimenting with time travel in a deluxe DeLorean, Arnold was terminating to fix the future, Rambo was blowing up the present and Bruce was spending Christmas mostly alone, one rival was moving closer and closer to its own goals.

About the same time when Hollywood began to glorify street vigilantes as the true antidote to an America that had become ridden with crime, in films like Clint Eastwood's *Dirty Harry* or Charles Bronson's *Death Wish*, former President Gerald Ford, then a US House of Representatives Minority Leader, wrote about his time in the People's Republic of China (1972). "If she (China) manages to achieve as she aspires, China in the next century can emerge as a self-sufficient power of a billion people…this last impression-of the reality of China's colossal potential-is perhaps, the most vivid of our journey. As our small party traveled through that boundless land, this sense of a giant stirring, *a dragon waking*, gave us much to ponder."[280]

Today, just over 100 years after Charlie Chaplin's brilliant film *The Kid* (1921) and 50 years since President Ford wrote those words in his journal, and Francis Ford Coppola's iconic film *The Godfather* made audiences an offer they couldn't refuse, the Chinese dragon has indeed awakened. And where the mighty Hollywood Kong once stood, the King of all he surveyed, the Chinese dragon now sits-atop the cinematic world for all to see. Long live the King, the Kong is dead.

It took 100 years, but Hollywood-at times admired by, resented, banned, in collaboration with, and now, partially owned by China, now looks to the East, to Beijing for approval and authority. The way of the Chinese dragon means always having to know where the dragon is and what he wants and does not want. What he will allow you to do and what he will not. What rewards you can hope for, what punishment you will receive if you anger the dragon.

Hong Kong and Taiwan found this undeniable truth out the hard way, politically and cinematically. China used its vast consumer market like a dragon's tail, at times dormant, at other times it moved with an astounding force, crushing its smaller rivals. China has run the gamut from banning films from Hong Kong and Taiwan over language, subject matter, cultural sensitivities, political and economic considerations, to forbidding its mainland Chinese films and filmmakers from exhibiting their films at Taiwanese and Hong Kong festivals, theaters or even traveling to discuss their films and craft. Despite brief periods when both regional rivals thrived, the dragon's tail could and did snap both into its place.

As for Hollywood, it was, for decades, fortunate to not be within the reach of the dragon and its volatile nature. Hollywood always seemed more about simply "putting fannies into the seats" and money into the till. Maybe it was always nothing more than making movies to make money and spending more money to make more movies to make even more money. A seemingly endless circle of creative energy, greed, and entertainment. Today, of course, it's about worldwide distribution rights, profit-sharing and streaming subscriptions. Is there still creative energy? Of course, but even Michelangelo had to get paid for his own brand of heavenly genius. A marriage of necessity if not love.

For China, art, and especially, film, has never had any inherent value. To the Chinese "art for art's sake" simply does not exist. Since its inception, profit-making has not been the sole or even primary driver of the Chinese film industry. Art, as Mao famously stated and Xi Jinping reiterated, must exist to serve a greater purpose. And for China, for the Chinese Communist Party (CCP), that greater purpose is to serve the Party and to continue to glorify the Communist Revolution, the "People's Revolution" and all it stood for, then and now.

Where Hollywood made more movies to make more money and self-consciously or not, its films became how America was perceived by millions around the globe, China takes no such chance with film. Films must reinforce the preferred national narrative while making profit to help advance its own ambitious plans of expanded global power and absolute domestic self-sufficiency. In past years, it was "Madame Mao" pulling and pushing the levers of artistic control as she saw fit to best express husband Mao's vision. Today, it is the CCP censors advancing the expansive and totalitarian rule of Xi Jinping. The names change but the script remains the same.

Where Hollywood offered a range of cinematic offerings, frequently probing the dark underbelly of American society and questioning the very fabric of its existence, China sees movies as an effective means to tell its story, but to tell it only in a good way. Let American films point out the many flaws, sins, and continued weakness of that nation. Chinese films will do no such thing. And any films wishing to enter the gates of China must never vilify or even question China, its people, its past, or its plans. It's a privilege to do business with China, not a right. And those are just some of its terms. It's one of the few areas the Communists and the Kuomintang Nationalists agreed. China must never be offended. Its sensitivities never insulted. Its pride never injured.

The same ground rules apply to filmmakers already within its gates. From big things to small, films must not show China in a bad light. Even films which showed litter in the Shanghai River got banned. Not because there was no litter there, because there is, but because showing it was unacceptable, inconsistent with telling the story of China "in a good way." Telling China's story in film also means that there is no crime in the streets, no sexual deviancy in the bedroom, no dissatisfaction with the Chinese way of life, no depression, no drugs, no dissident voices crying out. Let Hollywood spill its guts for all the world to see. Under the Chinese Communists, films have a specific purpose, and that purpose often has no relation to reality. Why should it?

Where Hollywood and its corporate giants have often been at loggerheads with the Government over its leftist leanings, its avowed sympathy for communism, and its graphic sexuality, violence and perversion in its films, Chinese Government brooks no opposition, no deviation from the approved and disseminated political narrative. Elon Musk gets to call out the US President Joe Biden on what he sees is the President's ignorance of even basic economic logic. Jack Ma takes issue with how Chinese banks handle business loans, and he gets toppled, all but banished from his own multi-billion company he founded and heads up.

To China under CCP rule, all businesses and those that manage them are merely pawns in a much larger game. Forget for even a second why you are allowed to operate and make the profit you do, forget the greater purpose and, like art, since you have no inherent value, you may just cease to exist.

This harsh reality, this very basic difference between the US and China, between Hollywood and the CCP-run film industry though profound, is frequently either ignored by many in America or dismissed as mostly rhetoric. The "We're really all the same" with just a few minor differences mantra is wildly naïve, dangerous, and inevitably self-defeating.

The Chinese dragon is different. The China of circa 2022 and beyond is not some innocuous relic of a deeply spiritual, dynastic past. Confucius may be the name on the hundreds of institutions established in schools around the globe but it's the CCP in charge not some ancient philosopher-priest. And the CCP are run by extremely sober, serious, and ruthless men and women who have absolute clarity on what they want, and what they are more than willing and ready to do to get it. This too, is the way of the modern Chinese dragon.

When the US FBI Director Christopher Wray cites the many ways in which the CCP pursues its global ambitions like industrial espionage, theft, extortion, coercion, intimidation, cyberattacks and even violence and terror, he is trying to ring an alarm to many in America who continue to see China and the CCP as a mostly, benign, well-meaning, even misunderstood rival. What those in law enforcement see as incredibly damaging, illegal activities, the CCP sees simply as means to a desired end.

When the Chinese finally chose to stop banning Hollywood films and pretending that it could somehow blunt the influence of America by ignoring it and decided to essentially beat Hollywood and America at its own game by joining them, both as partners in filmmaking and in the WTO, they have never looked back. The days of China blatantly appropriating Hollywood films like *Street Angels* starring Janet Gaynor and simply making its own *Street Angels* with Xuan Zhao, as if the original had never happened, seem long gone. So are the days when Madame Mao ruled film and a nation of 800 million would watch 8 films over and over again. Today, Hollywood legends like Scorsese adapt Chinese films like *Infernal Affairs* into Academy Award winners like *The Departed.* Now, it is Hollywood and America that may increasingly be looking back in regret.

Where the Chinese once played the role of student to its Hollywood mentor, their domestic film industry now accounts for 80-95% of its domestic movie box office. China has more movie screens, more box office, bigger film sets and enjoys final say on any films coming into or out of its nation.

When it comes to doing business with China it is largely a one-way street with traffic controlled by CCP censors and distributors. Unlike the US and Hollywood, China can and does turn on and off its spigot of films it allows into its vast, 1.4-billion-person market. Legends like Spielberg, Scorsese and more recently, Tarantino, have all felt the wrath of the dragon. There is no such creative and artistic censorship, control or restraints in Hollywood even approaching those thrown in one's path by the CCP.

Psychiatrists tell us that people with good intentions who seem to trust others often engage in a type of cognitive projection or transference. This leads to believing that others share the same values, intentions and good will that you do. Even if they do not.

Perhaps, this mindset, this tendency to project unto others how we feel internally, continues to dominate how we, as Americans, perceive and treat the Chinese collectively. We mean well, they must mean well too. We play fair, certainly they do, too. We value peace and stability above all else, why would they feel differently?

But China under CCP rule does not share our core American values of democracy, individualism, freedom of life, liberty, or artistic or political expression. China under CCP rule does not value the life of any citizen over what it sees as the collective good. That is why Hollywood films like *Saving Private Ryan* or *Captain Phillips* which both depicted a group risking its own collective life to save the life of another was either highly controversial or outright banned in China. That is not the communist mindset. That is not the way of the Chinese dragon. People exist to serve the needs of the government not the other way around. A simple truth with a historical track record of sustained evidence. Yet, many still prefer to deny and project.

And many in Hollywood continue to place profit or even just the chance at profitmaking in mainland China over people. Indifference to the consequences of helping advance the Chinese global narrative continues to be the coin of the realm. And those rare times when celebrities do speak their conscience over Chinese genocide and censorship, they better be prepared to pay a personal and professional price. Films once approved now don't get made. Finished films don't get released. Blockbusters about to premiere in China get pulled at the last second. No explanation forthcoming. Calls from their agent don't get returned. Budgets get cut. Stars who get ghosted tend not to have careers. So, they choose to do a different kind of "right thing." They grovel. They cook dim sum. They write scripts that bash America and praise China. They even have Captain America himself disgusted at the rot and corruption eating away his homeland. They apologize in Mandarin. They throw millions of people being "re-educated" under the bus. The lesson is clear-Do not anger the dragon. Let someone else with less to lose speak up for people and for basic human rights. That is, if they dare.

Of course, as we've seen, Hollywood is far from the only industry that cowers in fear of offending China and losing even a share of its vast consumer market. Whether it comes in the form of a cell phone, search engine, television network or an NBA basketball to name just a few, CEOs across the US go to bed in fear and wake-up in fear of somehow offending one of the many sensitivities of China. And we know intent makes no difference when it comes time for reprisals. "We Love China," yells James Harden across the Twitter Kingdom as he tweets safely ensconced in his sprawling 7,124 square foot palace at the Royal Oaks Country Club in Houston, Texas, some 7,120 or so miles from Beijing. I guess love really is blind.[281]

It took over 100 years to get here so does that mean that the next 100 years of film will be ruled by the Chinese dragon?

Will audiences around the globe continue to see only Chinese heroes but never villains, the kindness of communism and the corruption of capitalism, the purity of China and the poison of America, in short, the story of China told in a good way, the story of America told in a bad way?

Well, yes and no. If Hollywood stays on the path they have largely constructed for itself over the years, then yes, films will continue to be "Made in China" or at least approved by China, touting the Chinese way of life, often at the expense of its former moviemaking mentor.

But if this is indeed the way of the Chinese dragon, it need not be the only way for Hollywood moving forward. Don't get me wrong, I am suggesting Hollywood stop looking eastward to find a vast audience for its films, collaborative filmmaking opportunities, global star power, cutting edge technology or even a culture still curious and movie crazy, with unlimited potential.

I am however, suggesting Hollywood look slightly southeastward towards *Bharata*, better known as The Republic of India.

If I told you that as a Hollywood filmmaker, a producer, or even a deep-pocketed investor, you had a market consisting of over 1.4 billion people, on track to be the most populous nation in the world by 2030, outpacing even China, a market where English is spoken by nearly 12% of its people or close to 200 million possible moviegoers, and a market where movies are the number one form of entertainment despite only having less than 10,000 movie screens for the entire country, China has over 75,000 by comparison, what would you say? Would you at least be intrigued?

What if I sweetened the pot by mentioning that India is also the most populous democracy in the world? I see you have not asked me to leave the premises so let me also add that many Indian movie stars have global appeal and have enjoyed Hollywood success. Names like Priyanka Chopra (*Baywatch, Quantico*), Anushka Sharma (Xander Cage franchise), Anil Kapoor *(Slumdog Millionaire*, TV's *24, Mission Impossible*), Frieda Pinto (*Immortals*), Aishwarya Rai (*Pink Panther 2*), and Anupam Kher (*Bend it Like Beckham*), are, just to name a few, all megawatt stars in India and bankable stars even without the Hollywood movie marquee.

But do Indians truly love cinema, I mean, will they support film for years to come?

Well, Indian cinema releases more feature length films each year than anywhere else in the world. As for diversity and being open to many different stories being told, well, you should know that India itself is a diverse nation home to many different languages (26), cultures, and even movie genres.

Bollywood, formerly known as Bombay Cinema (now Mumbai), a playful word combination of Bombay and Hollywood, has, for decades, been synonymous with Indian cinema. With its dazzling dance choreographies, dramatic romance, pop songs, heart-stopping action and colorful sets, this genre ruled the industry. But times may be changing. This form of Hindi cinema now is part of a growing moviemaking landscape that varies greatly depending on whether one is in West Bengali, Jammu and Kashmir, or Punjabi. Films as varied as its land, its culture, its people.

Certainly, a long-lasting Hollywood-India marriage would not be a blessing without challenges. It does not offer the same profit opportunities which China currently does, at least to those films the CCP censors do not ban, and the relatively few it allows in each year. Sensitivity to the Indian culture and language would need to be shown for success. But then, we've seen the seemingly unlimited sensitivities of China constantly threaten to shut-down film productions and market access. And for such a large nation as India, there are relatively few movie screens though, unlike in the past, internet access and entertainment streaming services are now provided across India by both public and private companies.

Aside from the movie market opportunities for Hollywood's "Big Six Studios," independent filmmakers, largely shunned and blocked by China, would potentially stand to benefit greatly. Indie filmmaking, with its rich history dating back to pioneers like Orson Welles, release hundreds of wildly varied films each year. More formalized and codified trade relations when it comes to film could enrich film and audiences in both nations for years to come.

Politically, the US and India have enjoyed close relations since India gained its independence from the United Kingdom in 1947. Both democracies, India and the US are partners in a wide range of initiatives, including the Indo-Pacific Economic Framework for Prosperity, an alliance designed, in part, to counter China's regional aggressive ambitions. India and China are frequently bitter enemies. So, it will take skill and diplomacy to fully tap the potential of India. But then again, we continue to do business with China even as they publicly declare their long-lasting friendship for Russia, even as that nation declares its enmity and hostility towards the US. Life is complicated. Visionaries reap rewards while followers fall back.

Looking eastward to India would not be a short-term play by Hollywood, and would take a commitment of capital, creativity, and a willingness to cultivate relationships over time. But over the last several decades, as we've seen, a series of corporate and political miscalculations, blunders, and costly compromises, along with a naïve underestimating of China's prowess, its predatory nature, and its cunning, have all served to squarely place Hollywood in an inferior position to China.

Perhaps, it is time for leaders like President Joe Biden and his pal and former head of the Motion Picture Association of America (MPAA) Chris Dodd, to stop thinking in terms of immediate and short-term deals and quick "fixes." That type of thinking, built on promises not performance, and optimism not enforcement, helped make Hollywood the passenger and China the driver. Time to take back the steering wheel.

China thinks, plans, and acts for the long-term. It's how they approach the serious business of filmmaking along with everything else. It's in large part, how they reached the top of the mountain. So, why shouldn't Hollywood start do the same?

Every year it seems Hollywood loses just a little bit more of its creative independence, its pioneering soul, its legacy of leading. Every year we watch as China insists on telling the world its sanitized, pre-approved narrative of itself through film. And every year, more and more of Hollywood seems captured, no longer even resisting out of fear and futility. "It's just the way it is," insists one insider, reflecting the prevailing view across Hollywood and beyond, "and there's nothing that can be done."[282]

We all make choices. So do those in and out of the film industry. Choices are what got Hollywood into this mess and only bold and different choices will get them out.

Martin Scorsese has likened film to being an American art form, like jazz.[283] So, here's to Hollywood, let's hope they rediscover the creativity to start making beautiful, soulful jazz once again, the courage to share it with the whole world, and the unwavering commitment to tell its stories in its own voice in a good and honest way. Hooray for artistic freedom and human rights everywhere. Hooray for Hollywood.

END NOTES

1-Hollywood director Judd Apatow says Hollywood is now China's puppet: 'Chilling' censorship as China has 'bought our silence' - TheBlaze

2-Transcript of Attorney General Barr's Remarks on China Policy at the Gerald R. Ford Presidential Museum | OPA | Department of Justice

3-Martin Scorsese Quotes (Author of A Personal Journey with Martin Scorsese Through American Movies) (goodreads.com)

4-Quentin Tarantino Won't Recut 'Once Upon a Time in Hollywood' for China (Exclusive) – The Hollywood Reporter

5-Pompeo Praises Tarantino's Refusal to Appease Chinese Censorship - Loomered

6-China's Grip on Hollywood Began with Disney Apology for Scorsese's 'Kundun' (businessinsider.com)

7-Hollywood Executive Reveals How China's Politics Have Shaped Movie Industry (voanews.com)

8-Hollywood director Judd Apatow says Hollywood is now China's puppet: 'Chilling' censorship as China has 'bought our silence' - TheBlaze

9-Steven Spielberg - There is a fine line between censorship... (brainyquote.com)

10-TOP 25 QUOTES BY ALFRED HITCHCOCK (of 118) | A-Z Quotes (azquotes.com)

11-Joe Biden Quotes - BrainyQuote

Introduction: Confucius quote

47 Confucius Quotes That Still Ring True Today (thoughtco.com)

Chapter 1

1-Hollywood Sayings and Hollywood Quotes | Wise Sayings

2-Jack L. Warner - I don't want it good. I want it Tuesday. (brainyquote.com)

3-Shanghai's Last Stand - The '800 Heroes' of Sihang Warehouse (warhistoryonline.com)

4-Hollywood Sayings and Hollywood Quotes | Wise Sayings

5-Shanghai, Paris of the East - Travel - Chinadaily.com.cn

6-China Shanghai History: Timeline from 6,000 Years Ago to Preset (travelchinaguide.com)

7-The Early History of Motion Pictures | American Experience | Official Site | PBS

8-Puyi: The Last Emperor of China (thoughtco.com)

9-Gettysburg Address | National Geographic Society

10-Sun Yat-sen and 'Three Principles of the People' - CCTV News - CCTV.com English

11-Mandarin Ducks and Butterflies: Popular Fiction in Early Twentieth-Century Chinese Cities. By Perry Link. [Berkeley, Los Angeles and London: The University of California Press, 1981. x, 313 pp.] | The China Quarterly | Cambridge Core

12-Chinese culture and the spirits behind Chinese wuxia films - CGTN

13-A Golden Age of Chinese Cinema, 1947-52 | US-China Institute (usc.edu)

14-Benjamin Brodsky – first to open a Hong Kong film production company and "King of Chinese cinema" – The Industrial History of Hong Kong Group (industrialhistoryhk.org)

15-Lianhua Film Company aka United Photoplay Service Film Studio, registered in Hong Kong 1930 – The Industrial History of Hong Kong Group (industrialhistoryhk.org)

16-Eyes of the Buddha (1922) | MUBI

17-Genre, war, ideology: Anti-Japanese war films in Taiwan and Mainland China: Chinese Studies in History: Vol 49, No 4 (tandfonline.com)

18-A Century of Chinese Cinema: an introduction | BFI

19-A Short History of Film and Censorship in Mainland China (gvsu.edu)

20-The History of Hong Kong Action Cinema Pt. 1 - 1896-1930: The Pioneers - Film Inquiry

Chapter 2

21-Manchuria | historical region, China | Britannica

22-Mukden Incident | Summary | Britannica

23-China's Last Emperor: Who Was Puyi and Why Did He Abdicate? | History Hit

24-A Short History of Film and Censorship in Mainland China (gvsu.edu)

25-Sun Yat-sen and 'Three Principles of the People' - CCTV News - CCTV.com English

26-The politics of filmmaking: An investigation of the Central Film Censorship Committee in the mid-1930s | SpringerLink

27-Long March - HISTORY

28-Building a New China in Cinema: The Chinese Left-Wing Cinema Movement, 1932-1937 | MCLC Resource Center (osu.edu)

29-Ruan Lingyu: The Greta Garbo of China - BBC Culture

30-Ruan Lingyu: The Greta Garbo of China - BBC Culture

31-Ruan Lingyu Biography - Chinese silent film actress | Pantheon

32-"The Male Greta Garbo": Handsome Portrait Photos of Nils Asther in the 1920s and '30s ~ Vintage Everyday

33-John Howard Lawson | Peliplat

34-Shirley Temple Style Evolution: From The 'Good Ship Lollipop' To Bold and Beautiful (PHOTOS) | HuffPost Life

35-The Golden Age of Horror – The Best Horror Films of 30s-40s-50s

36-Shanghai's Last Stand - The '800 Heroes' of Sihang Warehouse (warhistoryonline.com)

37-China's Alamo: The real story behind 'the 800 heroes' – The China Project

38-The Rape of Nanking - HISTORY

39-Nanking Massacre - Facts, Denial & Cause - HISTORY

40-Shanghai Jewish Ghetto: a forgotten piece of history - Tristan Lavender Photography

41-Orphan Island Paradise (1939) Movie - CinemaCrush

42-White Terror Period - National Human Rights Museum (nhrm.gov.tw)

43-The Spring River Flows East | BAMPFA

44-The Spring River Flows East | BAMPFA

45-A Short History of Film and Censorship in Mainland China (gvsu.edu)

46-Module 11: Crows and Sparrows (1949) - Chinese Film Classics

47-Sugar Coated Bullets: Corruption and the New Economic Order in China | Office of Justice Programs (ojp.gov)

48-Chen Baichen (2004 edition) | Open Library

49-Double Tenth Agreement - Chinese Civil War - Historydraft

50-[Photo story] Failure of the Double Tenth Agreement and the beginning of the Chinese civil war, History News - ThinkChina

51-Book review of The China Mission: George Marshall?s Unfinished War, 1945-1947 by Daniel Kurtz-Phelan - The Washington Post

52-The Chinese Civil War (alphahistory.com)

Chapter 3

53-Cultural Revolution - Definition, Effects & Mao Zedong - HISTORY

54-Madame Mao: The White-Boned Demon by Ross Terrill (goodreads.com)

55-The Film Sufi: "Spring in a Small Town" - Fei Mu (1948)

56-Revolutionary opera — Google Arts & Culture

57-Rise of the Chinese Communist Party-approved blockbuster - CNN Style

58-Rise of the Chinese Communist Party-approved blockbuster - CNN Style

59-Zhang Chunqiao: Communist leader of China's Cultural Revolution – Liberation School

60-Jiang Qing (March 19, 1914 — May 14, 1991), Chinese politician, Revolutionary, actress | World Biographical Encyclopedia (prabook.com)

61-5 foreign movies Stalin watched in his home cinema - Russia Beyond (rbth.com)

62-Why Hitler watched Hollywood films – DW – 03/26/2019

63-'White-Haired Girl,' Opera Created Under Mao, Returns to Stage - The New York Times (nytimes.com)

64-Understanding Chinese media censorship: From Ming to Jinping | ORF (orfonline.org)

65-What Is the Hukou System in China? - Meaning, Pros, & Cons (nhglobalpartners.com)

66-Battle of Shangganling - China Military

67-The Death of 'Tailgunner Joe' McCarthy (historynet.com)

68-Galvan v. Press :: 347 U.S. 522 (1954) :: Justia US Supreme Court Center

69-What is "McCarthyism?" It's Ame... (freedommovement.info)

70-Hollywood Ten - HISTORY

71-archives.nypl.org -- Nora Sayre papers

72- City needs quality films, not Hollywood-formula flicks - SanBenito.com | Hollister, San Juan Bautista, CA

73- Letting a Hundred Flowers Bloom: What Coronavirus Teaches Us About Who We Are | Opinion (newsweek.com)

74- The Hundred Flowers campaign (alphahistory.com)

75- PR China - The Hundred Flowers Movement and the Anti-Rightist Movement 1956-1957 (www.chinaknowledge.de)

76- Great Leap Forward Facts | Britannica

77- Workers World [Sam Marcy]: Jiang Qing and the Cultural Revolution (June 20, 1991)

78- Why do revolutions "eat their own?" What is the sociological dynamic here? - History Stack Exchange

79- Mao's Great Leap Forward 'killed 45 million in four years' | The Independent | The Independent

80- The Hundred Flowers Movement was the first open criticism in the history of the People's Republic of China (thevintagenews.com)

81- Mao's Last Purge | News | The Harvard Crimson (thecrimson.com)

82- Mao's Hundred Flowers Campaign in China (thoughtco.com)

83- Mao Tse-tung (Mao Ze-dong) and the Sino-Soviet Dispute | US-China Institute (usc.edu)

84- Lin Biao Quote: "One word from Chairman Mao is worth ten thousand from others. His every statement is truth. We must carry out those we t..." (quotefancy.com)

85- Who, What, Why: What is the Little Red Book? - BBC News

86- Red Guards (alphahistory.com)

87- China: Confessions of a Red Guard | CNN

88-China: Confessions of a Red Guard | CNN

89-4th Generation of Chinese Directors, a list of films by chaarusu • Letterboxd

90-President Richard Nixon, Pat Nixon, Chou En-Lai, Jiang Qing (Madame Mao), William Rogers, Henry Kissinger, and Others Attend the Revolutionary Opera Performance of The Red Detachment of Women | DPLA

91-Dalton Trumbo (spartacus-educational.com)

92-Cultural Revolution | Definition, Facts, & Failure | Britannica

93-Interactive: Hollywood's 50 Greatest Producers of All Time (thedailybeast.com)

94-Young Bruce Lee, Part II: The Man Before the Legend (zolimacitymag.com)

95-Top 10 Bruce Lee Movies - IMDb

96-Gang of Four | Chinese politicians | Britannica

97-QUOTES BY JIANG QING | A-Z Quotes (azquotes.com)

Chapter 4

98-Deng's pragmatism is China's poison pill | Lowy Institute

99-Understanding China's One-Child Policy | The National Interest

100-True Story Behind Deng Xiaoping's South Tour Through the Eyes of a Historical Witness (theepochtimes.com)

101-Cinema of China - Cultural Revolution and Its Aftermath | Cultural Revolution Aftermath | Technology Trends (primidi.com)

102-Wu Tianming - Biography (liquisearch.com)

103-Wu Tianming dies at 74; Chinese director shook up state-run studio - Los Angeles Times (latimes.com)

104-Tiananmen Square: How the 'Goddess of Democracy' became a symbol of resistance - CNN Style

105-Tiananmen Square: How the 'Goddess of Democracy' became a symbol of resistance - CNN Style

106-President Reagan to Gorbachev: "Tear down this wall" - HISTORY

107-Foreign media at the 1989 Tiananmen Square protests and massacre - Wikipedia

108-Wu Tianming dies at 74; Chinese director shook up state-run studio - Los Angeles Times (latimes.com)

109-What's Hollywood's formula for making a blockbuster? | EW.com

110-Voting With Their Feet– The Story of Migration from East to West | Migration: Now and Then (musselmanlibrary.org)

111-Hollywood Branding Secrets That Entrepreneurs Can Use Too | HuffPost Impact

112-Keith Haring's Graffiti in New York Subway | DailyArt Magazine

113-Summer Blockbusters That Defined the 1980s (cbr.com)

114-Terminator Franchise Box Office History - The Numbers (the-numbers.com)

115-Tiananmen Square Protests: Timeline, Massacre & Aftermath - HISTORY

116-Deng Xiaoping's secret 'Southern Tour' and its enduring legacy – The China Project

117-Yinhe incident | Detailed Pedia

118-Portrait of an Laobaixing: The Post-Journey Interview (wildchina.com)

119-Shanghai Triad movie review & film summary (1996) | Roger Ebert

120-Agencies Responsible for Censorship in China | Congressional-Executive Commission on China (cecc.gov)

121-Kundun movie review & film summary (1998) | Roger Ebert

122-China's Grip on Hollywood Began with Disney Apology for Scorsese's 'Kundun' (businessinsider.com)

123-Crazy English - Harvard Film Archive

124-94 Best Confucius Quotes About Life (PHILOSOPHY) (graciousquotes.com)

125-'The White-Haired Girl': 70 years on [1]-Chinadaily.com.cn

Chapter 5

126-How Do You Say 'Boffo' in Chinese? 'The Fugitive': Movies: The first recent Hollywood blockbuster to be shown in

China in years has given a boost to the country's faltering movie theaters. - Los Angeles Times (latimes.com)

127-Agencies Responsible for Censorship in China | Congressional-Executive Commission on China (cecc.gov)

128-China Under Jiang Zemin - China Underground (china-underground.com)

129-China Under Jiang Zemin - China Underground (china-underground.com)

130-Ding Guan'gen (en-academic.com)

131-The Hollywood Business Model & Leadership - Be Human Project

132-Jim Carrey Was One of the First Actors to Get Paid $20 Million for a Role | Pulse Nigeria

133-How Much Did Leonardo DiCaprio Earn From His Role In 'Titanic'? (thethings.com)

134-10 Actors Who Were Paid Enormous Salary Per Word - FandomWire

135-The '90s: The decade that never ended - BBC Culture

136-Air Force One (1997) - Gary Oldman as Ivan Korshunov - IMDb

137-Disney's "Dark Age": How Disneyland Survived the Animation Slump - Duchess of Disneyland

Chapter 6

138-"Devils on the Doorstep": Film Censorship Up Close (chinadigitaltimes.net)

139- Transcript of Attorney General Barr's Remarks on China Policy at the Gerald R. Ford Presidential Museum | OPA | Department of Justice

140- China steps up censorship on films to suit CCP ideals amid growing rift with West | China (republicworld.com)

141- Deng Xiaoping: Biography & Policies | Study.com

142- What Happened When China Joined the WTO? | World101 (cfr.org)

143- What Happened When China Joined the WTO? | World101 (cfr.org)

144- What Happened When China Joined the WTO? | World101 (cfr.org)

145-China Tries to Close Gaps in WTO Talks Before Premier Zhu's Arrival to the U.S. - WSJ

146-The U.S.-China Relations Legacy of President George H. W. Bush - (bushchinafoundation.org)

147-Cisco sued for helping China monitor Internet (phys.org)

148-Cisco denies online censorship role in China (nbcnews.com)

149-China's Dangerous Step Toward Cyber Conflict – The Diplomat

150-WTO | 2021 News items - High-Level Forum marks 20 years of China's WTO membership

151-United States Files WTO Case Against China Over Treatment of U.S. Suppliers of Financial Information Services | United States Trade Representative (ustr.gov)

152-Ambassador Kirk Announces WTO Case Against China Over Export Restraints on Raw Materials | United States Trade Representative (ustr.gov)

153-MPAA's Dan Glickman hails WTO decision to open Chinese movie market - Business Of Cinema

154-Christian Bale controversy hurts China on Oscar night? | EW.com

155-Why Hollywood Hasn't Made a Tiananmen Movie (dailysignal.com)

156-Bide Your Time – Adam A. Azim (adam-azim.com)

157-Joe Biden Sold Out America to China While Working for Hollywood - The Washington Standard

158-Joe Biden Sold Out America to China While Working for Hollywood - The Washington Standard

159-A China Wins Twice Proposition: The Belt And Road Initiative – Analysis – Eurasia Review

160-Joe Biden Sold Out America to China While Working for Hollywood - The Washington Standard

161-AFM: Bruno Wu Launches $1.6 Billion Hollywood Fund with China's Ezubo (yahoo.com)

162-AFM: Bruno Wu Launches $1.6 Billion Hollywood Fund with China's Ezubo (yahoo.com)

163-Is 'Chinawood' the new Hollywood? - BBC Culture

164-MPAA getting involved in Hollywood's dispute with China - Los Angeles Times (latimes.com)

165-Hollywood's Mr China: Dan Mintz, DMG (forbes.com)

166-China's Xi declares US trip a 'full success' as Biden announces film deal | Fox News

Chapter 7

167-Alleged Chinese Spies Charged with Conspiring To Obstruct Prosecution Of China-Based Telecom Giant | The Daily Caller

168-FBI director calls Chinese students part of 'whole-of-society' threat to the US | by Shanghaiist.com | Shanghaiist | Medium (bing.com)

169-How Hong Kong Came Under 'One Country, Two Systems' Rule - HISTORY

170-Hong Kong fugitive Ted Hui talks life in exile (afr.com)

171-UK 'not giving up on Hong Kong', says Boris Johnson on 25th handover anniversary, accuses China of not keeping its promises (timesnownews.com)

172-The 25th anniversary of the handover on July 1 | Blinken: Hong Kong democracy has been eroded, the United States stands side by side with Hong Kong - The Limited Times (newsrnd.com)

173-Full text of Xi speech marking 25 years since Hong Kong's return to China - Nikkei Asia

174-Full text of Xi speech marking 25 years since Hong Kong's return to China - Nikkei Asia

175-Thousands of detained Uyghurs pictured in leaked Xinjiang police files | Uyghurs | The Guardian

176-Baerbock's comments on China met with unease – DW – 12/04/2021

177-Trove of leaked photos reveals China's abuses in Uyghur detention camps - Bulletin of the Atomic Scientists (thebulletin.org)

178-China's Uyghur 'shoot-to-kill re-education camps' as images blow apart propaganda - World News - Mirror Online

179-China: Leaked Xinjiang files likely accurate, experts say – DW – 05/24/2022

180-The cost of speaking up against China - BBC News

181-Qelbinur Sidik – A twisted life - Uyghur Times, Uyghur News

182-Qelbinur Sidik – A twisted life - Uyghur Times, Uyghur News

183-Ex-Detainee Describes Torture In China's Xinjiang Re-Education Camp : NPR

184-Ex-Detainee Describes Torture In China's Xinjiang Re-Education Camp : NPR

185-Ex-Detainee Describes Torture In China's Xinjiang Re-Education Camp : NPR

186-China: Draconian repression of Muslims in Xinjiang amounts to crimes against humanity - Amnesty International

187-Transplant tourism: understanding the risks - PubMed (nih.gov)

188-Sir Geoffrey Nice QC: Forced Organ Harvesting by the CCP Is a Threat to Mankind | Falun Dafa - Minghui.org

189-Sir Geoffrey Nice QC: Forced Organ Harvesting by the CCP Is a Threat to Mankind | Falun Dafa - Minghui.org

190-Fentanyl: China's Deadly Export to the United States | U.S.- CHINA | ECONOMIC and SECURITY REVIEW COMMISSION (uscc.gov)

191-Largest Seizure Of Fentanyl In Virginia State Police History | Leesburg Drug Crimes Defense Attorneys (simmsshowerslaw.com)

192-Fentanyl Awareness (dea.gov)

193-Trump accuses China's Xi of failing to halt fentanyl exports to U.S. (yahoo.com)

194-Chinese National Indicted for his Role in Distributing Fentanyl that resulted in four drug overdoses in Oregon | USAO-OR | Department of Justice

195-New report supports claim COVID-19 came from Wuhan lab (nypost.com)

196-Understanding China's Covid Propaganda - WSJ

197-China zero-Covid: Anger at the policy is rising, but Beijing refuses to change course | CNN

198-Shanghai's Two-Month Covid Lockdown Is Still Rippling Through Economy - Bloomberg

199-The Great Firewall of China: Background Torfox (stanford.edu)

200-China | OpenNet Initiative

201-» The Great Firewall of China: Background Torfox (stanford.edu)

202-Hu Jintao touts media freedom – Foreign Policy

203-China's New Cybersecurity Measures Allow State Police to Remotely Access Company Systems (recordedfuture.com)

204-Three Ways PEN's New Report Says China Is Compromising Free Expression (publishingperspectives.com)

205-Actors Who Are Banned From China (looper.com)

206-Tennis star Peng Shuai levels sexual assault allegation at ex-Chinese official (nbcnews.com)

207-Fan Bingbing Apology: 'I Feel Ashamed and Guilty for What I Did' - Variety

208-PEN America Report: Forbidden Feeds - PEN America

209-Influential LGBT Advocacy Group Shuts Down in China Amid Crackdown on Social Activism (newsweek.com)

210-Liu Xiaobo - PEN America

211-Who is Hu Xijin? Global Times Editor Resigns in Mysterious Circumstances (newsweek.com)

212-China Bans Effeminate Men On TV, Part of A Campaign To Tighten Social Control : NPR

213-Liu Xiaobo - PEN America

214-FBI Director Wray, MI5 chief raise alarm over China spying | CNN Politics

215-FBI Director Wray, MI5 chief raise alarm over China spying | CNN Politics

216-China Targets The Fed, Kat Cammack Responds · The Floridian (floridianpress.com)

217-DOJ Charges 2 Suspected Chinese Hackers Who Allegedly Targeted COVID-19 Research : NPR

218-UBC student uses satellite images to track suspected Chinese re-education centres where Uyghurs imprisoned - The Globe and Mail

219-U.S. spy chiefs warn of 'unparalleled' China threat in return to Congress | Reuters

220-The Confucius Institutes by Rachelle Peterson | NAS

221-China's Non-Traditional Espionage Against the United States: The Threat and Potential Policy Responses — FBI

222-China Never Was A Superpower—And It Won't Be One Anytime Soon | Hoover Institution China Never Was A Superpower—And It Won't Be One Anytime Soon

223-Iconic Films: 'The Manchurian Candidate': Director John Frankenheimer's Chilling and Timeless Masterpiece (theepochtimes.com)

224-Brain-Control Weapon Warning Show US Worry for China Military Research (businessinsider.com)

225-US Commerce Dept claims China has brain-control weaponry • The Register

226-Researchers in China claim they have developed 'mind-reading' artificial intelligence that can measure loyalty to the Chinese Communist Party, reports say (yahoo.com)

227-Researchers in China claim they have developed 'mind-reading' artificial intelligence that can measure loyalty to the Chinese Communist Party, reports say (yahoo.com)

Chapter 8

228-Who is Xi Van Fleet? Virginia mom who fled China Cultural Revolution slams critical race theory | MEAWW

229-A very good way to tell China's story to the world - Chinadaily.com.cn

230-“Xi Jinping’s Thought on the Rule of Law”: A New Tool of CCP (bitterwinter.org)

231-'Unsilenced': Chinese dissident film director details CCP threat (bizpacreview.com)

232-The China Threat — FBI

233-The Greatest Trick the Devil Ever Pulled Was Convincing the World He Didn’t Exist – Quote Investigator

234-Hollywood’s China Problem Goes Much Deeper Than CCP Censorship | The Daily Wire

235-Disney unapologetic over Mulan credit thanking Chinese Communist party | Walt Disney Company | The Guardian

236-Disney theme parks change welcome greeting to be more "inclusive" - (kusi.com)

237-Disney kids' show character: Men have periods, too – WND News Center

238-'Red Dawn' Changes Villains From Chinese To North Koreans | HuffPost Entertainment

239-Red Dawn Enemy Changes Addressed by Producer Tripp Vinson (movieweb.com)

240-Transformers: Age of Extinction Bigger in China than US (seibertron.com)

241-Looper Showed China Its Future to Get Time Travel Past Censors (bleedingcool.com)

242-Hollywood Executive Reveals How China’s Politics Have Shaped Movie Industry (voanews.com)

243-Doctor Strange: Why the MCU Changed The Ancient One's Race & Gender (screenrant.com)

244-Iron Man 3 Was Different In China: What Scenes Were Added (& Why)? (screenrant.com)

Chapter 9

245-The Gap sorry for T-shirts with China map that omits Taiwan - CBS News

246-LeBron James criticizes Morey tweet after NBA-China flap (yahoo.com)

247-The NBA: Where Amazing Happens | News, Scores, Highlights, Stats, and Rumors | Bleacher Report

248-Joe McCarthy and Lillian Hellman: The Hated Patriot vs. the Beloved Commie - American Thinker

249-Jack Ma: Traditional banks are operating with a 'pawn shop' mentality, Economy News - ThinkChina

250- Uyghur's in Turkey protest the Beijing Winter Olympics - AnalystNews

251- 'Django Unchained' Pulled from Theaters in China – Rolling Stone

252-'Django Unchained' Is Pulled From China's Theaters - The New York Times (nytimes.com)

253- Quentin Tarantino won't censor Once Upon a Time in Hollywood for China – report | Quentin Tarantino | The Guardian

254- Biden Secretary of State Condemns China's 'Acts Of Genocide' Against Muslim Uyghurs (forbes.com)

255- Biden Admin Responds to China's Atrocities and Genocide With "Diplomatic Boycott" of Beijing Olympics - The New American

256- Speaker Nancy Pelosi to U.S. Olympians: Shut Up & Don't Anger China | American Center for Law and Justice (aclj.org)

257- Ray Dalio Defends Investments in China Despite Human Rights Abuses: CCP Behaves Like a 'Strict Parent' - BFIA

258- Intel CEO Doubles Down on Xinjiang Apology: 'No Reason to Call Out One Region in Particular' | National Review

259- Why should we care about what's happening to the Uyghurs? | The Christian Century

260- James Harden apologizes to China after Daryl Morey's controversial tweet | Sporting News

261- LeBron says Morey 'wasn't educated' when he sent Hong Kong tweet (yahoo.com)

262- NBA in grovelling apology after China suspends broadcasts of Houston Rockets games over Hong Kong 'freedom' tweet | The Independent | The Independent

263- Houston Rockets Address Controversial Tweet from Team's GM - The Spun: What's Trending In The Sports World Today

264- Laura Ingraham to St. Louis Rams: 'Shut Up and Play' (mediaite.com)

Chapter 10

265- Made in Hollywood, Censored by Beijing - PEN America

266- The PEN Pod: Investigating Censorship in Hollywood with James Tager - PEN America

267-Made in Hollywood, Censored by Beijing - PEN America

268-Made in Hollywood, Censored by Beijing - PEN America

269-Made in Hollywood, Censored by Beijing - PEN America

270-Made in Hollywood, Censored by Beijing - PEN America

271-Angelina Jolie accused of ‘disrespecting China’s sovereignty’ after Ang Lee comment | The Independent | The Independent

272-John Cena Apologizes to China for Calling Taiwan a Country - The New York Times (nytimes.com)

273-Sen. Cruz to Introduce Legislation Cutting Off Hollywood Studios Over Complicity in Chinese Censorship | Senator Ted Cruz (senate.gov)

274-Sen. Cruz to Introduce Legislation Cutting Off Hollywood Studios Over Complicity in Chinese Censorship | Senator Ted Cruz (senate.gov)

275-Ted Cruz is right about getting Chinese censorship out of Hollywood movies (yahoo.com)

276-Sen. Cruz to Introduce Legislation Cutting Off Hollywood Studios Over Complicity in Chinese Censorship | Senator Ted Cruz (senate.gov)

277- Transcript of Attorney General Barr’s Remarks on China Policy at the Gerald R. Ford Presidential Museum | OPA | Department of Justice

278-Hollywood director Judd Apatow says Hollywood is now China's puppet: 'Chilling' censorship as China has 'bought our silence' - TheBlaze

279-Hollywood director Judd Apatow says Hollywood is now China's puppet: 'Chilling' censorship as China has 'bought our silence' - TheBlaze

280-Hollywood director Judd Apatow says Hollywood is now China's puppet: 'Chilling' censorship as China has 'bought our silence' - TheBlaze

281-Hollywood Executive Reveals How China’s Politics Have Shaped Movie Industry (voanews.com)

282-Hollywood Executive Reveals How China's Politics Have Shaped Movie Industry (voanews.com)

Conclusion: Flipping the Script

283- Transcript of Attorney General Barr's Remarks on China Policy at the Gerald R. Ford Presidential Museum | OPA | Department of Justice

284-James Harden's House in Houston, TX (Google Maps) (virtualglobetrotting.com)

285-Made in Hollywood, Censored by Beijing - PEN America

286-The Film Foundation (film-foundation.org)

Additional Sources Consulted:

Academic Freedom in China (2019) Jennifer Ruth and Yu Xiao, AAUP Press

America and the China Threat: From the End of History to the End of Empire (2022) Paulo Urio, Clarity Press

Ang Lee Interviews (2019) Karla Rae, University Press of Mississippi

Arresting Cinema: Surveillance in Hong Kong Film (2017) Karen Fang, Stanford U. Press

At Full Speed: Hong Kong in a Borderless World (2001) Esther Yau, University of Minnesota Press

Contemporary Chinese Politics: New Sources, Methods, and Field Strategies (2010) Edited by Allen Carlson, Mary E. Gallagher, et al., Cambridge U. Press

Crouching Tiger, Hidden Dragon: A Portrait of the Ang Lee Film (2000) Richard Corliss and James Schamus, New Market Press

Dark History of Hollywood: A Century of Greed, Corruption and Scandal Behind the Movies (2014) Kieron Connolly, Amber Book Co.

Drugs for the Mind: Censorship in China (2017) Solfie Sun, Eva Tas Foundation

Hollywood Cinema: An Introduction (1995) Richard Maltby, Wiley and Sons

Hollywood Politicos: Then and Now (2009) Greg Rabidoux, University Press of America

Hong Kong Film, Hollywood and New Global Cinema: No Film is an Island (2007) Gina Marchetti Editor, Routledge Press

Introduction to Film Studies (2012) fifth edition, Edited by Jill Nelmes, Routledge Publishing

John Woo: Interview (2005) Robert K. Elder, University Press of Mississippi

Looking at Movies: An Introduction to Film (2010) Richard Barsam and Dave Monahan, W.W. Norton and Sons

Made in Censorship: The Taiwanese Movement in Chinese Literature and Film (2022) Thomas Chen, Columbia U. Press

New Hong Kong Cinema: Transitions to Becoming Chinese in the 21st Century (2015) Ruby Cheung, Cambridge U. Press

New Taiwanese Cinema in Focus: Moving within and Beyond the Frame (2014) Flannery Wilson, Edinburgh University Press

Politics in China: An Introduction (3d Edition/2019) William A. Joseph, Columbia U. Press

The Cinema of Hong Kong: History, Arts, Identity (2002) Edited by Poshek Fu and David Desser, Cambridge U. Press

The Essential Directors: The Art and Impact of Cinema's Most Influential Filmmakers (2021) Sloan De Forest, Hachette Book Group/Turner Film Classics

*Thirty-Two Takes on Taiwan Cinema (*2022) Wenchi Lin, Emilie-Yu Yeh, Darrell William Davis, University of Michigan Press

US-China Economic and Security Review Commission: Directed by Hollywood, Edited by China: How China's Censorship and Influence Affect Films Worldwide (Sean O'Connor and Nicholas Armstrong) 2015

50 Interesting Facts About India - The Fact Site

A history of Hong Kong cinema through the ages | Localiiz

A History of Traditional Hong Kong Cinema (1913-1970) (theculturetrip.com)

Chinese cinema - Film Studies: National Cinemas - Research Guides at Dartmouth College

Chinese Cinema (mediahistoryproject.org)

China Box Office Ends Year With $6.77B – Deadline

China Box Office Grows Astonishing 48.7 Percent in 2015, Hits $6.78 Billion – The Hollywood Reporter

China Film Industry Report 2014-2015 (in brief) .pdf (entgroup.cn)

Entertainment News | Hollywood Reporter

Hong Kong Cinema - Cinema and Media Studies - Oxford Bibliographies

Indian Cinema - History & Evolution (culturalindia.net) The Chinese Cinema

The 10 Best Actors from India In Hollywood Movies & TV (screenrant.com)

The History of Hollywood: The Film Industry Exposed (historycooperative.org)

Threatened by the 'Chinese Oscars,' China rips the world of Chinese movies in two - Los Angeles Times (latimes.com)

Variety

LIST OF FILMS

Hollywood Films Mentioned:

24 (TV)
Ace Ventura: Pet Detective
Ace Ventura: When Nature Calls
A Corner in Wheat
Air Force One
Aladdin
All the President's Men
An American in Paris
A Space Odyssey
Avatar
Avengers
Back to the Future
Baymax (TV)
Baywatch
Beauty and the Beast
Bend it Like Beckham
Big Jim McClain
Bonnie and Clyde
Breakfast at Tiffany's
Bride of Frankenstein
Broken Arrow
Captain America
Captain Phillips
Casablanca
Casino
Champion

Chinatown

Citizen Kane

Cocoanuts

Death Wish

Die Hard Franchise

Dirty Harry

Django Unchained

Double Indemnity

Dr. Jekyll and Mr. Hyde

Dr. Strange

Dr. Strangelove

Easy Rider

Enter the Dragon

Face/Off

Fast and Furious

Fight Club

Fists of Fury

Forrest Gump

Foxy Brown

Frankenstein

Gone with the Wind

Goodfellas

Good Ship Lollipop

Gravity

Guess Who's Coming to Dinner?

Hercules in New York

Home Alone

Human Harvest

I Married a Communist

Immortals

Independence Day

Indiana Jones Franchise

Iron Man Franchise

It Happened One Night

I was a Communist for the FBI

Jaws

Jurassic Park Franchise

Kill Bill Vols. 1 and 2

King Kong

Kundun

Kung Fu Panda 3

Looper

Mr. Smith Goes to Washington

Man on a Tightrope

Martian

Men in Black 3

Midnight Cowboy

Mission Impossible Franchise

Mulan (Disney and Chinese Cinema titles)

North by Northwest

Once Upon a Time in Hollywood

On the Waterfront

Philadelphia Story

Pink Panther 2

Pirates of the Caribbean Franchise

Pixels

Pork Chop Hill

Pretty Woman

Psycho

Pulp Fiction

Quantico (TV)

Raging Bull

Rambo I, II
Red Dawn
Reservoir Dogs
Robin Hood
Rocky I, II and III, IV, V
Rush Hour
Rosemary's Baby
Saving Private Ryan
Seven Years in Tibet
Shadow of a Doubt
Sherlock Holmes
Silence
Silence of the Lambs
Singing in the Rain
Sixth Sense
Skyfall
Slumdog Millionaire
Snow White and the Seven Dwarfs
Spartacus
Spellbound
Star Wars Franchise
Steamboat Willie
Street Angel
Sudden Death
Tarzan: The Ape Man
Taxi Driver
Terminator Franchise
The Alamo
The Big Boss
The Big Sleep
The Birth of a Nation

The Bleeding edge
The Boy in the Plastic Bubble
The Buccaneer
The Dark Knight
The Departed
The Fugitive
The Godfather
The Gold Rush
The Graduate
The Great Dictator
The Great Gatsby
The Green Berets
The Green Hornet
The Hunchback of Notre Dame
The Irishman
The Jazz Singer
The Kid
The Last Emperor
The Lion King
The Maltese Falcon
The Manchurian Candidate
The Night of the Living Dead
The Passion of Joan of Arc
The Red Man
The Red Menace
The Single Standard
The Searchers
The Tramp
The Virginian
The Way of the Dragon
The Wizard of Oz

Titanic
To Catch a Thief
To Have and Have Not
To Kill a Mockingbird
Tomorrow Never Dies
Top Gun 1 and 2
Toy Story Franchise
Transformers
Vampyr
Viva Zapata
Way of the Dragon
Wizard of Oz
World War Z
Xander Cage Franchise
Xiu Xiu: The Sent Down Girl
X-Men Days of Future Past
Yankee Doodle Dandy

Chinese Films Mentioned:

800 Heroes
A Better Tomorrow
A Borrowed Life
A Brighter Summer Day
A Modern Woman
Arise United Toward Tomorrow
A Trip Through China
Beijing Bicycle
Bitter Tea of General Yen
Black Snow
Blue Kite

Center Stage
Chinese Box
Chong Po li gian de hei an
Chungking Express
City of Sadness
Crazy English
Crossroads
Crouching Tiger, Hidden Dragon
Crows and Sparrows
Daybreak
Devils on the Doorstep
Dingjun Mountain
East Palace/West Palace
Eat Drink Man Woman
Evening Rain
Eyes of Buddha
Fallen Angels
Farewell My Concubine
Father
Fight with Flood
Flowers of the Motherland
Full Moon in New York
Happy Together
Hibiscus Town
Hold You Tight
Hua Mulan Joins the Army
I Love Beijing
Infernal Affairs
Jiao Yulu
Ju Dou
Keep Cool

King of Masks
Legend of Tianyun Mountain
Life
Little Toys
Mambo Girl
Mulan Joins the Army
Mulan: The Rise of a Warrior
New Heroes and Heroines
New Women
Not One Less
Oil for the Lamps of China
Old Well
Once Upon a Time in Shanghai
Opium War
Purple Mountain
Pushing Hands
Raise the Red Lantern
Red Children
Red Sorghum
Revealed by the Pot
River Without Buoys
Rush Hour
Sense and Sensibility
Shanghai Express
Shanghai Triad
Shaolin Soccer
Shaolin Temple
Sing Song Girl: Red Peony
Sino-Dutch War
Song of China
Song of the Fishermen

Sparkling Red Star
Spring in a Small Town
Spring Silkworms
Street Angel (Chinese version)
Suzhou River
Tai Chi Master
Temptation of a Monk
The 8th Company of Nanking Road
The Battle of Shanggliang
The Burning of the Shaolin Temple
The East is Red
The Eight Hundred
The Flowers of War
The Founding of the Party
The Goddess
The Good Earth
The Great Road
The Homecoming
The Last Emperor
The Life of Wu Xun
The Married Couple
The Puppetmaster
The Purple Hairpin
The Red Detachment of Women
The Red Lantern
The Red Sorghum
The Replacement Killers
The Road Home
The Shaolin Temple
The Sport of Kings
The Spring River Flows East

The Wedding Banquet
The White-Haired Girl
The White Tiger Regiment
The Widowed Empress
Three Modern Women
Too Happy for Words
Vive L'Amour
Volga, Volga
Warmth of the Sun
Warriors of Virtue
Wildflower
Wild Rose
Wing Chun
Women's Basketball #5
Wonton Soup
Zuangzi Tests His Wife

Photo Credits:
All images used are royalty free, and are from either Pexels, Creative Commons or Google Free Public use images.
The Dragon neon sign on the back cover is credited to Ryutaro Tsukata.

ABOUT THE AUTHOR

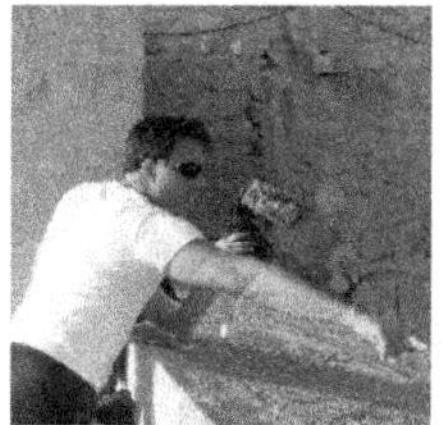

Greg Rabidoux is an award-winning documentary film director (*Stolen Babies of Spain*), the co-author of *Stolen Babies of Spain: The Book*, and author of *Hollywood Politicos: Then and Now*, theatrical plays including *Red Scared* and *The Diva*, and is currently developing the screenplay *My Sister, My Hero*. Greg has also appeared in several films, including *Death at Dinner* and numerous stage plays. He is a co-founder of ValMar Films and ValMar productions. He has been trained in film and directing at NYU Film, and the New York Film Academy, and has an earned Ph.D in politics and film, as well as a law degree. Greg and his film crew are currently in production for a documentary film about one man's quest to uncover a hidden truth which may affect hundreds of families which has taken him to the Vatican City steps and the Pope. When not working on film projects, he teaches film at Coastal Carolina University in South Carolina. Chants up!

For more Valmar Books publications please visit the following websites:

https://www.amazon.com/dp/B086JGLXCX
https://www.amazon.com/dp/B08NXWWNNZ
https://www.amazon.com/dp/B09Q556ZG3

To learn about the Valmar Productions award-winning documentary film Stolen Babies of Spain, the victims and their search for truth, justice and reconciliation or to learn how you can help please visit:

www.imdb.com/title/tt11219178/
www.stolenbabiesofspain.com
www.facebook.com/stolenbabiesofspain

The documentary can be watched in Amazon's Prime Video, Tubi TV, Roku, Vimeo on Demand and other VOD providers. Here are two of the sites:

https://www.primevideo.com/detail/Stolen-Babies-of-Spain/0L68NWCXKZI1J83E5FMFF8HWCW

https://tubitv.com/movies/677710/stolen-babies-of-spain?start=true

www.ingramcontent.com/pod-product-compliance
Lightning Source LLC
LaVergne TN
LVHW020537100826
845148LV00010B/1504

* 9 7 8 1 7 3 5 2 7 1 6 4 4 *